Lecture Notes in Computer Science　8456

Commenced Publication in 1973
Founding and Former Series Editors:
Gerhard Goos, Juris Hartmanis, and Jan van Leeuwen

More information about this series at http://www.springer.com/series/7409

Cathy Bodine · Sumi Helal
Tao Gu · Mounir Mokhtari (Eds.)

Smart Homes and Health Telematics

12th International Conference, ICOST 2014
Denver, CO, USA, June 25–27, 2014
Revised Papers

 Springer

Editors
Cathy Bodine
University of Colorado
Denver, CO
USA

Sumi Helal
University of Florida
Gainesville, FL
USA

Tao Gu
RMIT University
Melbourne, VIC
Australia

Mounir Mokhtari
CNRS IPAL (UMI 2955)
Singapore
Singapore

and

Institut Mines-Télécom
France

ISSN 0302-9743   ISSN 1611-3349 (electronic)
Lecture Notes in Computer Science
ISBN 978-3-319-14423-8   ISBN 978-3-319-14424-5 (eBook)
DOI 10.1007/978-3-319-14424-5

Library of Congress Control Number: 2014958661

LNCS Sublibrary: SL3 – Information Systems and Applications, incl. Internet/Web, and HCI

Printed on acid-free paper

Springer International Publishing AG Switzerland is part of Springer Science+Business Media
(www.springer.com)

Preface

It is our great pleasure to welcome you to Denver, Colorado, and to the 12th International Conference on Smart Homes and Health Telematics – ICOST 2014. This year the ICOST program offered exciting and high-quality sessions, including six technical sessions, a poster session, three keynotes from highly recognized researchers and visionary leaders in the industry in addition to two panels.

In addition to the technical program, an exciting social program was planned for all registrants. A welcome reception followed by a Gala Dinner kick-started our social program at the Denver Museum of Nature and Science on June 25. An evening of entertainment was also planned at the Denver Center for the Performing Arts, downtown Denver. Together, we enjoyed a sneak peek into the rehearsal process conducted by the Phamaly Theatre Company, as well as enjoyed musical pieces from the popular musical Joseph and the Amazing Technicolor Dreamcoat.

Putting together ICOST 2014 was a team effort. We would like to first thank the authors for submitting their best work and providing the content of the program in terms of papers and posters. We would also like to thank the panelists and the three keynote speakers for their contributions. We are grateful to the Organizing Committee and its dedication in making ICOST 2014 a success. Mounir Mokhtari provided invaluable guidance which was very helpful throughout the process. Tao Gu did a great job in assembling a world-class Program Committee for soliciting and reviewing the papers. Carl Chang did a great job guiding the process of forming the two panels in the program. Bessam Abdulrazzak did a great job with the conference publicity and for that we are very grateful. We also thank Elizabeth Woodruff for helping in many administrative and local arrangement issues.

Now we cannot forget to thank our sponsors: the Department of Bioengineering at the University of Colorado, Assistive Technology Partners at the Medical School, University of Colorado, the Coleman Institute for Cognitive Disabilities, the University of Florida, and the Institut Mines-Télécom, France. Their sponsorship and support were vital for the successful organization of this conference.

We wish you all a pleasant stay in Denver, and a memorable and rich experience in ICOST.

June 2014

Cathy Bodine
Sumi Helal

ICOST 2014 Organization

Organizing Committee

General Chair

Cathy Bodine — University of Colorado, Denver, USA

General Co-chair

Sumi Helal — University of Florida, USA

Program Chair

Tao Gu — RMIT University, Australia

Finance Co-chairs

Katherine Hoch — University of Colorado, Denver, USA
Jit Biswas — Institute for Infocomm Research, Singapore

Publicity Chairs

Bessam Abdulrazzak — Université de Sherbrooke, Canada

Publications Chair

Mounir Mokhtari — Institut Mines-Télécom, France

Local Organization Chair

Elizabeth Woodruff — University of Colorado, Denver, USA

International Liaison Chair

Daqing Zhang — Institut Mines-Télécom, France

Panels Chair

Carl Chang — Iowa State University, USA

Scientific Committee

Bessam Abdulrazak — Université de Sherbrooke, Canada
Z. Zenn Bien — Korea Advanced Institute of Science and Technology, South Korea
Carl K. Chang — Iowa State University, USA
Sylvain Giroux — Université de Sherbrooke, Canada

Sumi Helal   University of Florida, USA
Nick Hine   University of Dundee, UK
Ismail Khalil   Johannes Kepler University of Linz, Austria
Yeunsook Lee   Yonsei University/The Korean Gerontological
                                       Society, South Korea
Mounir Mokhtari   Institut Mines-Télécom, France/CNRS and Image
                                       & Pervasive Access Lab, Singapore
Chris Nugent   University of Ulster, UK
Tatsuya Yamazaki   NICT, Japan
Daqing Zhang   Institut Mines-Télécom/Telecom SudParis, France
Cristiano Paggetti   I+ S.r.l, Italy
William Cheng-Chung Chu   Tunghai University, Taiwan

Program Committee

Yves Demazeau   CNRS – Laboratoire LIG, France
Bin Guo   Telecom SudParis, France
Laurent Billonnet   University of Limoges, France
Lyes Khoukhi   University of Technology of Troyes, France
Margaret Hamilton   RMIT University, Australia
Jayachandran Maniyeri   Institute for Infocomm Research, Singapore
Nirmalya Roy   University of Maryland, Baltimore County, USA
Manfred Wojciechowski   Fraunhofer ISST, Germany
Daqing Zhang   Institut Mines-Télécom/Telecom SudParis, France
Jeffrey Soar   University of Southern Queensland, Australia
Joo-Hwee Lim   PI2R, A*STAR, Singapore
Hongbo Ni   Northwestern Polytechnical University, China
Duckki Lee   LG Electronics, South Korea
Hamdi Aloulou   Image & Pervasive Access Lab, Singapore
Fulvio Mastrogiovanni   University of Genoa, Italy
Natalia Díaz Rodríguez   Åbo Akademi University, TUCS, Finland
Amee Morgans   Monash University, Australia
Hyun Kim   ETRI, South Korea
Zhixian Yan   Samsung Research America, USA
Fabrice Peyrard   IRIT, France
Jit Biswas   Institute for Infocomm Research, Singapore
Zhiwen Yu   Northwestern Polytechnical University, China
Venet Osmani   CREATE-NET, Italy
Xianping Tao   Nanjing University, China
Johnny Wong   Iowa State University, USA
Abdallah M'Hamed   Telecom SudParis, France
Arkady Zaslavsky   CSIRO, Australia
Thibaut Tiberghien   Image & Pervasive Access Lab, UMI CNRS,
                                       Singapore
Ye-Qiong Song   LORIA – University of Lorraine, France

Mathieu Raynal   IRIT – University of Toulouse, France
Charles Gouin-Vallerand   Télé-Université du Québec, Canada
Nadine Vigouroux   IRIT, Université Paul Sabatier, France

Sponsored By

 Department of Bioengineering
UNIVERSITY OF COLORADO
DENVER | ANSCHUTZ MEDICAL CAMPUS

 Coleman Institute for Cognitive Disabilities
UNIVERSITY OF COLORADO
Boulder | Colorado Springs | Denver | Anschutz Medical Campus

 Assistive Technology Partners
SCHOOL OF MEDICINE
UNIVERSITY OF COLORADO ANSCHUTZ MEDICAL CAMPUS

 UF UNIVERSITY of FLORIDA

 INSTITUT Mines-Télécom

Keynotes

A New IT (Inclusive Technology) Revolution

Frances W. West

IBM, One Rogers Street, Cambridge, MA 02142, USA

Abstract. With more than one billion people with disabilities worldwide, in addition to the aging population, novice technology users, people with language, learning and literacy challenges, or any individual facing a situational impairment while using a device, the global demand for accessibility has made it a mainstream requirement for governments and businesses around the globe. And, the success of trends such as mobile, social, smart TVs, wearable devices and cognitive technologies will depend on the ongoing integration of adaptive, intuitive and accessible technology capabilities. This means that CIOs and IT leaders need to provide technology solutions to reduce barriers for people with disabilities and realize that these same accessible technologies can increase productivity and improve the overall user experience for the mass market. Attendees will learn how next generation solutions are complementing and supplementing the human senses to better optimize communications and make information more meaningful and consumable to everyone.

Short Biography

 Frances West is the worldwide director of the IBM Human Ability and Accessibility Center (HA&AC), a division of IBM Research. In this position, she advances IBM market leadership by driving technology innovation and solution development in the area of human ability and accessibility. Prior to her current assignment, Frances was director of Channels, Alliances and Business Development for IBM Lotus Software, where she recruited and managed IBM's global network of Business Partners specializing in Lotus software.

Frances joined IBM in 1979. Between 1979 and 1998, she held numerous management positions across the IBM sales and marketing organizations. In 1998, Frances became the Business Unit Executive of the Banking, Financial Services, Securities and Insurance Unit for the IBM Greater China Group. The following year, she was named the Director of Financial Services Sector Solutions for IBM Global Services, where she managed investment funding and executed financial services solution plans for ban king, insurance and financial markets. Since joining IBM Research to lead the HA&AC in 2003, Frances has become a globally-recognized expert in enabling human ability through accessible information and communications technology (ICT). She has served on the Board of Directors for numerous advocacy organizations, including the American Association of People with Disabilities, the Assistive Technology Industry Association and the U.S. Business Leadership Network (USBLN). She currently sits on the Board of Directors of the World Institute on Disability, is the board advisor to the National Business & Disability Council, and Founding member and Program Co-Chair of G3ict, an advocacy initiative launched by the United Nations Global Alliance for ICT and development in 2006.

Frances has become a sought after authority on the topic of global ICT accessibility trends and enablement. In 2010, she delivered remarks at policy forums hosted by the United Nation's Global Initiative for Inclusive Information and Communications Technologies; a U.S. Department of Labor, Office of Disability Employment Policy roundtable; and an international forum hosted by the São Paulo State Secretariat for the Rights of Persons with Disabilities in Brazil. Most recently, in November 2013, she testified on behalf of the IT industry to the U.S. Senate Committee on Foreign Relations in support of the ratification of the Convention on the Rights of Persons with Disabilities. Frances attended the Chinese University of Hong Kong, Washington & Lee University in Virginia and graduated with a marketing degree from the University of Kentucky. In 2011, she received an Honorary Doctor of Science degree from the University of Massachusetts Boston. Frances is married with two sons and currently resides in West Newton Hill, Mass.

10 Years of Reminding Technologies: What Have We Learnt?

Chris Nugent

Computer Science Research Institute, School of Computing and Mathematics,
University of Ulster, Rm 16J20, Jordanstown Campus,
Shore Rd., Newtownabbey, County Antrim, BT37 0QB, UK
cd.nugent@ulster.ac.uk

Abstract. People with mild dementia generally exhibit impairments of memory, reasoning and thought. As a result, they require varying levels of support to complete everyday activities to maintain a level of independence. The use of technological solutions to address such impairments have been recognized as being capable of providing a positive impact on the quality of life for both the patient and their carer. Specifically, the integration of cognitive prosthetics, technology based solutions to augment reminding functionality, into everyday lives of people with dementia has been shown to be a popular approach. This presentation will reflect upon the journey of the development and evaluation of cognitive prosthetics over the last 10 years, highlighting lessons which have been learnt. This will involve considering, through the use of a range of Case Studies, the evolution of cognitive prosthetics from a device perspective, the impact of adopting a user centred iterative design process, through to more recent efforts of aligning solutions with everyday technological platforms. The presentation will conclude by considering future trends, most notably highlighting user profiling in an effort to improve technology adoption.

Short Biography

Chris received a Bachelor of Engineering in Electronic Systems and DPhil in Biomedical Engineering both from the University of Ulster. He currently holds the position of Professor of Biomedical Engineering at the University.

His research within biomedical engineering addresses the themes of the development and evaluation of Technologies to support ambient assisted living. Specifically, this has involved research in the topics of mobile based reminding solutions, activity recognition and prompting, formats for data storage and more recently technology adoption modeling. He has published extensively in these areas with the work spanning theoretical, clinical and biomedical engineering domains.

He has been a grant holder of Research Projects funded by National, European and International funding bodies. Amongst these projects he was the Scientific co-ordinator of the European Union MEDICATE consortium, Technical co-ordinator of the European Union CogKnow consortium and Technical co-ordinator of the ESRC New Dynamics of Aging Well Consortium.

At present he is Group Leader of the Smart Environments Research Group which was established in 2009 and is co-PI of the Connected Health Innovation Centre at the University of Ulster. He currently holds the position of Visiting Professor of Mobile and Pervasive Computing at Lulea Technical University, Sweden.

The Challenge of Assistive Technologies in Developing Countries

Michael Lightner

Department of Electrical, Computer, and Energy Engineering,
University of Colorado – Boulder, Engineering Center,
Rm ECEE1B55, 425 UCB, Boulder, CO 80309-0425, USA
Michael.Lightner@colorado.edu

Abstract. The challenge of providing assistive technology (AT) to people with disabilities is one that is becoming a mainstream concern as presented in the keynote by Frances West and supported by specific case studies presented in the keynote by Chris Nugent. In this talk we address the challenges of providing these supports in developing countries. Most of the world's 1 billion people with disabilities do not live in the developed world, simply because most of the world's population is not in developed countries. Yet our technological solutions often require an infrastructure that is missing in villages with little or no electricity, where family units are the only support for those with disabilities, with schools having little effective infrastructure, where mainstreaming has never been heard of and where there are no support agencies. In this talk we will begin with a review of the demographics and associated economics of the developed and developing world. Then we will compare a number of ATs and their appropriateness in a variety of developing world situations. Examples of AT that are effective will be presented. The lesson is that there is a spectrum of technical sophistication in AT and this spectrum needs to be supported in order to span developing and developed countries. Some suggestions for understanding the ecosystem of AT and how that maps to developing countries will be presented. We will close with an example of a sophisticated solution to a simple, but difficult, problem and how a social entrepreneurship start-up is helping to bring this to developing countries.

Short Biography

Michael Lightner is Professor and Chair of Electrical, Computer and Energy Engineering at the University of Colorado, Boulder. He received his PhD from Carnegie-Mellon. He is Co-Director of the NIDRR funded Rehabilitation Engineering Research Center for Adv ancing Cognitive Technologies at the University of Colorado Health Sciences Center and Technology Director of Boulder Digital Works, an innovate postgraduate digital media program. He has also served as Associate Dean for Academic Affairs for the College of Engineering and Applied Science.

For many years his research was focused on electronic design automation including simulation, synthesis, test, formal verification and optimization. He has also worked in signal processing, most recently on multi-rate adaptive filters. The last ten years have been spent focusing on AT for people with cognitive disabilities. In this capacity he helped found and was Associate Executive Director of the University of Colorado Coleman Institute for Cognitive Disabilities, founded with a $250M gift from Bill and Claudia Coleman.

In these recent roles he has worked with a variety of government agencies and NGOs, and initiated the first IEEE Conference on the Future of Assistive Technology bringing together government, academia, industry, NGOs, public interest groups and the public to address the needs in AT over the next decade. He was made a Fellow of the IEEE for his contribution to computer-aided design. He is also a Fellow of the American Institute for Medical and Biological Engineering. Through his various roles in the IEEE, including 2006 President and CEO, and 2012–2013 Vice President for Education Activities, he has presented talks on Cognitive Assistive Technology in multiple locations in India, China, Africa, Indonesia, the EU and the USA. He has interacted with technology leaders in India on how cell phones can effectively be used in villages with little or no electricity.

Contents

Cognitive Technology

Activity Recognition

Context and Situation Awareness

Health IT

Short Contributions

Design and Usability

Designing a Multi-sided Health and Wellbeing Platform: Results of a First Design Cycle

W.J.W. Keijzer-Broers[1(✉)], G.A. de Reuver[1], and N.A. Guldemond[2]

[1] Delft University of Technology, Delft, The Netherlands
{w.j.w.keijzer-broers,g.a.dereuver}@tudelft.nl
[2] UMC Utrecht, Utrecht, The Netherlands
n.a.guldemond@umcutrecht.nl

Abstract. While worldwide several health and wellbeing products and services are being developed to support people to live comfortable and independently in their home environment, widespread adoption of these smart living solutions is still not envisioned. A hindering factor is that users are not aware of possible solutions or where to find them, which could be solved through promoting solutions on shared platforms. Designing such platforms is challenging as multiple stakeholders need to be satisfied and start-up problems need to be overcome. Most theory on platforms is explored in ex-post studies and there is a lack of knowledge on how platforms should be designed and implemented. In this paper, we elicit functional requirements for the design of a multi-sided health and wellbeing platform based on interviews with both end-users and stakeholders. These requirements provide the basis for future design cycles in which, the development and actual implementation of a platform is foreseen.

Keywords: Design science · Service platform · Health and wellbeing · Smart living · Matchmaking · Stakeholders · Social infrastructure

1 Introduction

Smart living services [1], aimed at people living at home, are not yet widely adopted [2–4]. Services can be seen as the non-material equivalent of a good, which is intangible by nature and is offered by a provider to its consumers as a value [5].

Two decades ago, Mark Weiser envisioned a world where numerous of interconnected intelligent devices and networks serve human in an unobtrusive way [6]. Despite the technological advancements in recent years [7] such vision still has to become reality in daily life [8] and can be explained by (1) the tools are missing for stakeholders to create awareness among end-users about existing solutions and (2) the highly fragmented market hinders end-users to find products and services that they need, and (3) the predominantly technological focus of service providers makes it difficult to understand how services fit end-user needs. Accordingly, a possible approach to solve issues like awareness, fragmentation and promotion, is to create a service platform (i.e., a social infrastructure) that connects providers and users of smart living products and services.

Our research is related to the European Ambient Assisted Living project Care@Home, that focuses on delivering connected ICT-based assistive living solutions

© Springer International Publishing Switzerland 2015
C. Bodine et al. (Eds.): ICOST 2014, LNCS 8456, pp. 3–12, 2015.
DOI: 10.1007/978-3-319-14424-5_1

involving multiple devices for elderly and enabling them to live an independent life as long as possible [9].

In this paper, we present the results of the first design cycle for the conceptual design of the platform, based on two series of exploratory interviews with potential end-users and relevant stakeholders in the Netherlands.

The paper is structured as follows: Sect. 2 provides a background on the health and wellbeing domain. In Sect. 3 we provide an overview of the platform literature. In Sect. 4, the method is described, followed by the results in Sect. 5. Then, in Sect. 6 the findings are discussed. Finally, in the last section the challenges and an outline of the next steps are provided.

2 Health and Wellbeing Domain

One of the main demanding markets in health and wellbeing is that of the elderly. The UN Population Division [10] foresees an increase of the global population over the age of 60 from 841 million in 2013 (11,7 % of the world population) to more than 2 billion in 2050 (21,2 % of the world population). Ageing population generates an increasing demand of healthcare resources due to the associated increase of chronic conditions. The World Health Organization, but also the European Commission and national governments promote the concept of 'active ageing' and define it as the process of optimizing opportunities for health, participation and security in order to enhance quality of life as people age [11]. There is largely consensus that innovative ICT solutions are required to both reduce costs and help people to stay at home as long as possible [12].

Although, technologies for smart living products and services are developing rapidly [13, 14], adoption of these technologies is not widespread. Generally, end-users are not aware of what smart living services are available and how these services could fulfil their needs. In addition, the highly fragmented market provides many services, but no integrated systems, which makes it difficult for end-users to find products and services. Moreover, especially in the health and wellbeing domain of smart living, end-users (i.e., elderly and disabled people) typically pass different stages of impairment, and they are often unaware as to what services they could use at what point in time. The predominantly technological focus of service providers makes it difficult for them to understand how services fit end-user needs. Especially technology-focused providers lack channels to reach users. Finally, besides end-users, there are other stakeholder groups, which need to be aware of health and wellbeing services (i.e., service and care providers, manufacturers, facilitators and government agencies).

In this paper, we focus on health and wellbeing services provided on the level of municipalities. The rationale behind this is that care services in the Netherlands, in which the study is conducted, are increasingly shifted to the municipal level. According to plans of the Dutch government, from 2015 onwards, the responsibility and the execution of healthcare will be even more shifted towards municipalities. Domestic help is being handed over to municipalities that will be free to decide for themselves how they will execute tasks and are accountable at a local level for their performance. A next step is 'age at place' either at home or in local communities rather than in care homes and other institutions. Although people prefer to stay at home as long as possible and deinstitutionalization is also based on the assumption that homecare services are less costly than institutional services, it also represents a major challenge, as increased support for homecare has to be provided somehow [15]. This transition will cause a paradigm shift in the Netherlands, because of the tension between keeping healthcare a universal good while harnessing costs [16]. Next to that it will have a huge effect on society and the social inclusiveness of elderly in particular. For that reason municipalities are searching for technical and organizational solutions to support them in the transition phase. For example, a service platform with monitoring features, that support the social intervention of citizens in the context of health and wellbeing, might be a helpful instrument.

3 Kernel Theory: Platform Theory

As this paper focuses on municipalities, service providers and end-user issues in establishing and governing a platform for health and wellbeing, we base the theoretical framework on concepts of platform theory from a multi-sided market perspective (i.e., different 'independent' providers provide complementary products and services on the platform [17]). Platform theory is relevant because it provides insights in (1) how service platforms come to exist and develop, (2) how to identify potential and patterns for collaboration and (3) how to organize users and form a foundation for their interactions. Platform theory enables us to clarify what has to be done when designing a service platform and how to involve different stakeholder groups in an early stage. Most of the theoretical and empirical research on multi-sided platforms has focused on mature platforms [18, 19] and less attention has been given to issues in starting up a new platform [20]. These issues include strategies for attracting different user groups of a platform and attaining a critical mass. From an economic point of view such a platform creates a multi-sided market and generally faces a critical mass constraint that must be satisfied if the business wants to be viable [18]. Therefore, the challenge is to find out if a health and wellbeing platform is a viable solution and generates value from bringing end-users and members of different stakeholder groups together. Platforms typically consist of features such as search functionality, payment administration, authentication, security, data-access and identity management. Previous studies show that the proliferation of platforms depends on several criteria such as satisfying multiple sides of the market [21], governing relationships with third party service providers [22] and maintaining a degree of openness in order to allow generativity [23]. Since trust in a platform and building up reputation are also important success factors, the process in which a platform is designed and stakeholders are involved is far from trivial. In summary, existing knowledge on platforms is merely based on ex post studies of successful cases and there is a lack of knowledge on the design of emerging platforms in the smart living domain [24]. In addition, the issues of how to involve and deal with external stakeholders during the design process is rarely discussed in literature on new service design [e.g., 25], service engineering [e.g., 26] or design science research [e.g., 27, 28]. In our design, we consider the five stages of the typical design cycle from Kuechler and Vaishnavi [29] (See Fig. 1).

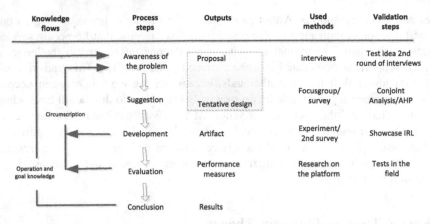

Fig. 1. Extended version design cycle Kuechler and Vaishnavi [29].

Comprising the stages of problem awareness, suggested solution, develop the artefact, implementation and evaluation as an overview of the patterns (i.e., generalized system design elements) of the platform design. Although in the design cycle of Kuechler and Vaishnavi, just one moment is included to measure the performance of the design, we entered the used methods and added validation steps (i.e., performance measures) for every phase (i.e., design step) in the design cycle.

4   Method

4.1   Design Science Research

This paper is positioned within the design science research paradigm [30, 31]; a fundamentally problem solving paradigm that has its roots in engineering and the sciences of the artificial world [32]. Design science research attempts to solve a specific problem and to generate and empirically test a design theory that can be reused in solving a class of related problems. We adopt a specific design science research method called Action Design Research (ADR) after a term first coined by Livari [31]. ADR provides explicit guidance for combining building, intervention, and evaluation in a concerted research effort. ADR contains two basic activities: building an artifact for a specific purpose and evaluation on performance of that artifact. We adopt Action Design Research because it has a dual mission: (1) to make theoretical contributions and (2) to assist solving current and anticipated problems of practitioners [33]. We use this approach in conducting our research as it provides a scientific research framework for designing a service platform, but taking into account that designing the platform is an iterative and sometimes 'messy' process.

4.2   Interview Method

In an earlier paper [34], we explored the problem awareness (i.e., first design step) for health and wellbeing. Through 11 exploratory interviews with different stakeholders, we found that end-users lack awareness of what smart living solutions are available and how they could fulfill their needs. At the same time, we found that service providers find it difficult to reach end-users and to market and promote their products and services. According to the interviewees a platform should solve this mismatch between demand and supply. In this paper, we analyze 59 semi-structured interviews with potential user groups and various stakeholders, to develop a solution (i.e., second design step) for the problem elicited and to address the mismatch between demand and supply. The results were used for analyzing and testing the first design step. Interviewees were selected in three stakeholder groups that each represents a different side of the platform: Two external stakeholder groups, like 23 strategic level stakeholders (i.e., knowledge institutes, government and funding partners), 17 affiliate level stakeholders (i.e., service and technology providers) and 19 end-users (i.e., care providers and citizens) on the other side. First, the aim of the interview was explained: the practical problem on the mismatch between demand and supply in health and wellbeing and the suggested solutions. Next, three questions were posed to every interviewee, followed by follow-up questions and discussion: (1) What should be the main purpose of a health and wellbeing platform? (2) Who would benefit from such a platform? (3) What are critical design issues when developing such a platform? Interview reports were summarized and coded into categories.

5   Results

5.1   Main Purpose of the Platform

To the question: *What should be the main purpose of the platform*, four main answers were given. (See Fig. 2).

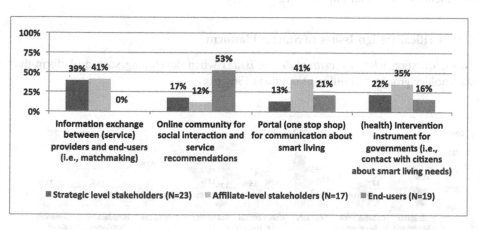

Fig. 2. Main purpose of the platform according to interviewees.

Most often mentioned functions are **information exchange** between providers and end-users. This was especially mentioned by the strategic and affiliate stakeholders, but strikingly not by end-users themselves. Besides exchanging information about services and products, interviewees pointed out that automatically matching end-user needs and services offered would add value, i.e. a recommendation feature. Affiliate stakeholders were mainly interested to communicate their offerings to potential user groups, rather than communication among end-users themselves. An **online community** for social interaction was often mentioned by end-users. Such a community should not only help end-users to find and recommend applications to each other but also to check on each other's social wellbeing. The main rationale behind this function is the need for social cohesion (i.e., staying in touch with other elderly people and the outside world). A **portal for communication** about solutions was mentioned often as well. Such a portal would be a marketplace for solutions and a 'one-stop-shop' to access services. Features mentioned less often were an **intervention instrument** for the municipality to get in contact with citizens about needs for services and questions about health care legislations. However, this feature was suggested by all five interviewees from government organizations to support this intervention role from municipalities in case of the health and wellbeing of citizens.

5.2   Benefited Users from the Platform

To the question *who would benefit from the platform* the strategic and affiliate stakeholders agree that the platform should be beneficial for both end-users and the industry. The platform could function as a 'one- stop-shop' for smart living needs and solutions, but also as an intermediary between the industry and end-users. The governmental interviewees argued that the platform should be merely beneficial for end-users only: like citizens in general, patients and elderly. End-users were more specific about the target group; they argue that the platform would be most beneficial for elderly who want to stay in their own home environment (i.e., ageing in place), citizens in general or patients with several impairments.

5.3   Critical Design Issues to Start a Platform

To the question *what are critical design issues* when developing such a platform the stakeholder groups had different opinions (See Fig. 3).

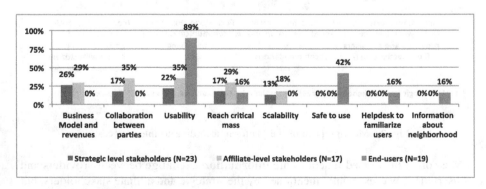

Fig. 3. Critical design issues for developing a health and wellbeing platform.

The strategic level stakeholders were mainly concerned over how a service platform for health and wellbeing could add value to different stakeholders, i.e. what would be sustainable **business models and** how to achieve **revenues.** They were concerned about the organization of such a platform (i.e., **collaboration between parties**) and how to reach **'critical mass'** (i.e., a sufficient number of adopters of the platform, to support further growth). This group had less attention for the **usability** of the platform, although they mentioned that easy access to the platform through multiple devices is required. The affiliate stakeholders raised issues about the **usability** for the consumers of such a platform and how to deal with the chicken-and-egg problem to reach **critical mass.** They were skeptical about the **revenues** and **collaboration between different parties,** especially because of competitive considerations (i.e., linking content with databases, free-riding issues). On the other hand they consider that such a platform could help them to reach customers in the domain. The external stakeholders preferred a local (i.e., postal code based) but **scalable** platform, starting on a micro-scale before rolling out on a national level. The end-users had more concerns about practical issues, like the **usability** of the platform (i.e., ease of use, full filling needs, practical, accessible), **safety and privacy**, if the online platform combines online with offline information (i.e., information about gatherings in the **neighborhood**) and finally if there would be a **helpdesk** for the platform.

6 Discussion and Interpretation

We propose an interactive service platform to (1) satisfy the requirements of end-users, service-providers and municipalities; (2) create awareness among end-users on what products, services and technologies can help them and (3) assist in matchmaking between (latent) needs and (yet unknown) services. The interviews lead to a first requirement elicitation from a stakeholder perspective. The main findings of the interviews were that a service platform could provoke various experts to be active in the health and wellbeing environment and that such a platform could be an accelerator for further developments and accelerate the diffusion process of applications in the smart living domain. According to the interviews the main purpose of the health and wellbeing platform, should be to provide: (1) an **online community** for contact, solutions, social wellbeing, interaction with the neighborhood and a digital marketplace for applications (consumer to consumer). The need for this functionality is driven by the need for social cohesion; and (2) an **information exchange platform** between providers and end-users (business to consumer), driven by the need for matchmaking between service providers and end-users; and (3) a **portal** for bundled services and solutions (business to consumer), driven by the one-stop-shop philosophy for 'ageing in place', were end-users can find all relevant applications in the smart living domain, but also can create a personal profile; and (4) an **intervention instrument** for the municipality (government to consumer) to get in contact with citizens about needs for services and questions about health care legislations (i.e., AWBZ, WMO legislations) and to get insight in transaction costs. During the alternating cycles of discussions this input from different angles lead to a general first idea about a novel artifact that can be applied in the health and wellbeing domain. Although it is not clear yet if all features elicited by the interviewees can be included in one and the same platform, it is a feasible option to combine suggestions to create, retain, transfer and exchange information in the smart living domain. Ultimately, such a platform should (1) enable end-users to enhance their quality of life, and (2) support matchmaking between different stakeholders. While end-users stress the social and communication element of an online platform for health and wellbeing, providers focus on information exchange and transaction features. To attain a critical mass of both providers and end-users, the platform should thus integrate the communication, information and transaction features. Another potential tension results from the focus of stakeholders on the governmental level. The currently changing regulations on care in the Netherlands lead to a more narrow focus of government stakeholders on tools that support the regulatory transition. The results indicate that such narrow focus may not be acceptable by the more commercial providers and end-users. Our results illustrate the multiplicity requirements for platform functions, ranging from basic information exchange towards active recommendations for services and matchmaking, and from pure focus on transactions towards communication among users on one side of the platform. Strategic and affiliate stakeholders and end-users stress rather different design issues that warrant most attention for designing the platform. To a large extent, these differences can be explained through the interests and objectives of these stakeholder groups. However, the findings do suggest that a viable platform for health and wellbeing will require taking into account a variety of design issues.

7 Conclusions and Next Steps

This paper elicits four main features of a platform for health and wellbeing: (1) online community, (2) information exchange, (3) portal, and (4) (health) intervention instrument. It illustrates the multifaceted nature of platforms and the diversity of features they may support. Importantly, we show that different stakeholder groups emphasize different platform features as a focus point. This complexity is increased by regulatory transitions that make especially government stakeholders have a narrow focus on the platform features. The study contributes to design knowledge of digital platforms, by showing what could be possible platform features and indicating the critical design issues in the design of such a service platform. We argue that designing a multi-sided platform can only be done by addressing end-users' as well as external stakeholder needs in concert, and addressing the value proposition as well as the business model. Considering the first hunch of a matchmaking platform it demands collaboration of stakeholders in multiple sectors to contribute required resources and to find catalyst innovators to start and accelerate a catalytic reaction. To get multi groups on board at the same time to create value in an exchange platform is already partly covered by stakeholder groups (i.e., government, providers and end-user groups) that want to participate in the project. Next to that, issues such as access methods, but also user-adoption and usability are important topics.

Our future research aims to study this issue using Action Design Research (ADR) to develop design knowledge on how to develop and launch a multi-sided platform while dealing with end-users as well as external stakeholders.

To test if the interviews are rigorous and valid, multiple focus groups, a workshop and a survey will be conducted (i.e., mixed method) to validate the first two steps of the design cycle (i.e., awareness of the problem and first suggestion) and to elicit the technical specifications of the platform. Taken into account that we are at the start of our research, these steps will be used to develop the tentative design of a health and wellbeing platform and to prototype a social infrastructure based on agile scrum.

References

1. Nikayin, F., De Reuver, M.: Opening up the smart home: a classification of smart living service platforms. Int. J. E-services Mob. Appl. **5**(2), 37–53 (2013)
2. Peine, A.: Technol. Forecast. Soc. Chang. **76**(3), 396–409 (2009)
3. Wichert, R., Furfari, F., Kung, A., Tazari, M.R.: How to overcome the market entrance barrier and achieve the market breakthrough in AAL. In: Wichert, R., Eberhardt, B. (eds.) Ambient Assisted Living. ATSC, vol. 2, pp. 349–358. Springer, Heidelberg (2012)
4. Solaimani, S., Bouwman, H., Baken, N.: The smart home landscape: a qualitative meta-analysis. In: Abdulrazak, B., Giroux, S., Bouchard, B., Pigot, H., Mokhtari, M. (eds.) ICOST 2011. LNCS, vol. 6719, pp. 192–199. Springer, Heidelberg (2011)
5. Grönroos, C.: Service logic revisited: who creates value? And who co-creates? Eur. Bus. Rev. **20**(4), 298–314 (2008)
6. Weiser, M.: The computer for the 21st century. Palo Alto, Research Center: Xerox, CA, USA (1991)
7. Pung, H.K., et al.: Context-aware middleware for pervasive elderly homecare. IEEE J. Sel. Areas Commun. **27**(4), 510–524 (2009)
8. Solaimani, S., Keijzer-Broers, W., Bouwman, H.: What we do - and don't - know about the Smart Home - An analysis of the Smart Home literature (IBE-13-0120) Indoor and Built Environment (2013)
9. Fitrianie, S., Huldtgren, A., Alers, H., Guldemond, N.A.: A SmartTV platform for wellbeing, care and social support for elderly at home. In: Biswas, J., Kobayashi, H., Wong, L., Abdulrazak, B., Mokhtari, M. (eds.) ICOST 2013. LNCS, vol. 7910, pp. 94–101. Springer, Heidelberg (2013)
10. UN_Population_Division, World Population Ageing 2013, in ST/ESA/SER.A/348. 2013, United Nations, Department of Economic and Social Affairs, Population Division
11. Eurostat, Active ageing and solidarity between generations. A statistical portrait of the European Union, E. Commission, Editor (2012)
12. EC, CoR, and AGE. How to promote active ageing in Europe: EU support to local and regional actors (2011). http://europa.eu/ey2012/BlobServlet?docId=7005&langId=en (cited June 2013)
13. Aldrich, F.K.: Smart homes: past, present, and future. In: Harper, R. (ed.) Inside the Smart Home, pp. 17–39. Springer, London (2003)
14. Barlow, J., Venables, T.: Smart home, dumb suppliers? The future of smart homes markets. In: Harper, R. (ed.) Inside the Smart Home, pp. 247–262. Springer, London (2003)
15. Jacobzone, S., Cambois, E, Robine, J.M.: The health of older persons in OECD countries: is it improving fast enough to compensate for population ageing?. In: Labour Market and Social Policy Occasional Papers, pp. 149–190. OECD, Paris (1999)
16. Da Roit, B.: Long-term care reforms in the Netherlands. In: Ranci, C., Pavolini, E. (eds.) Reforms in Long-Term Care Policies in Europe, pp. 97–115. Springer, New York (2013)

17. Hagiu, A.: Proprietary vs. Open two-sided platforms and social efficiency (2006)
18. Evans, D., Schmalensee, R.: Failure to launch: critical mass in platform businesses. Soc. Sci. Res. Netw. (2010)
19. Gawer, A.: Platform dynamics and strategies: from products to services. In: Gawer, A. (ed.) Platforms, Markets and Innovation, pp. 45–76. Edward Elgar, Northampton (2009)
20. Evans, D.: How catalysts ignite: the economics of platform-based start-ups. In: Gawer, A. (ed.) Platforms Markets and Innovation. Elgar Publishing, Cheltenham (2009)
21. Boudreau, K.J., Hagiu, A.: Platform rules: multi-sided platforms as regulators. In: Gawer, A. (ed.) Platforms, Markets and Innovation, pp. 163–191. Edward Elgar Publishing Limited, Cheltenham (2009)
22. Tilson, D., Lyytinen, K., Sørensen, C.: Research commentary-digital infrastructures: the missing is research agenda. Inf. Syst. Res. 21(4), 748–759 (2010)
23. West, J.: How open is open enough? Res. Policy 32(7), 1259–1285 (2003)
24. Nikayin, F.: Common platform dilemmas: collective action and the internet of things. In: Technology, Policy and Management - Engineering, Systems and Services 2014. Delft University of Technology, The Netherlands (2014)
25. Smith, A., Fischbacher, M., Wilson, F.: New service development: from panoramas to precision. Eur. Manag. J. 25(5), 370–383 (2007)
26. Räisänen, V.: Service modeling: principles and applications. Wiley, Chichester (2008)
27. Hevner, A., et al.: Design science in information systems research. MIS Q. 28(1), 75–105 (2004)
28. Verschuren, P., Hartog, R.: Evaluation in design-oriented research. Qual. Quant. 39(6), 733–762 (2005)
29. Kuechler, W., Vaishnavi, V.: On theory development in design science research: anatomy of a research project. Eur. J. Inf. Syst. 17(5), 1–23 (2008)
30. Van Aken, J.E.: Management research based on the paradigm of the design sciences: the quest for field-tested and grounded technological rules. J. Manage. Stud. 41(2), 219–246 (2004)
31. Livari, J.: A paradigmatic analysis of information systems as a design science. Scand. J. Inf. Syst. 19(2), 39–64 (2007)
32. Simon, H.: The Sciences of Artificial, 3rd edn. MIT Press, Cambridge (1996)
33. Sein, M., et al.: Action design research. MIS Q. 35(1), 37–56 (2011)
34. Keijzer-Broers, W.J.W., de Reuver, M., Guldemond, N.A.: Designing a matchmaking platform for smart living services. In: Biswas, J., Kobayashi, H., Wong, L., Abdulrazak, B., Mokhtari, M. (eds.) ICOST 2013. LNCS, vol. 7910, pp. 224–229. Springer, Heidelberg (2013)

Design and Usability of a Smart Home Sensor Data User Interface for a Clinical and Research Audience

Mary Sheahen[1](✉) and Marjorie Skubic[2]

[1] Department of Computer Science, University of Missouri,
Columbia, MO 65211, USA
misq4f@mail.missouri.edu
[2] Department of Electrical and Computer Engineering,
University of Missouri, Columbia, MO 65211, USA
skubicm@missouri.edu

Abstract. Motion, bed, and gait analysis sensors are installed in the homes of seniors and monitored continuously for the purpose of detecting early signs of health change and functional decline. Automated health alerts are sent to clinical staff as part of a clinical decision support system. Embedded in each health alert is a link to a web interface for interactively displaying the sensor data patterns. The health alerts facilitate early interventions; however, the design and usability of the web interface greatly affect the effectiveness of the clinical decision support system. Here, we present the analysis and redesign of the interactive web-based interface for displaying the in-home sensor data. The current design is analyzed for inconsistencies and potential user frustrations, and a new design is proposed to correct these problems.

Keywords: User-centered interface · Iterative design · Web interface design · Usability

1 Introduction

In this paper, we discuss the analysis and redesign of a web-based interface for displaying in-home sensor data. Different types of sensor data are collected in the homes of seniors in order to capture health status and activity [1]. Sensors installed in the home include passive infrared (PIR) motion sensors, a bed sensor for capturing pulse, respiration, and sleep patterns, and a Microsoft Kinect device for capturing in-home gait and fall risk. Using these sensors, our team of engineers, computer scientists, and clinicians has developed algorithms that recognize changes in sensor data patterns that correspond to possible declines in health status or functional ability. When such a decline is detected, a health alert is automatically generated and sent to the clinical staff and research team via email [2]. Embedded in the health alert email is a link to a web-based interface for viewing the sensor data interactively. This allows for efficient access to the data and, with a well-designed interface, effective interpretation of the sensor data and the context in which the alert was generated.

© Springer International Publishing Switzerland 2015
C. Bodine et al. (Eds.): ICOST 2014, LNCS 8456, pp. 13–20, 2015.
DOI: 10.1007/978-3-319-14424-5_2

The system functions as a clinical decision support system. Health alerts showing early signs of health change or functional decline allow the clinical staff to assess the seniors at the beginning of the problem and offer timely interventions [3]. Health changes are addressed early before they become serious health problems. Thus, it is important that the interface be intuitive, interactive, and flexible to accommodate different views and allow the clinicians to display the sensor data in the context of individualized behavioral and activity patterns.

Recently, our team has added sensors to the health alert system, namely a new bed sensor that captures quantitative pulse, respiration, and restless in bed [4–6] as well as the Kinect-based in-home gait analysis system [7]. With the addition of the new sensors, we started a redesign effort to integrate the new, more finely grained sensor data into our web interface. The interface has been evaluated on a weekly basis by the research team, and changes are made in order to improve usability. In a continuing study, this interface will eventually be modified so that senior residents themselves are able to view their data. Since most of the seniors are over the age of 70 and have varying levels of sensory limitations, the differences in user expectations and capabilities must be taken into account when designing an efficient interface.

Other research teams have developed in-home sensor systems for the purpose of early detection of health change, e.g., [8] but not all rely on user interfaces as part of a clinical decision support system. Hussain et al. proposed an architecture and a web application design for a monitoring network [9]. Cuddihy et al. introduced a visualization display as a summary for activity [10]. As part of our team's earlier work, Wang et al. proposed the density map as a visualization and summary of motion density and out of home activity patterns [11]; Galambos et al. showed how these can be used clinically [12]. Alexander et al. presented results of a usability study on the user interface [13]. In more recent work, Le et al. and Reeder et al. have explored visual displays of in-home sensor data that are suitable for elderly users [14, 15]. These related studies show the possibilities in using a variety of sensors for in-home monitoring and visualization.

In this paper, our focus is on designing a user interface that supports the health alerts as a means of early detection of health change and functional decline such that early interventions are possible. We begin in Sect. 2 by first analyzing the Version 1 system for inconsistencies and potential user frustrations. In Sect. 3, we present our improved design. We conclude in Sect. 4 with a discussion of future work.

2 Analysis of Previous System and Components

The previous web-based interface (Version 1) displays data on a series of time based graphs. Researchers are able to log in to the web system, select a research subject's ID, and then query the sensor database to return data given a date range. This interface has been used for several years in previous studies of evaluating in-home sensor data in the past [2, 3]. By default, the user is shown data over a 2 week period which gives an aggregate or average value for each day. When the user wants to see more precise data, she can click on a data point and then is taken to a chart which shows data for each hour. The previous interface also contains information about the smart homes and senior residents, such as what sensors each resident has installed, floor plans, and a history of health alerts for that resident.

2.1 Inconsistent Grouping of Controls and Poor Navigation Between Charts

Once users choose a resident, they are shown a web page of varying charts, each one showing a different measure, yet colors and styles of charts are displayed almost exactly the same, causing extra cognitive load on the user by having to inspect each title carefully to find the chart they are looking for [16]. The charts are labeled with the measure they are presenting; however, it is not prominent. For example, see Fig. 1. Users have reported that this is a problem.

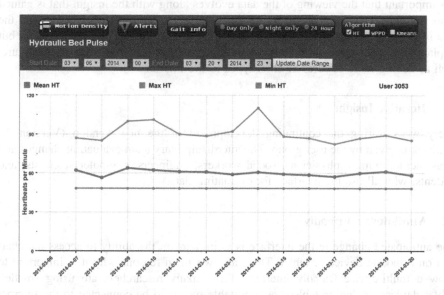

Fig. 1. Screen-shot of chart for viewing pulse captured from the hydraulic bed sensor. Note that the use of space seems cluttered, and that the navigation bar contains date ranges with multiple drop-downs. Many unrelated buttons are placed at the top of the page

Another problem is that the bar above each chart contains several buttons that have no correlation to each other and have different types of functionality. For example, one button labeled alerts will redirect you to another page, yet toggling check buttons labeled algorithm will affect the actual chart data. This leads to extra visual search by the user to determine what each button does and can cause fatigue in the user [17].

2.2 Frustrations in Navigating Through Time Data

Possibly the largest frustration for research users is that, in the Version 1 system, navigating through time can be cumbersome. The user must continually select a date range in which to view (using a cumbersome interface), and then re-submit the page. Having to go through these steps every time does not result in a flexible navigation system because it forces the user to use mental math to compute which dates are relative to the ones currently being displayed [16].

Another frustration is that if there are no data present for that user during the requested time period, the site will simply show an orange screen, with no other information other than an error loading the chart. This is not an effective use of feedback, which further adds to user frustration [17].

3 Version 2

As the research of the in-home sensor network expands and more measures are added, it is important that the viewing of the data evolves along with the insight that is gained from studying. Development of a new user-interface is an ongoing process, and the idea is to not only improve upon issues that were present in the Version 1 system, but to plan for expansion and better accommodate changes that may arise in the future, such as adding more features or chart types to the interface.

3.1 Iterative Insight

Every week during the continuing development of the new version (Version 2), feedback is given by the user group. The interdisciplinary team evaluating changes and ideas include nurses, physicians, social workers, engineers, computer scientists, and students, who all use the interface for evaluating data.

3.2 Multi-device Friendly

One anticipated change in the interface is to implement the ability to access the chart data on a mobile device or tablet. There are two main reasons why it is important to allow a multi-device friendly interface. First, many researchers are using smaller, lighter devices, including tablets, as a portable means to be connected to the Internet while they are on the move. Making the website tablet-accessible allows research to be more convenient to these types of users, decreasing the likelihood of user frustration. The other reason is that with a touch screen, it may be easier for some users to access data; accessing the interface with a mouse or keyboard may cause more strain on users with limited mobility, such as those with arthritis.

In order to satisfy the need for a multi-device interface, a few major changes in design and tools were made in Version 2. First, the charting library now uses HTML5 and Javascript libraries including Flot.js instead of a Flash based product. Adobe Flash is not supported on mobile devices, whereas using HTML5 allows easy porting across browsers and platforms. Another change that was necessary was to make the website sensitive to different device and window sizes using Responsive Web Design [17] and media queries placed in the CSS. Responsiveness in the website will allow the same page to be viewed on varying devices, and look proportionate and relevant as the screen size decreases.

3.3   Improvement on Time Navigation

In order to reduce frustration in time navigation and to enable the user to have better control over date ranges, a range selection tool is used in Version 2. Allowing a user to adjust and move a window easily without having to re-load the page is an efficient interaction [16, 17] because it reduces the time and thought put into changing the date range as was required for Version 1. The new date range selection bar is shown in Fig. 2.

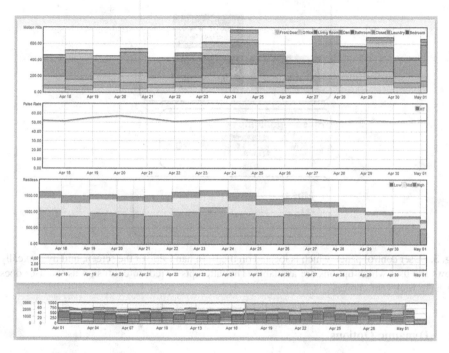

Fig. 2. View of sensor data on the improved Version 2 interface showing motion data (row 1) pulse rate (row 2), and bed restlessness (row 3). Notice the time range selection bar at the bottom (row 4). The highlighted date range is the range displayed in the large view.

3.4   Visual Controls

The improved user-interface uses visual controls in order to tell the user what is selected (Fig. 3). The user can see by referencing the control panel, which can be seen at all times on the right hand side of the screen. Features of the graph which are plotted have been highlighted, indicating that they are on. To turn a feature on or off, the user simply has to click the button to toggle it. The logical organization and consistency of these controls reduces the visual search required, leading to a more user-centered design [17].

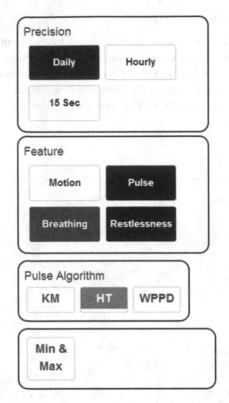

Fig. 3. User control panel, which is located on the right hand side of the screen, and dynamically shows the user which options are available. This attempts to reduce confusion as the user does not have irrelevant choices.

3.5   Dynamic Options

One feature of the Version 2 interface is that users have control over what measures to add to the graphical display. For example, Fig. 2 shows stacked histograms of motion sensor data, a graph of pulse rate below, and stacked histograms of bed restlessness below that. Viewing features together was a suggestion made by the research team during the iterative design process. However, there are still measures that the user is more likely to want to see than others. This leads to the decision of what to put as defaults. The use of defaults can increase the pace of work [17] by anticipating the most likely scenario that the user will want.

One problem that may arise from dynamic options is that the user may be overwhelmed by too many options, causing mental fatigue and frustration. As the study continues, there will be more insight into how much control by the user is too much control. For now, one way of helping the user to not get overwhelmed is to only show options on the control panel that are relevant to the current display. For instance, if users view a chart showing the restlessness, breathing rate, and pulse rate for a senior, they will have the option to change the pulse algorithm. However, if they are only viewing restlessness and breathing rate, the 'Pulse Algorithm' sub-panel will be hidden. This reduces irrelevant information as well as unnecessary visual search [16, 17].

For the Version 2 interface, once a research subject ID is selected, the default is to show only the motion sensor data for the past month calculated at the daily precision level. The reason for this default is that researchers generally like to see a view of the senior resident's general activity patterns over a broad time period if the interface is accessed from an alert email [3].

4 Future Work

The analysis and redesign have brought numerous improvements to the web interface design. However, there are still aspects that will need to be improved, as it is an ongoing development project. As the interface continues to evolve, more specific features for varying user types will be formed. Usability testing will be performed on both tablet and desktop configurations, and adjustments will be made. Ultimately, we will investigate usability for senior users who may have cognitive, mobility, or visual impairments.

4.1 Accommodating Different User Types and Motivations

Viewing health-related data may have significant usability differences depending on the types of users that are accessing it. For this particular interface, there are at least three types of users: clinical researchers, technical researchers, and consumers (elderly users and their family members). The technical researchers tend to want access to precise data, as well as raw signals from the sensors, in order to easily see if their devices are working properly and how they work under different conditions. Clinical researchers also like to see a wide variety of measures, but less detailed information than the technical researchers. Consumers are the most different from the other two types. Generally, too much information for these users can be fatiguing, as raw signals or extra data are likely meaningless. However, general trends in health such as seeing the trend line of the average heart rate can be very meaningful. User differences such as these will be investigated as part of our future work.

References

1. Skubic, M., Alexander, G., Popescu, M., Rantz, M., Keller, J.: A smart home application to eldercare: current status and lessons learned. Technol. Health Care 17(3), 183–201 (2009)
2. Rantz, M.J., Skubic, M., Koopman, R.J., Alexander, G., Phillips, L., Musterman, K.I., Back, J.R., Aud, M.A., Galambos, C., Guevara, R.D., Miller, S.J.: Automated technology to speed recognition of signs of illness in older adults. J. Gerontological Nurs. 38(4), 18–23 (2012)
3. Rantz, M., Scott, S.D., Miller, S.J., Skubic, M., Phillips, L., Alexander, G., Koopman, R.J., Musterman, K., Back, J.: Evaluation of health alerts from an early illness warning system in independent living. Comput. Inform. Nurs. 31(6), 274–280 (2013)

4. Heise, D., Rosales, L., Sheahen, M., Su, B.Y., Skubic, M.: Non-invasive measurement of heartbeat with a hydraulic bed sensor: progress, challenges, and opportunities. In: Proceedings of the 2013 IEEE International Instrumentation & Measurement Technical Conference, Minneapolis, MN, pp. 4356–4360 (2013)
5. Rosales, L., Skubic, M., Heise, D., Devaney, M.J., Schaumburg, M.: Heartbeat detection from a hydraulic bed sensor using a clustering approach. In: Proceedings of the International Conference on IEEE Engineering in Medicine and Biology Society, San Diego, CA, pp. 2383–2387 (2012)
6. Su, B.Y., Ho, K.C., Skubic, M., Rosales, L.: Pulse rate estimation using hydraulic bed sensor. In: Proceedings of the International Conference on IEEE Engineering in Medicine and Biology Society, San Diego, CA, pp. 2587–2590 (2012)
7. Stone, E., Skubic, M.: Unobtrusive, continuous, In-HomeGait measurement using the microsoft kinect. IEEE Trans. Biomed. Eng. 60(10), 2925–2932 (2013)
8. Kaye, J., Maxwell, S., Mattek, N., Hayes, T., Dodge, H., Pavel, M., Jimison, H., Wild, K., Boise, L., Zitzelberger, T.: Intelligent systems for assessing aging changes: home-based, unobtrusive and continuous assessment of aging. J Geron. B Psych. Sci. 66B, 180–190 (2011)
9. Hussain, S., Enrdogen, S., Park, J.: Monitoring user activities in smart home environments. Inf. Syst. Front. 11, 539–549 (2009)
10. Cuddihy, P., Hinman, R.T., Avestruz, A., Lupton, E.C., Livshin, G., et al.: Successful aging. Pervasive Comput. 3(2), 48–50 (2004)
11. Wang, S., Skubic, M., Zhu, Y.: Activity density map visualization and dis-similarity comparison for eldercare monitoring. IEEE J. Biomed. Health Inf. 16(4), 607–614 (2012)
12. Galambos, C., Skubic, M., Wang, S., Rantz, M.: Management of dementia and depression utilizing in-home passive sensor data. Gerontechnology 11(3), 457–468 (2013)
13. Alexander, G.L., Wakefield, B.J., Rantz, M., Skubic, M., Aud, M., Erdelez, S., Ghenaimi, S.A.: Passive sensor technology interface to assess elder activity in independent living. J. Nurs. Res. 60(5), 318–325 (2011)
14. Le, T., Reeder, B., Chung, J., Thompson, H., Demiris, G.: Design of smart home sensor visualizations for older adults. Technol Health Care, July 2014
15. Reeder, B., Chung, J., Le, T., Thompson, H., Demiris, G.: Assessing older adults' perceptions of sensor data and designing visual displays for ambient environments: an exploratory study. Meth. Inf Med. 53(3), 152–159 (2014)
16. Smelcer, J.B., Miller-Jacobs, H., Kantrovich, L.: Usability of electronic medical records. J. Usability Stud. 4(2), 70–84 (2009)
17. U.S. Dept. of Health and Human Services. The Research-Based Web Design & Usability Guidelines, Enlarged/Expanded edition. Washington: U.S. Government Printing Office (2006)

EasiSocial: An Innovative Way of Increasing Adoption of Social Media in Older People

Kyle Boyd[(✉)], Chris Nugent, Mark Donnelly, Roy Sterritt,
Raymond Bond, and Lorraine Lavery-Bowen

School of Computing and Mathematics, Computer Science Research Institute
and Centre for Flexible and Continuing Education,
University of Ulster, Jordanstown, Northern Ireland, UK
boyd-k5@email.ulster.ac.uk,
{cd.nugent,mp.donnelly,r.sterrit,rb.bond,
l.lavery-bowen}@ulster.ac.uk

Abstract. Online Social Networking has become one of the biggest successes of the Internet. Facebook is the most popular service with over 1.23 billion users. Online Social Networks have the potential to combat feelings of social isolation amongst the aging population. Nevertheless, many older people do not use online social networks given the barriers resulting from a lack of understanding and perceived usefulness. This paper presents the findings from a ten week training course were participants were trained in the use of Facebook and EasiSocial, a newly introduced web application which displays Facebook in a manner which is more suitable for older people. An evaluation study was undertaken of both applications in an effort to gain insight into the reasons why older people (50–80 years old) do not use social media. Findings demonstrated that EasiSocial was statistically easier to learn and easier to use than Facebook and therefore potentially helpful to increase the adoption of Social Media technologies.

Keywords: Social isolation · Technology adoption · Web 2.0 · Social media · Online social networks · Facebook

1 Introduction

Kaplan and Haenlein [1] define Social Media as a group of Internet technologies built on the platform of Web 2.0 technologies that allows the creation and exchange of user generated content. Web 2.0 can be categorised as a number of different types: collaboration, blogs and microblogs, content communities, social networking sites, virtual game worlds and virtual social worlds. Also included are picture sharing, email, instant messaging and voice over Internet protocol (VOIP) based communications. All of these can be integrated into online social networking (OSN) sites such as Facebook, which is currently the world's largest OSN with 1.23 billion users [2]. Facebook allows users to interact with friends. An interaction is defined as being a status update, making a comment, liking a comment or sharing a post.

Currently, in the United Kingdom (UK), 10.3 million people are aged 65 and over [3]. This represents 16 % of the total UK population. Latest figures show this will

© Springer International Publishing Switzerland 2015
C. Bodine et al. (Eds.): ICOST 2014, LNCS 8456, pp. 21–28, 2015.
DOI: 10.1007/978-3-319-14424-5_3

increase to 15 million over the next 20 years and is predicted to nearly double to around 19 million by 2050 (23 % of the UK population) [3, 4]. Traditionally "old age" has been associated with negative stereotypes of frailty, ill health and social and economic dependency, which can lead to social isolation. Previous research has suggested [5] that Information and Communication Technology (ICT) could be used to help connect those who are socially isolated to enable them to stay connected with family and friends. Social interactions allow people to share knowledge, expertise, new skills and help them feel that they are contributing to society as a whole. Nevertheless, the uptake of these socially enabled technologies is not always significant. Reasons for this can be partly attributed to poor education and training in the technologies available [6]. Boyd et al. have already considered how to increase Social Media adoption amongst elderly carers via training [7] and have conducted a usability test with Facebook [8]. Results from this study have indicated that such an OSN did not meet the needs of older people. The aim of the current work was to investigate if it was possible to change perceptions by explaining how Social Media works and to discover if training aids adoption by looking at a participants' abilities to engage with a light version of Social Media.

2 EasiSocial

In an effort to try and address these needs a web application was developed referred to as EasiSocial. This solution was designed to run in a web browser on a tablet. This application is a skin, which can be placed over the current Facebook interface and re-purposes the information from the OSN, which may be more suitable for use by older participants. To access Facebook, the Facebook SDK (Software Development Kit) for PHP was employed. This supports server side functionality to access the Facebook Graph Application Programming Interface (API) allowing developers to access and query user's data and newsfeeds from their Facebook profiles in addition to posting status updates and commenting upon updates. This supported EasiSocial with the ability to provide update status, commenting and viewing photos through the EasiSocial application.

Creation of EasiSocial was carefully undertaken following a combination of recommendations in designing user interfaces for older people as outlined by Caprani, O'Connor and Gurrin [9] in addition to the five golden rules written by SAP (Systems Analysis and Program Development):

- **Speed:** Make sure application runs fast
- **Intuitiveness:** Avoid making the user think about what they have to do
- **Choices:** Limit choices
- **Guidance:** Guide the user through the application
- **Testing:** Test the application with focus groups or observations

Designing for the Web can be problematic with inconsistent window widths, screen resolutions and user preferences being a number of the key challenges to overcome before the solution can be released. In addition, the plethora of devices currently available offer further challenges accommodating for differences in both hardware and software. Responsive Web design uses a combination of CSS 3 media queries.

These media queries allow the inspection of the physical characteristics of the device rendering the design. Media queries serve up a tailored style sheet for any device whether desktop, laptop, tablet or mobile.

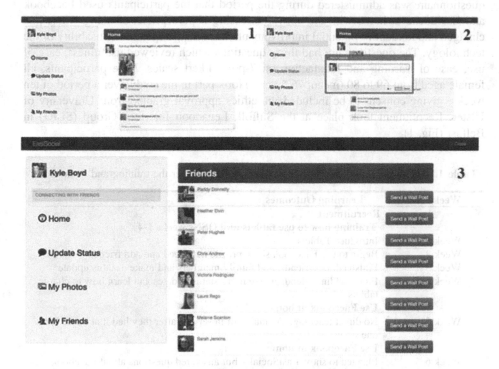

Fig. 1. Screenshots of the EasiSocial Web application (1) home news feed (2) Update status window and (3) Friends list with message button which was used by participants.

EasiSocial simplifies the regular Facebook interface by displaying a newsfeed, friends list and photos. Participants can write a status update, comment and send messages to friends. The numbers of steps to complete these interactions are shorter than on Facebook.

3 Method

An evaluation of both Facebook and EasiSocial was conducted over a 10 week period between December 2013 to February 2014 with 9 participants. All participants had never previously used Social Media or a tablet device and rated their mean computer literacy as 1.33 (1 being Novice, 7 being Expert). Participants were invited to undertake training using a Nexus tablet in how to use Facebook with a number of predefined tasks (update status, send a message and upload a photo and add friends) and then take the tablet home and use Facebook for the ensuing two weeks. At the end of the two week period the same process was completed, however, this time using EasiSocial as opposed to Facebook. The structure of the evaluation is presented in Table 1. A pre-evaluation questionnaire was administered to gather information in relation to the participant's background, gender, age and experience/level of usage with Social Media. A usability questionnaire was administered during the period that the participants used Facebook and EasiSocial at home with the aim of assessing if perceptions of using OSNs had changed and to identify potential improvements from the perspective of usability of the technology. The questionnaire had thirty questions which reviewed usefulness, ease of use, ease of learning and satisfaction on 7-point likert scales. Nine participants, all female aged from 69 to 80 (mean: 76.5 years) took part in the study over a period of ten weeks, giving consent to be included via ethics approval granted from University of Ulster. Recruitment took place at the Suffolk Lenadoon Interface Group (SLIG) in Belfast (Fig. 1).

Table 1. The weekly tasks completed by the participants over the training and evaluations.

Week	Learning Outcomes
	Recruitment
	Training how to use tablets and OSNs weeks 1-4
Week 1	Introduce Tablets
Week 2	Begin to use Facebook show profile newsfeed and add friends
Week 3	Finish adding friends, add family members and make a status update
Week 4	Finish adding friends, make more status updates and learn how to charge tablets
	Use Facebook at home
Week 5	No direct teaching. A small call in service after they had it at home for one week.
	Use Facebook at home
Week 6	Planned to show EasiSocial – but answered questions about Facebook and issues
	One week break
Week 7	Show EasiSocial – how to look at newsfeed, update status and reply to updates through comments
	Use EasiSocial at home
Week 8	Show EasiSocial – how to look at newsfeed, update status and reply to updates through comments
	Use EasiSocial at home
Week 9	Answer Queries on EasiSocial demo status update, messaging friends and commenting
Week 10	Administer last questionnaires

4   Results

All participants were provided training on how to use tablets and OSNs from weeks 1–4. Participants then took the tablets home for four weeks. Weeks 4–6 were intended for use with Facebook while weeks 7–9 prescribed the use of EasiSocial. The results from the evaluations are presented in the follow Sections.

4.1   Total Interactions per Participant

During the course of the study the number of interactions completed by each participant were recorded. An interaction was defined as being a status update, a comment, a share and a like. Participant P8 and P9 had the most interactions with 11 and 13, respectively.

4.2   Total Time Spent Using Facebook and EasiSocial

Comparing the usage of the two applications, as presented in Fig. 2, it is evident that Facebook had more usage in the first week than in other weeks, however, following this it decreased. The usage for EasiSocial peaked in the first week of usage, however, again usage was reduced to a similar level of Facebook to three and a half hours per week.

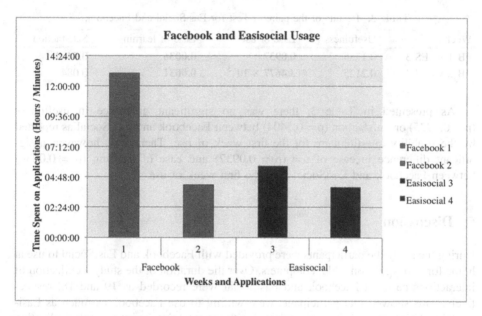

Fig. 2. Total time spent using Facebook and EasiSocial during the two evaluation periods for both applications by all participants.

4.3   The Usability Questionnaire

During the period when the participants used the tablets at home a usability question-naire was administered at the end of each week. This was used to understand how usable both applications were. The participants completed the same questionnaires for the two weeks they used Facebook (FB) at home and the two weeks when they used EasiSocial (ES) at home. The mean and standard deviation of each week is shown in Table 2.

A paired *t-test* (significance level 0.05) was conducted to compare the usefulness, ease of use, ease of learning and the satisfaction of use between Facebook and Easi-Social. These results are presented in Table 3.

Table 2. The mean and standard deviation of the responses from the usability questionnaire for each week Facebook and EasiSocial were used.

Weeks	Usefulness	Ease of use	Ease of learning	Satisfaction
FB 1 Mean	5.0286	4.2545	3.5000	5.0286
ST DEV	1.2264	0.6662	0.5863	0.8043
FB 2 Mean	4.0000	3.1455	2.2000	4.3143
ST DEV	1.8378	0.5126	1.1779	1.7391
ES 3 Mean	5.8000	5.2000	5.5000	5.4286
ST DEV	0.6194	0.6906	0.9186	1.1429
ES 4 Mean	5.3714	5.6909	5.7000	6.1714
ST DEV	0.8244	0.4921	0.6937	1.0222

Table 3. Results of the paired t-Test for EasiSocial and Facebook.

Weeks	Usefulness	Ease of use	Ease of learning	Satisfaction
FB 1 vs ES 3	0.1735	**0.0937**	**0.0036**	0.5404
FB 2 vs ES 4	0.2125	$\mathbf{3.4677 \times 10^{-5}}$	**0.0031**	0.0841

As presented in Table 3, there was no significant difference in usefulness (p = 0.1735) or satisfaction (p = 0.5404) between Facebook and EasiSocial as reported by the usability questionnaire for the first week of use. There was, however, a significant difference in ease of use (p = 0.0937) and ease of learning (p = 0.0036) between Facebook and EasiSocial after the first week of use.

5   Discussion

During the study the participants were provided with Facebook and EasiSocial to use at home for two weeks on tablet computers. Over the duration of the study a collection of interactions between Facebook and EasiSocial were recorded as 19 and 18, respectively. This showed that participants were willing to use Facebook as much as EasiSocial and vice versa. This also correlated with the total time spent on each application as depicted in Fig. 2 which showed the time spent on each application. Week 1 of the study was reported to have had considerable usage. This is understandable given that this was the first week that participants had the tablets at home. The uniqueness of having Facebook and a tablet encouraged use. Nevertheless, if one examines weeks 2, 3 and 4 it can be noted that all participants recorded similar levels of usage of between 3–5 h per week between both applications.

Usability questionnaires were administered over the four weeks that the applications were used at home. When a paired *t-test* was conducted on each application for the two weeks of use no significant findings were found. When the first week versus the third week was compared (these were the first time each application was used at home) and the second and fourth week there was a significant difference in the ease of use and ease of learning, with EasiSocial scoring better on both occasions. This is representative that for first time use EasiSocial was easier to learn and easier to use. The average age of participants was 76 and all owned and used a mobile phone to receive and make calls, two also reported to use their phones to send and receive text messages. In Fig. 2 the interactions of the nine participants are presented. Both P8 and P9 have the most interactions with 11 and 13 during the two evaluation periods at home weeks 4–6 and 7–9. Both P8 and P9 texted on mobile phones whilst the other participants did not. P8 was a medical receptionist and had some experience of computers before retirement. P9 had a very large family with many of them Facebook users. This encouraged P9 to use EasiSocial more and stay in contact. P9's profile grew more rapidly than the other participants as family members tagged them in photos they uploaded. P2 and P6 also had large families, however, their previous jobs, while skilled, did not include any use of technology. There sheer willingness to learn about Social Media and particularly OSNs was what made them so willing to participate. At the end of the study, all nine participants completed a post evaluation questionnaire. When asked outright which application they preferred three liked EasiSocial, three liked both and one liked Facebook better. They liked to keep up to date with family and look at family pictures, just to allow them to communicate, especially with family living abroad. Compared to Facebook they felt that EasiSocial was easier to use and less complicated, making it easier to find friends and send them messages. Of all the participants 71 % said that they would continue to use OSNs and 86 % thought that EasiSocial was a good way to start using OSNs given its simplicity. P9 said:

"I liked using EasiSocial because I missed one of the weeks and it allowed me to get up to speed, but then as I got better I preferred to use Facebook. So I would say EasiSocial is a great way to learn about Social Media and to learn about it but once the penny drops move to Facebook."

At the end of the evaluation period three of the participants had purchased tablets during the training and two were considering purchasing them upon its conclusion. They stated they hadn't realised how useful tablets could be if it hadn't been for the training. Three participants did not finish the evaluations or training, lack of interest and perceived usefulness was the most common outcome. Due to technical constraints there were some limitations. It was necessary for participants to have a Facebook account before they could use EasiSocial. Therefore participants trained how to use Facebook first and then EasiSocial. This gave them some previous experience in using Facebook. When planning the study it had been suggested to test two groups one with Facebook, the other with EasiSocial. It was, however, not possible to do so due to the low number of participants who consented to take part in the study. Future work may look at this possibility.

6 Conclusion

To conclude, in this study we have demonstrated the potential of training older people to use Web 2.0 technology and OSN to help alleviate the problem of social isolation in older people. By giving special training and consideration to usability in technology design, which suits older users needs, it is possible to increase adoption. Results from the study conducted demonstrated that EasiSocial, a web based application, was both statistically easier to learn and easier to use than regular Facebook. This could be used as a training application prior to moving to regular Facebook. Participants who engaged in the study, which was undertaken had never used a tablet or Social Media before, however, by the end of the evaluation period three had purchased tablets. This is a clear indication that the introduction to Social Media increased adoption to both contemporary technology and social networks. The findings from the study will be used in the future to continue developing the EasiSocial application and further usability evaluations are planned along with recommendations for developing training materials for older people regarding Social Media. Nevertheless the study did have some limitations. Due to technical restraints it was necessary for participants to have a Facebook account before they could use EasiSocial. Therefore participants trained how to use Facebook first and then EasiSocial. This gave them some previous experience and bias in using Facebook. When planning the study it had been suggested to test two groups one with Facebook, the other with EasiSocial. It was however not possible to do so because of the low number of participants who consented to take part in the study.

Acknowledgements. The authors wish to acknowledge the Self Management project at the University of Ulster who provided the tablets used within this study. Invest Northern Ireland is acknowledged for supporting this project under the R and D grant RD0513844.

References

1. Kaplan, A.M., Haenlein, M.: Users of the world, unite! The challenges and opportunities of Social Media. Bus. Horiz. **53**, 59–68 (2010)
2. Facebook, 24 January 2012. Facebook Home Page. http://www.facebook.com
3. Rutherford, T.: Population ageing: Statistics, House of Commons, London, Technical report SN/SG/3228, 0/02/12 (2012)
4. Office for National Statistics. "Population ageing in the united kingdom, its constituent countries and the european union," 02 March 2012
5. Goswami, S., Köbler, F., Leimeister, J.M., Krcmar, H.: Using online social networking to enhance social connectedness and social support for the elderly (2010)
6. Independent Age, "Older people, technology and community: The potential of technology to help older people renew or develop social contacts and to actively engage in their communities," Calouste Gulbenkian Foundation (2011)
7. Boyd, K., Nugent, C., Donnelly, M., Bond, R., Sterritt, R., Gibson, L.: Investigating methods for increasing the adoption of social media amongst carers for the elderly. In: Roa Romero, L.M. (ed.) XIII Mediterranean Conference on Medical and Biological Engineering and Computing 2013. IFMBE Proceedings, vol. 41, pp. 1439–1442. Springer, Heidelberg (2014)
8. Boyd, K., Nugent, C., Donnelly, M., Sterritt, R., Bond, R.: A usability protocol for evaluating online social networks. In: Donnelly, M., Paggetti, C., Nugent, C., Mokhtari, M. (eds.) ICOST 2012. LNCS, vol. 7251, pp. 222–225. Springer, Heidelberg (2012)
9. Caprani, N., O'Connor, N.E., Gurrin, C.: Touch screens for the older user. In: Auat Cheein, F. (ed.) Assistive Technologies, pp. 95–118 (2012)

Agile Development for the Creation of Proper Human-Computer Interfaces for the Elderly

Drew Williams[1](✉), Mong-Te Wang[2], Chih-Hung Chang[3],
Sheikh Iqbal Ahamed[1], and William Chu[2]

[1] Department of Mathematics, Statistics and Computer Science,
Marquette University, Milwaukee, WI, USA
{drew.williams, sheikh.ahamed}@marquette.edu

[2] Department of Computer Science, Tunghai University, Taichung, Taiwan
{shaka, cchu}@thu.edu.tw

[3] Department of Computer Science and Information Engineering,
Hsiuping University of Science and Technology, Taichung, Taiwan
chchang@mail.hust.edu.tw

Abstract. While computers may greatly enhance the lives of the elderly, many software developers fail to create human-computer interfaces that properly appeal to elderly users. Developers often fail to take into consideration the elderly user from the beginning, and the elderly now face a variety of challenges when using most applications. We believe that the adoption of a modified agile development workflow when developing human-computer interfaces for the elderly will assist in better integrating an inclusive design into applications as early as possible. Agile development relies heavily on user feedback, which is imperative in the development of elderly-friendly human-computer interfaces where the target audience has a diverse set of abilities.

Keywords: Human computer interfaces · Elderly people · Agile development · Software engineering practices · Software development

1 Introduction

In recent years, the everyday use of desktop and mobile computers has grown in leaps and bounds. Such devices hold great usefulness for the elderly, though manufacturers of applications and devices often fail to adapt their user interfaces for the elderly user. Buttons that are too small or strangely placed may not be optimal for those with visual impairments or differing abilities in regard to their motor skills, and alert tones that are not of proper volume may be lost on those with hearing loss. In addition, if an interface is too cluttered for a user to figure out how to edit features, allowing a user to adjust settings might end up causing more problems than solutions!

The best way to address the problem of developing elderly-friendly human-computer interfaces would be to take steps in working such requirements into applications early in the development process. While a variety of different development strategies exist, agile development is one strategy that perfectly coincides with the requirements of developing for the elderly individual. As a rule, agile development

© Springer International Publishing Switzerland 2015
C. Bodine et al. (Eds.): ICOST 2014, LNCS 8456, pp. 29–38, 2015.
DOI: 10.1007/978-3-319-14424-5_4

workflows insist on adaptability, collaborative efforts, simplicity, and customer feed-back [1], all of which make it an understandable choice for developing for the elderly. Adaptability means the developer can react to the variety requirements they will need to consider, as well as new hardware that might assist users with varying abilities. Collaboration between the user and the developer, in addition to acquiring prompt customer feedback, can help a developer properly assess how to adjust user interface designs to make them more intuitive, while avoiding overestimating *or* underestimating the elderly users' knowledge of computers [2, 3]. Simplicity is desirable in interfaces for the elderly as well – many elderly users are not experienced with computers.

However, it should also be mentioned that agile development process might further be adapted so it caters in particular to the development of human-computer interfaces for the elderly. The existing agile process breaks the development of applications into a series of weeks, where a number of tasks are given high focus so they may be com-pleted and working software is pushed at the end of the time period [1]. Adapting the sprint workflow to allow a period of user testing between individual sprints, as well as a set timeframe for implementing tutorials at the end of the application's 'completion', would also allow for verification of the app's ease of use, and allow feedback from the target audience to be gathered.

In this paper, we propose the use of an adjusted agile development workflow when developing human-computer interfaces for the elderly. We begin by briefly giving our motivation for this conclusion, and an explanation of the agile development process. We then discuss the different development goals the agile development process helps one achieve via the goals of the agile development process. After this, we discuss the steps of a modified agile development plan, which includes communication with a diverse group of potential users, setting aside extra time for tutorials and user testing, and rapid inclusion of useful implementations for accessible interfaces. Finally, we give a brief case study to illustrate the process overall, and set about drawing conclusions overall about utilizing agile development in creating elderly-friendly human-computer interfaces.

2   Motivation

Our general motivation for using the process of agile development when creating human-computer interfaces for the elderly is to ease developers into the notion of creating more elderly-friendly human computer interfaces. This has great benefits for both parties. For the elderly user, it allows them to benefit from the application-based assistance, and use new varieties of technology in their everyday lives. For the developer, it allows them to expand the target market for a given application, and thus help a wider number of people with their apps and devices. In particular, we're con-centrating on the following goals.

New target markets for an existing application. The elderly population in many countries is on the rise [4, 5], and as a result creating elderly-friendly human-computer interfaces can assist new startups and established companies alike in selling their applications.

Ability for the elderly user to use a wider variety of applications. If application development takes into account the fact that an elderly user might want to use an app from the start, it will be easier for an elderly as well as a younger user to use popular applications at the same time. This means that an elderly adult and their grandchildren, for instance, could together use a messaging or communications app with little difficulty and stay in touch in an easier fashion, without the elderly user being embarrassed by their lack of knowledge, which is often a problem [6] or the younger user being exasperated by an overly-simplified interface.

Ability for the elderly user to stay independent in their old age. Elderly users benefit greatly from application-based assistance - especially mobile applications. Age is linked to a number of sensory disabilities, including vision, hearing and cognitive impairments [7]. Utilization of applications to help elderly users remember things they have to do or assist them in getting to places they need to go can positively affect their independence, which can be quite hurt by having sensory impairments [8].

By focusing on creating a development methodology that best accompanies development for the elderly user, these goals stay in sight without any extra work on the part of the developer. This makes developing for the elderly user easier for the developer, and ensures that it will take priority in the developer's mind.

3   Goals of Agile Development

In more recent years, there has been an influx of support for agile development methodologies. Instead of previous software development methodologies, which prioritize business developments such as contracts over interaction with people and proper requirements gathering, agile expects rapidly changing requirements, and prioritizes proper communication and constant, frequent deliverables. While there are multiple types of agile development methodologies, all of them keep several major goals in mind when developing software.

3.1   Adaptability

Agile software development seeks to be adaptive to new and changing requirements as a rule; changing requirements are welcomed, even late in development [1]. In this way, agile software development truly is agile; it adapts to new obstacles as they pop up. Requirements must be properly talked over with the customer and fully decided upon in a series of meetings. Software is developed in short bouts and is expected to be delivered frequently, while adapting to user needs [1]. This means that goal-setting procedures often need to be adjusted accordingly [1]. The agile process of quick bouts of development continues until a project is fully completed, and may extend as bug fixes may require.

3.2   Simplicity

While one should pay attention to technical excellence and great design, the simplest solution for a problem should be used. Maximizing the amount of work that does not need to be done is important for keeping development timely and efficient [1]. Requirements should also be confined to what a customer states - additional requirements will be mentioned (and adapted to) as needed [1].

3.3   Communication

It is often suggested that collaboration should occur face-to-face [1], which will assist in reducing miscommunications so regularly seen otherwise. This is especially important in making sure that progress continues to be made in development - in agile development methodologies, progress is determined by working software, so teams need to work quickly to finish software so that it can be verified by other members of the team, and progress can continue.

While agile downplays other aspects of software development, such as documentation, keeping these people-oriented goals in mind can greatly assist in the timely development of quality software. Furthermore, these goals remain priority, even when one is involving themselves in other agile methodologies - differences between the tactics exist, but they don't detract from the overall agile goals.

4   Applying Agile Development Workflows to Creating Proper Applications for Elderly Users

While keeping these goals in mind for any software project has proven to be a good strategy, they become quite handy in particular when designing elderly-friendly human-computer interfaces. Particular goals of agile development line up perfectly with requirements to consider when developing for the elderly user. In particular, the following aspects of the agile methodology can assist with the following unique goals of developing proper interfaces for elderly adults.

4.1   Adaptability and Diversity of Elderly Ability

An elderly person might encounter a variety of problems when using a computer app. For one, declination in visual ability is common with old age, including but not limited to a decline in visual acuity, peripheral vision, color contrast, and dark adaptation [9, 10]. As a result, small buttons, poor color choices, flashy animations/popups and dim screens can lead to frustration on part of the user. In addition, by the age of 65, half of men and 30 % of women experience some degree of hearing loss that affects their ability to interact with others [9]. The range of pitches the ear can detect also may decrease [10]. Auditory displays that do not sound at a proper volume and pitch can easily be lost on the elderly user, causing apps that do things such as remind an elderly user to take medication or alert an elderly user to problems in traffic, to become less useful in the long run. However, complicating efforts to solve human factors problems like these is the variety of abilities found in the elderly – not all encounter the poor vision and frailty that some have! This means that software developed with older users in mind should be adaptable for a variety of users.

The adaptability of the agile work environment thus makes it a perfect fit for developing for the elderly user! Developers taking part in agile development methodologies seek to communicate with the target audience to best determine requirements – something that is required in elderly interface development. Furthermore, as new requirements come up as a result of user testing (i.e. a color scheme not having enough contrast) an agile development team will find themselves better able to adapt to such things. Adapting to include new physical interfaces for an application – such as pen tablets, haptic touchscreens [11] or gesture-based input – would also be favorable, as a newly developed input, although unfamiliar, may offer a better experience for the elderly user than an existing one.

4.2 Communication and Working with Your Target Audience

Because in part of the diverse ability set of the elderly mentioned above, communication with the elderly users within your target audience is essential. A study carried out in 2011 by Valentine, et al. showed that communication with elderly users allowed developers to better understand not only their abilities, but also morals and mindsets, which can be important in developing proper applications for the elderly [12]. In fact, groups in the study who did not carry out the aforementioned communication later wished they could have done it, and some set out to interview people they knew in lieu of the official interviews [12].

As one of the core principles of agile development is communication with one's target audience, such helpful communication will be expected of those developing with agile methodologies in mind. However, one should also consider that they should not ask just one person, but many elderly users in their target market – the aforementioned study interviewed 29 users [12]. For ease of statistical evaluation, we would suggest at least 30 elderly users be consulted when developing elderly-specific software. This will ensure the interface is suitable for a wide variety of elderly users.

4.3 Simplicity and Computer Skill Levels

Elderly users typically experience a degree of cognitive decline, making multitasking harder for them [9]. Things such as being faced with a multitude of error messages can be distressing for an elderly user [10] and make them feel helpless in the face of these errors, or hurt their confidence in using computers in general. However, agile development strives for simplicity; excess requirements only serve to distract and deter from higher priorities, and can lead to confusing software once it's deployed. Striving for simplicity in developing software is greatly beneficial to the elderly user, as it reduces clutter in app, resulting in easier to understand (and easier to use) applications! Plus, approaching this matter from the start of development is much preferred to simplifying existing software – often the simplification of existing software is assumed to be beneficial for elderly users wishing to use the software; this is not a tactic that always works. An app that is cluttered with useless features, despite being "easy to use," can be just as problematic to understand and use by older adults [3] (Table 1).

Table 1. Goals of agile development and corresponding elderly interface development goals.

Agile development goal	Application to elderly interface development
Adaptability	Adapting to various user abilities and interface requirements. Adapting to criticism regarding interfaces of applications and new requirements
Simplicity	Simple designs save time, create more understandable user interfaces for elderly users
	Simplifying from the start is preferable from simplifying an existing app
Communication	Communication between older users and younger developers to determine best requirements, user morals/ideas
	Communication between multiple older users to understand range of abilities to develop for

5 Modifying Agile Development Tactics for Elderly HCI Design

While agile development methodologies have a variety of fantastic focuses that make them ideal for use in developing for the elderly, they also set aside little to no time for user testing, and do not prioritize things such as development of tutorials regardless of requirements and user interface simplicity. As a result, we offer the following modifications for those seeking to utilize agile software development methodologies in developing elderly-friendly human computer interfaces.

Set aside extra time post-sprints for user testing and feedback. Agile development prioritizes listening to customer concerns and implementing them as new requirements, and adapting to said new requirements smoothly and easily. It's imperative that the developers seek feedback from users of the application, whether through a closed beta or other such program. Between sprints, talk with not only any specific customer for your application for feedback, but reach out to possible users of your application and let them walk through the app to determine whether or not it would be useful in its current state. This is the best way to gauge whether or not your app is usable by elderly users. As mentioned previously, interviewing at least 30 people within your target market is a good idea for developing for elderly users.

When requesting user feedback, listen to a wide variety of users for your app, not just the customer. Keep in mind that the elderly population is quite diverse, and includes a wide variety of abilities. Make sure you talk to a wide variety of elderly people to get a feel for ways to improve your app so it is accessible for a variety of users. For example, a hearing-impaired user might point out that the auditory display that a seeing-impaired user enjoyed is pitched incorrectly for their use - meaning that the developers should either adjust the pitch, or work in a mechanism so the user can adjust a pitch as required for those with hearing disabilities.

Be prepared to add requirements as needed for increasing app ease of use for the elderly user. Rather than making excuses for your application or attempting to explain troublesome features to the elderly user, adjust so that the application is easier to use right away for the elderly user. This might include repositioning options and toolbars and adding new tutorials so that an elderly user feels the flow of the application is more intuitive, or simply adding a mode that makes adjustments for older users based on the feedback gathered. However, the important thing to do is to actually make changes as requested!

Prioritize simplicity in your user interface designs as well as your programming. Agile development prioritizes simplicity in programming; that is, the simplest possible implementation for a programming problem should be used. This should also be the motto in developing interfaces for users. Rather than going for flashy backgrounds and obtrusive color schemes, take a simpler route. Only add new notifications or interface elements as required by the design of the app - unnecessary uses of swipes and gestures, or strange settings, may unnecessarily confuse the elderly user. Good design can be implemented in a minimalist fashion.

After the completion of all requirements, set time aside to implement a tutorial. Finally, when the project reaches a level of completion where it can be released, set aside a special sprint to create a variety of in-depth tutorials. Never assume that a user will simply know how to use the application - the addition of tutorials has shown to be incredibly useful in helping an elderly user use applications! But also make sure that these receive the round of user testing and feedback as the other requirements have: tutorials should not be confusing, and any confusion that a tutorial might cause should be eliminated by clarification or simplification as soon as possible.

By integrating these strategies with existing agile development methodologies, software developers can take steps towards building more elderly-friendly human computer interfaces, and helping elderly users use their applications.

6 Case Study: Creating a Grocery Shopping Application

In order to further illustrate the development process explored in this paper, we offer a case study regarding a simple grocery shopping application targeted at elderly adult users. The application is mobile, runs on smartphones, and hopes to achieve the following goals:

- Show a user a variety of popular grocery stores in a 15 mile radius from their current location.
- Allow a user to browse sale papers available at each of these grocery stores.
- Allow the creation of shopping lists based on these sale papers, and items available at each of these grocery stores.

With these goals in mind, the application developers decide to use an agile development methodology in order to achieve these goals and develop the application so it's understandable and easy to use for older adults. The developers understand that agile development's goals go hand-in-hand with requirements for developing for elderly users, hence their decision.

The first stage of development involves gathering requirements. As is expected with agile development, several meetings with potential customers are orchestrated and attended – a particular nursing home in the area has sponsored development of the application, and thus the developers meet frequently with various residents from the home in order to understand the expectations a user would have of such an application. However, instead of limiting focus to the "customer" so to speak, focus groups involving other elderly users in the community are held as well. In this way, the developers are listening to a wide variety of users.

After the initial stage of requirements-gathering is complete, the sprints of development begin. Within each sprint, developers set aside a limited number of tasks and declare that they will finish these tasks within a particular period of, say, two weeks. Because the sprint time period is so short, simplicity is prioritized in programming. The developers look over the various features they have planned for the application, and decide which are worth it in order to simplify the amount of development they have to do. Complicated features that were suggested, such as social network integration, that may not intrigue their targeted users can be dropped to make the application less complicated. However, simplifying the programming in this manner also simplifies the user interface - fewer options mean less information to parse on individual screens. A simpler user interface can be easier to use for elderly users.

Between sprints, extra time for testing and feedback is set aside. Rather than the traditional post-sprint meeting where the developers and customers discuss their next steps, the developers return to their sponsoring nursing home and conduct meetings with a variety of users to obtain feedback on the development of the application. They *also* conduct focus groups with those potential users not involved with their customer (again, the nursing home). All in all, they get a few complaints about the method of adding sale items to a grocery list, and instead of explaining how to perform the action and leaving it as is, the developers add additional clarification for the user, *adapting* to the new requirements.

At last, the application is complete. In order to ensure that future users have no trouble using the application, the developers create an intricate tutorial in their last few sprints, explaining how to use individual portions of the application (the grocery list feature, the grocery store search feature, and so on). The tutorial is set to activate the very first time the application opens, without user intervention, to ensure that the user understands the application. Although the traditional agile process did not require this step, setting aside this special sprint ensures that elderly users who may be less experienced with technology easily understand the application. The result is an application tailored for the older adult computer user which had a abundance of feedback from potential elderly users during the development process, a thought-out design based on this feedback, a simple interface that does what needs to be done (and not more than that), and an application with an in-set tutorial, that explains the features and workflows of the application to new elderly users.

7   Conclusions

In conclusion, an agile method of engineering applications will assist greatly in getting the user feedback necessary to properly develop accessible apps for the elderly. This method of development also may be useful for disabled users of all ages – the same rules of proper testing and user feedback apply no matter what the age group for disabled users. Future considerations include investigating this framework when used to develop for the disabled of various age groups, as well as using this framework of increased user feedback when developing for children. Children are another growing target market for applications; and getting feedback about what is intuitive and what is not when using an application would be quite useful in ensuring that children are familiar with technology from a young age.

Acknowledgements. This work is sponsored by TUNGHAI UNIVERSITY 'The U-Care ICT Integration Platform for the Elderly – No.102 GREEnS004 – 2', 2013. We also would like to offer a special thanks to Mohammad Arif Ul Alam, who offered many helpful comments on this paper via his experience with the subject of developing for elderly users [13].

References

1. Paulk, M.C.: Agile methodologies and process discipline. CrossTalk J. Def. Softw. Eng. **15** (10), 15–18 (2002). (Lumin Publishing, Salt Lake City)
2. Newell, A.F.: HCI and older people. Presented at the HCI and the Older Population Workshop at British HCI 2004, Leeds, UK, September 7 (2004)
3. Durick, J., Robertson, T., Brereton, M., Vetere, F., Nansen, B.: Dispelling ageing myths in technology design. In: Proceedings of the 25th Australian Computer-Human Interaction Conference: Augmentation, Application, Innovation, Collaboration, pp. 467–476. ACM, New York (2013)
4. Cracknell, R.: The ageing population. Report, House of Commons Library Research, London (2010)
5. Sealey, G.: U.S. elderly to double in 25 years. ABC News (2014). http://abcnews.go.com/US/story?id=91943
6. Kantner, L., Rosenbaum, S.: Usable computers for the elderly: applying coaching experiences. In: Proceedings of the 2003 IEEE International Professional Communication Conference, pp. 92–100. IEEE (2003)
7. Williams, D., Ul Alam, M.A., Ahamed, S.I., Chu, W.: Considerations in designing human-computer interfaces for elderly people. In: 2013 13th International Conference on Quality Software (QSIC), pp. 372–377. IEEE (2013)
8. Raina, P., Wong, M., Massfeller, H.: The relationship between sensory impairment and functional independence among elderly. BMC Geriatr. **4**, 3 (2004)
9. Nunes, F., Silva, P.A., Abrantes, F.: Human-computer interaction and the older adult: an example using user research and personas. In: Proceedings of the 3rd International Conference on Pervasive Technologies Related to Assistive Environments, pp. 49:1–49:8. ACM, New York (2010)
10. Phiriyapokanon, T.: Is a big button interface enough for elderly users?: towards user interface guidelines for elderly users. Thesis, Malardalen University, Sweden (2011)
11. Nishino, H., Fukakusa, Y., Hatano, A., Kagawa, T., Utsumiya, K.: A tangible information explorer using vibratory touch screen. In: 2012 IEEE 26th International Conference on Advanced Information Networking and Applications (AINA), pp. 671–677. IEEE (2012)

12. Valentine, E., Bobrowicz, A., Coleman, G., Gibson, L., Hanson, V.L., Kundu, S., McKay, A., Holt, R.: Narrating past to present: conveying the needs and values of older people to young digital technology designers. In: Stephanidis, C. (ed.) Universal Access in HCI, Part II, HCII 2011. LNCS, vol. 6766, pp. 243–249. Springer, Heidelberg (2011)
13. Alam, M.A., Wang, W., Ahamed, S.I., Chu, W.: Elderly safety: a smartphone based real time approach. In: Biswas, J., Kobayashi, H., Wong, L., Abdulrazak, B., Mokhtari, M. (eds.) ICOST 2013. LNCS, vol. 7910, pp. 134–142. Springer, Heidelberg (2013)

Assistive and Sentient Environments

Testing Real-Time In-Home Fall Alerts with Embedded Depth Video Hyperlink

Erik E. Stone$^{(\boxtimes)}$ and Marjorie Skubic

Department of Electrical and Computer Engineering,
University of Missouri, Columbia, MO 65211, USA
{stoneee, skubicm}@missouri.edu

Abstract. A method for sending real-time fall alerts containing an embedded hyperlink to a depth video clip of the suspected fall was evaluated in senior housing. A previously reported fall detection method using the Microsoft Kinect was used to detect naturally occurring falls in the main living area of each apartment. In this paper, evaluation results are included for 12 apartments over a 101 day period in which 34 naturally occurring falls were detected. Based on computed fall confidences, real-time alerts were sent via email to facility staff. The alerts contained an embedded hyperlink to a short depth video clip of the suspected fall. Recipients were able to click on the hyperlink to view the clip on any device supporting play back of MPEG-4 video, such as smart phones, to immediately determine if the alert was for an actual fall or a false alarm. Benefits and limitations of the technology are discussed.

Keywords: Fall detection · Fall alerts · Kinect

1 Introduction

The Center for Disease Control and Prevention states that one out of three older adults (those age 65 and older) falls each year [1]. Of those who fall, many suffer serious injuries which reduce their mobility and independence. The direct medical cost of falls among older adults in the United States in the year 2000 was over $19 billion [2], and this cost does not account for the decreased quality of life many individuals experience after suffering a fall. Beyond the injuries and costs incurred as a result of the fall itself, studies have also found an increased risk of physical and physiological complications associated with prolonged periods of lying on the floor following a fall, due to an inability to get up [3]. Older adults living alone, or in independent settings, are at great risk of delayed assistance following a fall.

Many methods for reporting or detecting falls have been developed. This includes wearable devices, such as manual push buttons and automatic fall detection systems based on accelerometers [4, 5]. However, wearable devices must be continuously worn, may be forgotten, and require battery changes or charging. Studies have also indicated a preference for non-wearable sensors among older adults [6]. For these reasons, many researchers have investigated the use of environmentally mounted sensors, such as passive infrared (PIR) sensors [7], acoustic sensors [8], and video-based sensors [9–13], among others. Although privacy is always a concern with video-based sensors, studies

© Springer International Publishing Switzerland 2015
C. Bodine et al. (Eds.): ICOST 2014, LNCS 8456, pp. 41–48, 2015.
DOI: 10.1007/978-3-319-14424-5_5

have found that privacy concerns may be alleviated by use of appropriate privacy preserving techniques such as the use of silhouettes [14].

This work investigates the use of a fall detection system (described in [15]) that uses an inexpensive depth imaging sensor, the Microsoft Kinect, to send real-time email-based fall alerts to staff members of a senior housing facility. Each alert contains basic information about the suspected fall, such as time and location, as well as an embedded hyperlink to a short depth video clip viewable on smart phones carried by staff members. The video clip allows recipients to immediately determine whether the alert corresponds to an actual fall, or a false alarm, without the need to go physically investigate the alert, significantly reducing the cost of false alarms and unnecessary disturbances.

2   Related Work and Motivation

Few automatic fall detection systems have undergone significant, real-world, real-time testing in older adult housing. In [21], the authors evaluated a custom vest with an attached tri-axial accelerometer in a nursing home. The vest was worn by 10 elderly subjects for 8 h a day, 6 days a week, for approximately 4 weeks. In total 833 h of monitoring was recorded. Alert messages were sent to a care-taker terminal. A total of 42 fall alerts were generated; however, no actual falls were reported, yielding an overall false alarm rate of 1.2 per day for the vest. Feedback from subjects and staff indicated they did not appreciate the vests in their current form, stating they were uncomfortable and bulky.

In a recently published study [22], the authors used previously recorded acceleration data on a set of high fall risk patients to evaluate 13 published acceleration-based fall detection algorithms. The data contained 29 actual falls of older adults that were used for analysis. Results indicated that the algorithms performed worse in terms of sensitivity and specificity as compared to what was originally reported on simulated data. Mean sensitivity was 57 %, with a maximum of 83 %. Additionally, the number of false alarms generated during 24 h (based on three representative fallers) ranged from 3 to 85.

As with other sensing technologies, a number of methods for fall detection using the Microsoft Kinect sensor have been published [15–20]. Although all these studies show encouraging results, the major limitation of most is the lack of sufficient (if any) evaluation in real-world settings. In [15], the authors compared their method to five previously published methods [12, 17–20] developed and evaluated using laboratory data. All six methods were evaluated on a combined 9 years (80,939 h) of previously recorded depth data collected in 13 actual older adult apartments. The data contained 445 falls performed by trained stunt actors and 9 real falls. All five previously published methods performed worse than originally reported, generating many false alarms at relatively low detection rates. This is not surprising given the wide range of conditions and issues that occur in complex, dynamic, real-world settings, which make it virtually impossible to create a realistic data set in the lab.

Although the fall detection method described in [15] was developed and evaluated on 9 years of previously recorded real-world data, further real-time evaluation of the system is critical for a number of reasons, including: (1) to better assess performance on real falls, (2) to get feedback from facility staff, and (3) to further assess performance in untrained settings. The previously recorded data almost exclusively contained stunt actor falls. Only 9 falls (less than 2 %) were real falls. System performance (detection rate vs. false alarm rate) could be significantly different on only real falls. Additionally, real-time evaluation, in which alerts are actually sent to caregivers, is the only way to assess the perceived benefits and costs of the system by end users. If the perceived benefits are low and costs high, it will not be used. Finally, testing in new, untrained settings will help determine whether the previously recorded data is sufficient, or whether additional training may be necessary in new settings.

3   Methodology

Figure 1a shows the Kinect sensor installed in one apartment included in the study. The Kinect is placed on a small shelf a few inches below the ceiling (height 2.75 m), above the front door. A small computer (Acer Veriton N2620G) is placed in a cabinet above the refrigerator. Readers are referred to [15] for a description of the fall detection algorithm and system operation.

A fall confidence is computed for each possible fall event identified by the algorithm in [15] within 6–8 s of the initial event trigger. The confidence is immediately compared against an alert threshold (specified individually for each apartment), and if the confidence is greater than or equal to the alert threshold an email alert is generated and sent to a list of recipients defined in a configuration file. A sample email-based fall alert is shown in Fig. 1b. The alert contains basic information regarding the suspected fall, including: fall confidence, the research ID associated with the apartment, the IP address of the system, the date and time the fall occurred, and whether another individual was detected walking in the room during (or immediately following) the fall. In addition, a hyperlink to a 10 s depth video clip centered on the fall impact is embedded in the alert. The depth video clip can be viewed, following secure password

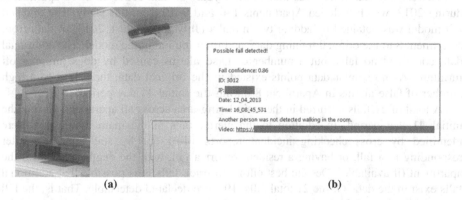

Possible fall detected!

Fall confidence: 0.86

ID: 3012

IP:

Date: 12_04_2013

Time: 16_08_45_531

Another person was not detected walking in the room.

Video: https://

(a)   (b)

Fig. 1. (a) Kinect and computer (inside cabinet) installed in an apartment. (b) Sample email-based fall alert with embedded hyperlink to depth video clip of the suspected fall.

authentication, on any device supporting playback of MPEG-4 video. This includes smart phones carried by staff members while in the facility, as well as laptop or desktop computers. Selected frames from two depth video clips of alerted falls are shown in Fig. 2.

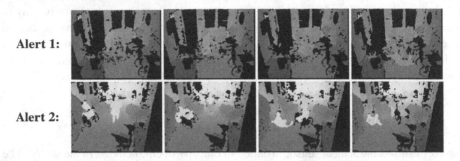

Fig. 2. Selected frames from two depth video clips. Ground is shaded blue, while foreground objects are shaded yellow, red, and/or green, based on segmentation and distance (Color figure online).

4 Evaluation

As part of an IRB approved study, a Kinect sensor and computer where installed in the main living area (in a similar fashion as shown in Fig. 1) of 12 apartments in a senior housing facility. Ages of the 14 residents ranged from 68 to 98 and 6 were male. Informed consent was obtained from all. Tables 1 and 2 contain alert and real fall statistics for the apartments for two time periods totaling 101 days. The first time period covers the initial 41 days when alerts were active. The second time period, beginning October 2, 2013, covers the final 60 days. At approximately midnight on the evening of October 1, 2013, an updated version of the fall detection model was installed on each system.

The original fall model was trained on 9 years of data collected in 13 apartments during 2012, which included Apartments 1–6 and 9–10 from this study. The updated fall model was obtained by adding two months (July and August, 2013) of data from Apartment 8 to the original training data, and then retraining the model. The additional data contained no falls, but a number of false alarms caused by dogs jumping off furniture. As no similar data points existed in the original data, these lead to a high number of false alarms in Apartment 8 during the initial 41 day period.

A total of 21 falls occurred in the main living area across all apartments during the initial 41 day period. In addition to the alerts, falls in the main living area were identified by cross checking incident reports filled out by staff members after responding to a fall, or having a resident report a fall, with the depth video from the apartment (if available). Despite best efforts to track falls, it is possible that additional falls exist in the data. Of the 21 total falls, 19 were declared detectable. That is, the fall occurred in view of the Kinect, and occurred when the system was operational. Of the 19 detectable falls, 15 triggered an alert email, yielding a combined alert rate of 79 %.

Table 1. Main living area, Aug. 22, 2013 – Oct. 1, 2013, 41 days, original fall model

Ap. #	Up Time (Days)	Alert Threshold	Target FA rate (FA/month)[1]	Total Falls[2]	Detectable Falls[3]	Alerted Falls	Missed Falls[4]	Alert Rate[5]	False Alarms	FA rate (FA/month)[6]
1	41	0.55	1.0	0	0	0	0	--	0	0.00
2	41	0.55	1.0	0	0	0	0	--	4	2.97
3	41	0.55	1.0	0	0	0	0	--	0	0.00
4	32	0.55	1.0	0	0	0	0	--	1	0.95
5	41	0.55	1.0	0	0	0	0	--	0	0.00
6	41	0.55	1.0	0	0	0	0	--	2	1.48
7	41	0.55	1.0	0	0	0	0	--	0	0.00
8	33	0.55	1.0	0	0	0	0	--	7	6.45
9	32	0.55	1.0	0	0	0	0	--	0	0.00
10	41	0.45	2.0	2	2	1	1	0.50	3	2.23
11	41	0.45	2.0	5	5	3	2	0.60	4	2.97
12	40	0.45	2.0	14	12	11	1	0.92	7	5.32
Total	465	--	--	21	19	15	4	0.79	28	1.83

Table 2. Main living area, Oct. 2, 2013 – Nov. 30, 2013, 60 days, Updated fall model

Ap. #	Up Time (Days)	Alert Threshold	Target FA rate (FA/month)[1]	Total Falls[2]	Detectable Falls[3]	Alerted Falls	Missed Falls[4]	Alert Rate[5]	False Alarms	FA rate (FA/month)[6]
1	60	0.55	1.0	0	0	0	0	--	0	0.00
2	55	0.55	1.0	0	0	0	0	--	0	0.00
3	54	0.55	1.0	0	0	0	0	--	0	0.00
4	24	0.55	1.0	0	0	0	0	--	0	0.00
5	60	0.55	1.0	0	0	0	0	--	0	0.00
6	60	0.55	1.0	0	0	0	0	--	1	0.51
7	60	0.55	1.0	0	0	0	0	--	0	0.00
8	55	0.55	1.0	0	0	0	0	--	2	1.11
9	32	0.55	1.0	1	0	0	0	--	0	0.00
10	48	0.45	2.0	1	1	0	1	0.00	1	0.63
11	54	0.35	3.0	4	4	4	0	1.00	8	4.51
12	60	0.35	3.0	26	21	15	6	0.71	2	1.01
Total	622	--	--	32	26	19	7	0.73	14	0.68

Meanwhile, 28 false alarms were sent during this period across all apartments, yielding a combined false alarm rate of 1.83 per month per apartment.

During the final 60 day period, a total of 32 falls occurred in the main living area across all apartments. Of the 32 falls, 26 were declared detectable. Of the 26 detectable falls, 19 triggered an alert email, yielding a combined alert rate of 73 %. Meanwhile, 14 false alarms were sent, yielding a combined false alarm rate of 0.68 per month per apartment.

4.1   Apartments 11 and 12

Apartment 11 had two residents, one of whom is a relatively frequent faller and used an assistive walking device on a regular basis when moving around the apartment.

Over the final 60 day period (with the updated fall model in place), this resident suffered 4 detectable falls in the main living area, all of which were alerted. Of the 4 falls, 3 were standing falls that occurred after the resident bent over to pick something up off the floor, and 1 was a sitting fall that occurred when the resident attempted to get up from a wheel chair. Of the 8 false alarms sent during the final 60 days, 2 were the result of children dropping to the floor while playing, and 6 were the result of items being dropped or placed on the floor by the residents or staff. A retrospective analysis found that all falls would have been alerted at a false alarm rate of roughly 2.5 false alarms per month. Figure 3a shows the floor plan of Apartment 11, along with the position of the Kinect and its field of view, and the location of the alerted and not alerted but detectable falls (all falls were alerted).

Apartment 12 had a single resident who is a very frequent faller and used an assistive walking device almost exclusively when moving around her apartment. Over the final 60 day period, this resident suffered 21 detectable falls in the main living area, 15 of which were alerted. Of the 21 falls, all were standing falls that occurred while the resident was using her walker. The 2 false alarms sent during the final 60 day period were both caused by staff members placing or moving large items on the floor. A retrospective analysis found that all falls would have been alerted at a false alarm rate of roughly 23 false alarms per month. Figure 3b shows the floor plan of Apartment 12, with the position of the Kinect and the location of the alerted and not alerted but detectable falls.

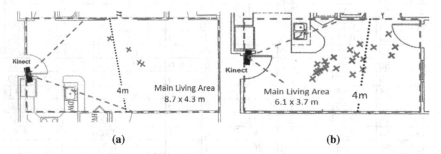

(a)   (b)

Fig. 3. Floor plan of (a) Apartment 11 and (b) 12. Position, field of view, and 4 meter distance reference for Kinect are overlaid, along with location of alerted (red +) and not alerted (blue x) detectable falls during final 60 day period. Dashed blue rectangle covers main living area (Color figure online).

5   Discussion

Kinect-based fall detection systems installed in 12 older adults' apartments successfully sent real-time fall alerts via email to facility staff members. Results over a 101 day period showed an overall alert rate of roughly 75 % with a false alarm rate of 1 per month per apartment. It should be noted that no data from Apartments 7, 11, or 12 were ever used to train the fall detection system. In these apartments, a total of 21 false alarms were generated. Given the target false alarms rates, 20 false alarms would have been expected. Although the false alarms were somewhat unequally distributed among the apartments, the results indicate that the previously recorded data from [15] is likely sufficient training data for many senior housing settings. However, inclusion of additional unique false alarms (such as dogs jumping off furniture) could likely improve performance in certain cases.

Better results (a higher alert rate at a lower false alarm rate) could almost certainly have been achieved by training on a few of the real falls from Apartment 12, due to the fact they tended to differ considerably from the falls in the training data. During these falls, the resident typically used her walker as a point of support, leading to significantly reduced vertical velocity and acceleration compared to falls in the training data. Although the training data contained sitting falls, none of the falls in the training data involved individuals using a walker, or using any object as a point of support during a standing fall. The seven missed falls in Apartment 12 were largely due to this issue, in combination with partial occlusion by the walker in some cases.

Feedback from staff members was quite positive. The embedding of a hyperlink to a depth video clip of the suspected fall (that could be viewed on a smart phone) was seen as a major benefit over other approaches. Removing the need to physically investigate false alarms significantly reduces the costs, both in terms of time and frustration, associated with false alarms for staff members and residents. Staff members could potentially review 10 to 15 video clips in the time it would take to physically investigate a single alert, depending on a facility's size. Out of 76 alerts sent, there was not a single case in which it was not obvious to all recipients whether the alert was for an actual fall or a false alarm. There was some desire to operate at a higher false alarm rate, perhaps upwards of 5 per month per apartment, to achieve higher alert rates. The videos also provide a record of what happened before the fall, which creates new opportunities for fall analysis and prevention strategies in senior living facilities. Meanwhile, the use of only depth video, and not traditional color video, helps preserve the privacy of users.

References

1. Center for Disease Control and Prevention (CDC): Falls among older adults: An overview. www.cdc.gov/homeandrecreationalsafety/Falls/adultfalls.html. Accessed 13 Dec 2013
2. Stevens, J.A., Corso, P.S., Finkelstein, E.A., Miller, T.R.: The costs of fatal and non-fatal falls among older adults. Inj. Prev. 12(5), 290–295 (2006)
3. Tinetti, M.E., Liu, W.L., Claus, E.B.: Predictors and prognosis of inability to get up after falls among elderly persons. JAMA, J. Am. Med. Assoc. 269(1), 65–70 (1993)
4. Noury, N., et al.: Fall detection-principles and methods. In: 29th Annual International Conference of the IEEE Engineering in Medicine and Biology Society, pp. 1663–1666 (2007)
5. Bourke, A.K., O'brien, J.V., Lyons, G.M.: Evaluation of a threshold-based tri-axial accelerometer fall detection algorithm. Gait Posture 26(2), 194–199 (2007)
6. Demiris, G., et al.: Older adults' attitudes towards and perceptions of smart home technologies: A pilot study. Inf. Health Soc. Care 29(2), 87–94 (2004)
7. Sixsmith, A., Johnson, N., Whatmore, R.: Pyrolitic IR sensor arrays for fall detection in the older population. J. Phys. IV France 128, 153–160 (2005)

8. Li, Y., Zeng, Z.L., Popescu, M., Ho, K.C.: Acoustic fall detection using a circular microphone array. In: 32nd Annual International Conference of the IEEE Engineering in Medicine and Biology Society, pp. 2242–2245 (2010)
9. Rougier, C., Meunier, J., St-Arnaud, A., Rousseau, J.: Robust video surveillance for fall detection based on human shape deformation. IEEE Trans. Circ. Syst. Video Technol. 21, 611–622 (2011)
10. Miaou, S.G., Sung, P.H., Huang, C.Y.: A customized human fall detection system using omni-camera images and personal information. In: Transdisciplinary Conference on Distributed Diagnosis and Home Healthcare, pp. 39–42 (2006)
11. Lee, T., Mihailidis, A.: An intelligent emergency response system: preliminary development and testing of automated fall detection. J. Telemed. Telecare 11(4), 194–198 (2005)
12. Anderson, D., Luke, R.H., Keller, J., Skubic, M., Rantz, M., Aud, M.: Linguistic summarization of activities from video for fall detection using voxel person and fuzzy logic. Comput. Vis. Image Underst. 113(1), 80–89 (2009)
13. Auvinet, E., et al.: Fall detection with multiple cameras: An occlusion-resistant method based on 3-d silhouette vertical distribution. IEEE Trans. Info. Tech. Biomed. 15(2), 290–300 (2011)
14. Demiris, G., Parker, O.D., Giger, J., Skubic, M., Rantz, M.: Older adults' privacy considerations for vision based recognition methods of eldercare applications. Technol. Health Care 17, 41–48 (2009)
15. Stone, E., Skubic, M.: Fall detection in homes of older adults using the microsoft kinect. IEEE J. Biomed. Health Inf. (2014). doi:10.1109/JBHI.2014.2312180
16. Kepski, M., Kwolek, B., Austvoll, I.: Fuzzy inference-based reliable fall detection using kinect and accelerometer. In: Rutkowski, L., Korytkowski, M., Scherer, R., Tadeusiewicz, R., Zadeh, L.A., Zurada, J.M. (eds.) ICAISC 2012, Part I. LNCS, vol. 7267, pp. 266–273. Springer, Heidelberg (2012)
17. Marzahl, C., Penndorf, P., Bruder, I., Staemmler, M.: Unobtrusive fall detection using 3D images of a gaming console: concept and first results. In: Wichert, R., Eberhardt, B. (eds.) Ambient Assisted Living. ATSC, vol. 2, pp. 135–146. Springer, Heidelberg (2012)
18. Mastorakis, G., Makris, D.: Fall detection system using Kinect's infrared sensor. J. Real-Time Image Process. 9(4), 635–646 (2014)
19. Rougier, C., Anvient, E., Rousseau, J., Mignotte, M., Meunier, J.: Fall detection from depth map video sequences. In: International Conference on Smart Homes and Health Telematics, pp. 121–128 (2011)
20. Planinc, R., Kampel, M.: Introducing the use of depth data for fall detection. Pers. Ubiquit. Comput. 17(6), 1063–1072 (2012)
21. Bourke, A.K., Pepijn, W.J., Chaya, A.E., Olaighin, G.M., Nelson, J.: Testing of a long-term fall detection system incorporated into a custom vest for the elderly. In: 30th Annual International Conference of the IEEE Engineering in Medicine and Biology Society, pp. 2844–2847 (2008)
22. Bagalà, F., et al.: Evaluation of accelerometer-based fall detection algorithms on real-world falls. PLoS ONE 7(5), e37062 (2012)

ShowMeHow: Using Smart, Interactive Tutorials in Elderly Software Development

Drew Williams[1(✉)], Mong-Te Wang[2], Chih-Hung Chang[3],
Sheikh Iqbal Ahamed[1], and William Chu[2]

[1] Department of Mathematics, Statistics and Computer Science,
Marquette University, Milwaukee, WI, USA
{drew.williams,sheikh.ahamed}@marquette.edu
[2] Department of Computer Science, Tunghai University, Taichung City, Taiwan
{shaka,cchu}@thu.edu.tw
[3] Department of Computer Science and Information Engineering,
Hsiuping University of Science and Technology, Taichung City, Taiwan
chchang@mail.hust.edu.tw

Abstract. Many elderly users fail to use technology simply because of the fear of failure, and perceiving themselves as "too old" to use new technology. Studies show that coaching is helpful in assisting the elderly with learning new technology, but unfortunately many do not like to ask for help. We propose the development of smart tutorials that detect user frustration by tracking various affective markers, communicate with the user clearly and offer customized tutorials for the users' convenience. We hope that such a system will benefit the elderly by giving them on-demand, customized assistance while allowing them to retain their independence.

Keywords: Human computer interfaces · Elderly people · Tutorials · Intelligent interfaces

1 Introduction

With the advent of touch screens and multimodal interfaces, computers - capable of doing more things than ever - are becoming easier and easier to use. To flick through a series of images, a user can simply swipe the images they are viewing left and right; making an image smaller or larger involves a quick pinching motion applied to the screen. On devices, labels for power and volume buttons are becoming smaller, or nonexistent, as users pick up on the common places for such buttons to be located. Expectations take over and reduce the need for labels.

Unfortunately, as users become more accustomed to particular design or interface trends, developers spend less time explaining the trends with the assumption that the user understands it from prior exposure and experience. Web applications can update too rapidly for the paper instruction manuals of old to keep up with, and thus are not necessarily the best choice for software guides. For some population groups, prior knowledge is lacking and thus computers remain difficult to understand and use. Elderly adults may have little computer experience coupled with interest in using

© Springer International Publishing Switzerland 2015
C. Bodine et al. (Eds.): ICOST 2014, LNCS 8456, pp. 49–58, 2015.
DOI: 10.1007/978-3-319-14424-5_6

computers for various things in their lives – but find the process intimidating. Without proper instructions, these older adults may be reluctant to try and use the software – there will be less of a benefit to using the software if it takes more time to use! However, older adults are some of those who may benefit the most from modern software – it can promote lifelong learning, social connections, and help people remain productive in old age [1].

The implementation of smart, interactive tutorials would strongly benefit older adults who seek to use these new applications, but require a bit of guidance in doing so. An assistance system that speaks with a user in a clear, understandable way free of jargon, automatically reacts to a users' emotional state/use patterns to determine if a user may be having difficulty with a previously-taught task, and guides a user to further help if necessary without the user needing to seek it out themselves will help ensure that older adults receive the help they need. Such a system may even help them take steps in learning how to use computers better on their own.

In this paper, we propose the development of ShowMeHow – an intelligent computer assistance and support system – tailored for the older adult. ShowMeHow works via a combination of automatic emotional state detection, recognition of a user's location in the application, and conversational language use when communicating with the user. We start by outlining our motivations in creating ShowMeHow, and looking at related works in the field of intelligent education systems. We then discuss the development of ShowMeHow and how it hopes to revolutionize how older users interact with computers. Finally, we conclude by going through some future directions we may consider regarding ShowMeHow.

2   Motivation

Helping older adults become more comfortable with using computers is our highest priority, and our strongest motivator. As the number of older adults in the world increases [1], it's a good strategy to develop ways of improving the attitudes of the elderly towards technology. There are a number of things that would help with this – developing proper human-computer interfaces that take into account elderly abilities, for example [2] – but proper help screens and tutorial software would go a long way in helping developers make their existing software a bit more user-friendly for all users. In particular, we hope ShowMeHow can assist in preventing some of the scenarios listed as follows:

Frustration in Computer Use. A user often may avoid computers due to the association of frustration and other negative emotions accompanying their use. As an example, while elderly users can learn how to perform certain tasks, often they encounter problems remembering said tasks later [3] or using interfaces that were not designed with a variety of users in mind [2]. Such experiences can make elderly users frustrated when using computers, and see no benefit in their use. As lack of perceived benefit is a major reason for lack of computer use in older adults, [4] this can perpetuate the cycle of elderly users refusing to use computers. The ShowMeHow system remains sensitive to user frustration via the utilization of affective computing: detecting and parsing user emotional states and adjusting its teaching strategies depending on the users' mood. This way a user can obtain help, even if they're not sure how to ask for it.

Age in Relation to Properly Using Technology. Elderly users often report feeling as if they are "too old" for technology, as a result of societal reinforcement regarding older adults and technology use [4]. It has been a complaint in the literature that current efforts to develop programs for elderly abilities puts more emphasis on what they cannot do, reinforcing such notions in the minds of younger and older people. This in and of itself can hurt the development of applications that include elderly users in their target market, and reinforce stereotypes of elderly users as stubborn and resistant to new things. In order to combat this problem, the ShowMeHow system developed does not single out the elderly user by way of expecting an elderly user, but rather expects a novice user first, and adds adaptations that an elderly user would find useful.

Perceived Loss of Independence via Technology. In addition to feeling "too old", some users may find themselves feeling a lack of independence for turning to technology. Durick, et al. (2013) described the idea that a clear line exists between the accommodation and assimilation of technology – and that technology may not be associated with positive feelings when a user feels they have been forced to adopt it due to personal (physical or other) shortcomings [4]. By using technology designed for the elderly, they may feel identified by their age, rather than their status as users of technology. However, the ShowMeHow system works to empower a user versus taking away their independence, by helping them use technology and understand how it works instead of oversimplifying applications and reducing them to that which "the elderly user" can digest.

By helping an older user learn best practices for using computers right away, we ensure that an older user sees computers in a positive light, and remains more open to using them in everyday life.

3 Related Work

A variety of work has been done in the realm of developing intelligent systems, intelligent tutoring systems, and methods of picking up on emotions via affective computing. The following list is not intended to be a complete list of all related solutions, but rather a sampling of similar solutions.

3.1 Adaptive and Intelligent User Interfaces

Adaptive and intelligent interfaces are those that frequently go through the act of adjusting visual content based on users' abilities. One notable example, SUPPLE, adjusts the arrangement of a graphical user interface depending on a users' motor abilities (determined via a questionnaire) [5]. MyUI adapts to a user's abilities based on a series of design patterns developed in application [6]. HAIL adapts to a users' motor abilities and adjusts the graphical interface of a given website accordingly, coupling this with input from a device that converts head motion to onscreen pointer motion [7]. Most of these asked the user for some sort of direct input, instead of picking up on user habits, for interface changes to occur.

3.2   Intelligent Tutoring Systems

In addition to general intelligent response systems, intelligent tutoring systems (ITS) have also been explored, typically for children. These systems seek to educate in a similar manner to adult teachers – by picking up on nonverbal cues from students that can be detected via sensors [8]. This allows interactions to be customized for the particular student, based on the learning methods that cause the most positive reactions [8]. The computer can then create a model of the best strategies to use with the learner, based on the nonverbal feedback and answers to questions given during the tutoring session [8]. Intelligent assistants specifically for web pages have also been developed, with the intent of using a neural network taking user input to adjust magnification and keyboard settings for a web browser accordingly [9]. This project was one of few that offered assistance that adjusted users' settings automatically based on actions taken by the user in-program. While this assistance did not explain to a user what they needed to do in order to make the changes, it did provide a stress-free solution for editing a user interface to be more in line with a user's abilities.

3.3   Engagement Detection Systems

Ongoing work is also being conducted in the field of detecting user engagement. Systems that track boredom via keystrokes showed some accuracy when compared to random guessing regarding the user [10]. Studies detecting user emotional state (in this case, frustration) based on characteristics of pen strokes have also been conducted, and show promising results – notably, an ability to detect frustration with a precision of 87 % [11]. Finally, some promise has been shown in detecting posture accuracy via cameras such as the Microsoft Kinect [12] which could give hint to exhaustion or frustration in a user. In fact, another study mapped particular postures detected by the Microsoft Kinect to affective states, proving that this sort of engagement detection solution may be useful in future ubiquitous environments [13].

While various applications of engagement detection systems, intelligent tutoring and adaptive interface systems existed; we did not find a project that combined these individual research topics with the notion of development for the elderly user. It's certainly understandable why each of these things would be beneficial to the elderly user. Adaptable interfaces allow for customization for the benefit of individual users, and intelligent tutoring systems and engagement detection work together to understand when a user wants to learn and when they are encountering stress in their efforts to learn. For that reason, in developing ShowMeHow, we brought each of these things together to make a fully educational tutoring system for an elderly user wishing to learn how to properly use an application.

4   ShowMeHow: An Intelligent Computer Assistance System

ShowMeHow is an intelligent computer assistance system, developed to help elderly users learn how to better use their computers. It would be able to assist users by taking in information about the different options a user has available to them from within an application on a per-screen basis. Paired with multiple tutorial options (i.e. a long, explanatory way for describing how to take a picture, and a shorter way), ShowMeHow can use the information learned about the user in making decisions regarding what a user is attempting to do in a ShowMeHow application, and how best to assist them.

ShowMeHow would be developed for both Windows and Mac computers, and in both cases would exist as two separate applications. The first application, which is active even when tutorials are not being parsed through and common to all applications using ShowMeHow technology, runs in the background as the affective computing layer of the system. This part of the app uses the camera, microphone and keyboard of users' computer and tracks input trends. This includes facial expressions and posture from the camera, utterances from the microphone, and keyboard input. These trends are analyzed for known data patterns that imply particular moods. For example, if a user is expressing frustrated facial expressions, erratic typing and a hunched posture, they may have a displeased or disgruntled mood.

The second application gathers the logged emotion information data from the first, and uses it to influence the appearance of and contents of a series of developer-scripted tutorials for a particular application. Developers can script information about a given application on a per-screen basis - transitions between different screens in their applications trigger alerts in ShowMeHow that change the tutorial information shown. That data is then loaded into ShowMeHow where, depending on a users' mood and other data, different sorts of tutorials are shown via an on-screen overlay (overlaying the scripted application) to a user. After all, if a user is relatively new to an application, they should be shown a different set of tutorials versus a user who has used an application frequently but just appears to have forgotten a series of steps they've previously used in a fit of frustration.

ShowMeHow Tutorials operate on a hierarchical basis; they give the user a series of options that depend on the screen the user currently has selected. These options can be broken down into two series of questions: what does this screen do, and what could this screen lead to. For example, the tutorial for the home screen of an application would explain that the home screen functions as a "landing page" for the application as a whole, and explain the different pages the buttons on the home screen lead to. Language used in these tutorials would be easily understandable by those even without a technical background.

Finally, there are several methods of triggering these tutorials. The overlay with these tutorials can be trigged with a keyboard shortcut, but manual searches can be completed, and tutorials can also be triggered by the monitored affective data. If a confused or anxious look is detected, the overlay can trigger automatically in an effort to provide help to a confused user *without* confusing them more (i.e. forcing them to then find the help section in the application).

5 Evaluation

Now that we've discussed the overall system proposed, we can explore how it benefits the older adult user in particular. Earlier in the paper, we suggested particular problems currently in elderly interface development that we were hoping to solve with the development of the aforementioned tutorial system. In this section, we'll explore how various unique features of ShowMeHow go about solving those different problems we previously proposed.

5.1   Simplified Language

One of the common problems encountered by elderly users is the lack of knowledge of the computer vocabulary - there can be a lot of confusion regarding what terms apply to what parts of the system. When coaching users, some coaches even end up modifying their own vocabulary to properly communicate problems and solutions with the users [3]. This said, especially in a system designed for novice users, great efforts should be taken to avoid overly technical detail in favor of simple, understandable sentences. As previously mentioned, ShowMeHow opts for simplistic language and understandable metaphor if necessary to explain functions and the reasons for doing what needs to be done as part of the tutorials. Instead of asking a user to go to their desktop, explicit instructions to click on the small picture of a computer representing the desktop might be given, with an explanation of the desktop as the "main display" of the computer, where one can access all other programs and settings. One could imagine an elderly computer user being relieved to have such simple and understandable instructions for doing things within an application. Also, both of the text included in the overlay and voice augmentation should use this style of communication. Voice augmentation in particular, when used correctly, can reduce the cognitive load on a user [14] – but used incorrectly, this benefit is lost [14].

This style of communication seeks to overcome the previously mentioned user frustration with using applications. Instead of expecting that the user has previously used computers and will understand what a "Recycle Bin" or "icon" refers to, the application will explain everything to the user and help them form decisions about the actions they want to take. In addition to reducing user frustration, this also helps an elderly user feel more independent when using computers – thanks to the explanations provided within the tutorials, they no longer have to ask friends or family for definitions of various technical terms.

5.2   Hierarchical System

All applications have a hierarchy of screens: one 'home' or 'desktop' screen leads to a series of other screens, each of which may have options of their own. Thus, in favor of keeping things simplified, users only receive tutorials in ShowMeHow relating to the screen they are currently on. As previously mentioned, manual search will allow a user to look up particular actions, but by default ShowMeHow will give an explanation of the features of the particular screen the user is on at that point in time, in addition to what the application is capable of from that particular point within the app. For most users, this method of distributing options will suffice.

If the user chooses some particular action and is taken to the next screen, the same hierarchical options show relative to the next screen. There may exist some special actions that may take a user through several screens will also be included, and will continue to guide a user until the action (say, taking a photo and uploading it to a social network) is complete – however, these will be very commonly executed workflows and not common.

An elderly user would be very pleased with this system of tutorial, as it reduces the amount of information a user needs to parse when initiating the tutorial system by not giving all possible action options within the application, and structures the options available via a particular screen in an understandable fashion. In addition to streamlining the information presented to a user, structuring the tutorials in this way allows for a user to better make a decision in the application by analyzing each option and choosing the best path among them. This, like the jargon-free text mentioned previously, facilitates a sensation of independence. An older user will have the steps of an application explained to them thoroughly (and in an understandable manner) before they make a decision on how to proceed. Furthermore, by explaining how to parse through an application instead of presenting the user with an overly simplified interface, the application does not explicitly expect a user to be elderly – rather, simply inexperienced. This means the application is not implying old age on the part of the user – and this can be beneficial in how the application is perceived, as users may not want to be associated with being "old," due to the stigma the word has associated with it [4].

5.3   Adaptation Based on Affective State

Although a user could go through the tutorials based on the hierarchical system, the most helpful feature for most users will be the dynamic tutorials, which are activated based on the affective state of the user.

Every time an application with ShowMeHow support scripted in is launched, the affective layer will begin to read data from the microphone, camera, and input devices (keyboard, mouse, tablet, etc.). This data can be used to detect frustration or other negative emotions that may imply a user is unable to properly use the computer. If several trends indicate a user is encountering frustration, such as erratic keyboard input and a tense posture, the tutorial overlay can pop up on its own and ask the user if they need help with the application in questions. Furthermore, time, program and screen trends will also be saved. In the event that trends relating a user to having negative emotions in relation with a particular screen in an app come about, the next time the user attempts to use that app, the tutorial display may pop up automatically. Depending on how much trouble a user has with a particular app, the text of the tutorial may adjust itself to being more detailed as well, seeking to further educate the user in how to use the app rather than giving just a quick overview. Finally, in order to ensure that the tutorials are having a positive affect on the users' computing experience, reactions from the user will be monitored in relation to tutorials. These will also be taken into consideration, and ultimately a profile of the user will be built depending on how they respond to interactions from the application.

Finally, as a security and privacy precaution, while data will be read per session, it transmitted nowhere and immediately deleted. The application will only save trends and instances of poor mood, timestamps, and the like – no recordings, video or audio, of the user will be saved.

The affective data is one of the more unique features of ShowMeHow; instead of leaving users to fend for themselves, attempting to find their own solutions to problems, we detect the first signs of frustration on part of an elderly user, present them with solutions, and then verify (again via affective data) whether or not the solutions were applicable. While it may be surprising to an older adult user who is not used to the computer making judgments like this itself, overall it would most likely make the user quite happy to know the computer could pick up on frustration and stop to explain how to proceed to a novice user. This act of responding to and confirming the correct response to user need would do wonders for user frustration! It also – as the other features mentioned – would allow elderly users to feel more independent and reduce the number of questions asked of their grandchildren and friends regarding how to use computers.

Now, it is possible that users could run into problems that ShowMeHow would not be able to assist them with – such as problems related to viruses or hardware issues within the computer they are using. However, for the most part ShowMeHow would be able to educate and guide users through applications they otherwise might not have been able to use. This allows older adult users to retain their independence while learning how to use computers, and feel less targeted due to their age and more like a novice computer user, while overall reducing user frustration.

6   Conclusions

In conclusion, the development of an interactive, smart tutorial system would benefit not only older adults, but also many other novice computer users struggling to make sense of a world increasingly filled with new technical masterpieces. Tutorials have been around for as long as computers have – but they have remained static and plain, as they were when they first debuted. Current applications need an enhanced tutorial system to guide users with little computer experience, like the elderly population, through applications while teaching them the logic behind a given interface. Overlays that take the time to educate, in understandable terms, a user in use of an application (and know to stop or suggest that a break might be taken in accordance with user emotional state) would be fantastic in all cases. Furthermore, the ability to script in ShowMeHow functionality is especially important; in a world where interfaces change frequently, scripted support would ensure that an update didn't destroy the usefulness of ShowMeHow, while allowing it to be removed in the event a user feels secure enough with the application after some time.

In terms of where to take this idea in the future, the potential for a system as we are describing here to be used in a larger environment – such as a smart home – does exist! In this case, weaving in a full-fledged ubiquitous computing framework, such as one that takes into account user location and feeds this data into the system for emotional analysis, would be useful in this case [15]. Determining whether frustration with a particular segment of the system – say, in a connected house, a particular television versus another one – would allow the system to make intelligent troubleshooting decisions like suggesting that a device be taken to a shop to be fixed.

Acknowledgements. This work is sponsored by TUNGHAI UNIVERSITY 'The U-Care ICT Integration Platform for the Elderly – No.102 GREEnS004 – 2', 2013.

References

1. Alm, N., Gregor, P., Newell, A.F.: Older people and information technology are ideal partners. In: Proceedings of the International Conference for Universal Design (UD2002), Yokohoma, Japan, pp. 1–7 (2002)
2. Williams, D., Ul Alam, M.A., Ahamed, S.I., Chu, W.: Considerations in designing human-computer interfaces for elderly people. In: 2013 13th International Conference on Quality Software (QSIC), pp. 372–377. IEEE (2013)
3. Kantner, L., Rosenbaum, S.: Usable computers for the elderly: applying coaching experiences. In: Proceedings of the 2003 IEEE International Professional Communication Conference, pp. 92–101. IEEE (2003)
4. Durick, J., Robertson, T., Brereton, M., Vetere, F., Nansen, B.: Dispelling ageing myths in technology design. In: Proceedings of the 25th Australian Computer-Human Interaction Conference: Augmentation, Application, Innovation, Collaboration, pp. 467–476. ACM, New York (2013)
5. Gajos, K., Christianson, D., Hoffmann, R., Shaked, T., Henning, K., Long, J.J., Weld, D.S.: Fast and robust interface generation for ubiquitous applications. In: Beigl, M., Intille, S.S., Rekimoto, J., Tokuda, H. (eds.) UbiComp 2005. LNCS, vol. 3660, pp. 37–55. Springer, Heidelberg (2005)
6. Peissner, M., Schuller, A., Spath, D.: A design patterns approach to adaptive user interfaces for users with special needs. In: Jacko, J.A. (ed.) Human-Computer Interaction, Part I, HCII 2011. LNCS, vol. 6761, pp. 268–277. Springer, Heidelberg (2011)
7. Magee, J., Betke, M.: HAIL: hierarchical adaptive interface layout. In: Miesenberger, K., Klaus, J., Zagler, W., Karshmer, A. (eds.) ICCHP 2010, Part 1. LNCS, vol. 6179, pp. 139–146. Springer, Heidelberg (2010)
8. Sarrafzadeh, A., Alexander, S., Dadgostar, F., Fan, C., Bigdeli, A.: How do you know that I don't understand? A look at the future of intelligent tutoring systems. Comput. Hum. Behav. **24**(4), 1342–1363 (2008)
9. Hunter, A., Sayers, H., McDaid, L.: An evolvable computer interface for elderly users. In: Support Human Memory with Interactive Systems; HCI Conference, Lancaster, UK, pp. 29–32 (2007)
10. Bixler, R., D'Mello, S.: Detecting boredom and engagement during writing with keystroke analysis, task appraisals, and stable traits. In: Proceedings of the 2013 International Conference on Intelligent User Interfaces - IUI '13, pp. 225–234. ACM Press, New York (2013)
11. Asai, H., Yamana, H.: Detecting student frustration based on handwriting behavior. In: Proceedings of the Adjunct Publication of the 26th Annual ACM Symposium on User Interface Software and Technology - UIST '13 Adjunct, pp. 77–78. ACM Press, New York (2013)
12. Obdrzalek, S.A.N., Kurillo, G., Ofli, F., Bajcsy, R., Seto, E., Jimison, H., Pavel, M.: Accuracy and robustness of Kinect pose estimation in the context of coaching of elderly population. In: 2012 Annual International Conference of the IEEE Engineering in Medicine and Biology Society, pp. 1188–1193. The Printing House, Wisconsin (2012)

13. Tan, C.S.S., Schoning, J., Luyten, K., Coninx, K.: Informing intelligent user interfaces by inferring affective states from body postures in ubiquitous computing environments. In: Proceedings of the 2013 International Conference on Intelligent User Interfaces - IUI '13, pp. 235–246. ACM Press, New York (2013)
14. Sato, D., Kobayashi, M., Takagi, H., Asakawa, C., Tanaka, J.: How voice augmentation supports elderly web users. In: The Proceedings of the 13th International ACM SIGACCESS Conference on Computers and Accessibility - ASSETS '11, pp. 155–162. ACM Press, New York (2011)
15. Mantoro, T., Johnson, C.W., Ayu, M.A.: A framework in ubiquitous computing environment for providing intelligent responses. In: 2009 Third International Conference on Mobile Ubiquitous Computing, Systems, Services and Technologies, pp. 289–294. IEEE Computer Society, Washington (2009)

Actimetry@home: Actimetric Tele-surveillance and Tailored to the Signal Data Compression

Jacques Demongeot$^{(\boxtimes)}$, Olivier Hansen, Ali Hamie, Hana Hazgui,
Gilles Virone, and Nicolas Vuillerme

AGIM (Ageing, Imaging & Modelling) Laboratory, Faculty of Medicine,
FRE 3405 CNRS-UJF-EPHE, 38700 La Tronche, France
Jacques.Demongeot@yahoo.fr,
{Olivier.Hansen,Ali.Hamie,Hana.Hazgui,
Gilles.Virone,Nicolas.Vuillerme}@agim.eu

Abstract. An early diagnosis of a neurodegenerative process like the Alzheimer's disease needs a tele-surveillance at home based on the recording of
pathologic signals coming both from the cardiac activity (for detecting the loss
of the sinus respiratory arrhythmia) and from the repetition of tasks of the daily
life (signing a pathologic behavior called perseveration), whose non-invasive
detection can lead to an early diagnosis, if it triggers secondly a battery of tests
based on brain imaging, clinical neurology and cognitive sciences to confirm the
suspicion of neuronal degeneration. For increasing the efficiency of alarms
triggering these tests, we use dedicated tailored data compression methods,
whose two examples will be presented, the Dynalets method for quantitative
compression of the physiologic signals and the monotonic signature for qualitative compression.

Keywords: Tele-surveillance at home · Alarm triggering · Tailored to the
signal data compression

1 Introduction

The worldwide population is ageing, this phenomenon being accompanied by a dramatic
increase of the neurodegenerative diseases: in 2050, the number of elders aged 65+ in
the world will have increased by 100 % compared to the year 1950 [1]. The prevalence
of neurodegenerative diseases in developed countries has been found to double with
every five-year increase in age, from 3 percent at age 70 to 25 percent at age 85, the
increase per year ranging from 0.84 to 3.50 percent [2]. Hence, new pervasive technologies have been developed for smart homes or smart residences for seniors [3, 4] with
assistive technologies [5]. Experimental platforms and living labs are a prototype support for conducting experiments taking normally place in these healthcare facilities. This
offers advantages such as the ability to pre-validate prototypes before their use in
the real-world. In case of infrastructure absence, computer simulations [5–12] can play a
key role, for simulating different activity trends based on heterogeneous parameters
(*e.g.,* age, education, seasons, etc.) [13–16], testing uncommon scenarios of everyday
life on demand (instead of waiting for unpredictable real-life apparitions), and assessing

© Springer International Publishing Switzerland 2015
C. Bodine et al. (Eds.): ICOST 2014, LNCS 8456, pp. 59–70, 2015.
DOI: 10.1007/978-3-319-14424-5_7

specific algorithms invented and used in the area of activity or cognition [17–20]. We have for example modeled a persistence in certain tasks of daily life to infer a more generalized decline induced by a neurodegenerative disease. This persistence, also known as perseveration, in performing common tasks already completed successfully, but repeated pathologically was already the subject of comment in Romans, who willingly quoted the proverb: "errare humanum est, perseverare diabolicum"… The basis of such scenarios of daily living implemented in our computer simulations started from a previous research described in [14]. The present article deals with two methodologies of compression tailored to the physiologic or pathologic mechanisms generating the signal used to follow the person at home: (i) first concerns ECG signal, whose loss of the sinus respiratory arrhythmia is a good marker of the entrance in a neurodegenerative disease and (ii) second is a qualitative method for interpreting a sequence of increase/ decrease of an activity, by focusing only on its successive intervals of monotony. Note that samples used for validating these methods are essentially simulated using random numbers generator, bootstrapping data from already observed empirical distributions [3, 4].

2   History: Magical Medicine, Hermetic and Mysterious Numerology

Greek and Romanesque medicine have used commonly tables for predicting the fatal (resp. happy) evolution of a patient, if a mysterious calculation involving his age and pulse frequency belonged to a certain "lethal" part of an arithmetic table (Fig. 1 top left). Heir of Aristotle, hermetic pre-Roman and early Middle Age physicians gave rise to tables such as the "secret of secrets" (from an apocryphal letter by Aristotle to Alexander, attributed to Rhazes (circa 900), but probably from Hermes Trismegistus (circa 100)) showing on Fig. 1 in its center the number 22 (number of vertebrae in humans, nucleic bases in a microRNA,…). The table by G. d'Auberive (1180) [21], however, remains of more obscure origin usefulness in medicine, but shows also the intention to condensate health predictions in hermetic numerology.

3   Data Compression: From Tailored to Signal Physiology Towards Alarm Adapted Schematized Information

As the ancient Greeks, today's physicians, who seek to follow the evolution of a patient at home, need fast calculation of physiological parameters derived from clinical, biological or imaging records. For this, methods of rapid real-time processing must be developed to quickly compare patient evolutions with those from databases containing comparable patients. We give here two examples of the compression needed to quickly extract relevant parameters, in order to trigger an early and reliable alarm: one concerns an ECG signal decomposition closer to the genesis of the physiological signal that the Fourier transform, and the other deals with actimetric data reduced to their signature monotony (i.e., to the sequence of the signs of their derivative).

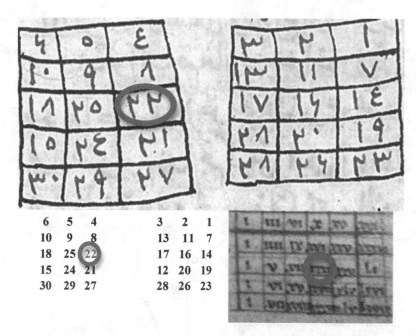

Fig. 1. Top: Table of secret of secrets and its translation into modern Arabic digits in the bottom left. A patient was declared fatal prognosis, if a formula with its age and the numerical value of the name belonged to the left side of the table. Bottom right: G. d'Auberive table, with the sum of the first integers in first row and the cumulative sum of multiples of the previous amount in column.

3.1   The Compression of the ECG Signal: The Dynalets Method

We propose in the following a new method of compression of the QRS wave of the ECG based on its mechanism of generation inside the sinus node of the heart.

The method, called Dynalets decomposition, consists of three main steps:

- we have represented together in the phase plane (amplitude, speed), the physiological signal (Fig. 2) and the approximation function belonging to a family of approximating selected functions (adapted to the mechanism of genesis of the physiological signal), and their proximity is maximized by minimizing a given distance in the phase plane (distance "delta", which minimizes the area between the curves, quadratic distance, which minimizes the sum of the distances between points chosen on the curves, or Hausdorff distance between the inner subsets of the curves) (Fig. 3)
- we subtract the function thus obtained, called fundamental signal, to the experimental signal, so as to obtain a second function, which we seek to approximate in the selected functional family
- iterations are stopped when the quadratic relative error (QRE) is below 0.1 and the SNR (signal to noise ratio) is over 20 dB, where:

a)   b)

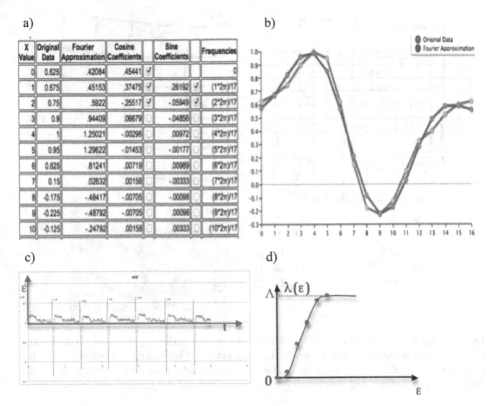

c)   d)

Fig. 2. Top left a): first coefficients of the Fourier transform of the QRS complex: the fundamental and two first harmonics are labeled. Top right b): original QRS complex of the ECG (green) and Fourier (blue) reconstruction with two harmonics matching. Bottom left c): experimental ECG. Bottom right d): evolution of the Lévy time $\lambda(\varepsilon)$ corresponding to the duration time the signal has passed between 0 and ε during 7 cycles (Colour figure online).

$$QRE = \left(\sum_{i=1,K} (X_i - Y_i)^2 \Big/ \sum_{i=1,K} X_i^2\right)^{1/2} \text{and SNR} = -20\, Log_{10}QRE \quad (1)$$

For ECG or the signal of the pulse, the chosen family is the solutions of the Liénard equations, specifically one called van der Pol equation. In the example of the Figs. 2 and 3, the QRS part of the ECG is approximated, after identification and extraction of the values less than $\inf\left(\lambda^{-1}(\{\Lambda\})\right)$ from the inter-beats base line, by using successively Fourier transform and then the family of the limit cycles (having a polynomial approximation [22]) of the van der Pol equation (called Dynalets transform). In the example of Fig. 3, QRE (resp. SNR) is equal to 8 % with Fourier transform and 9 % with Dynalets decomposition (resp. 22 % and 21 %). We can notice that Fourier transform used in Fig. 3 needs 6 parameters (including the value of the period), while the Dynalets transform requires only 5 parameters.

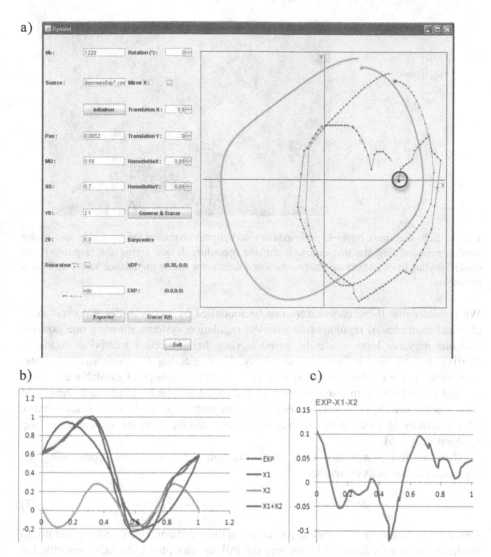

Fig. 3. Top (a): original ECG (red) and van der Pol (green) signal matching, after translation of the origin of the (xOy) referential and localization of the points of the base line (blue circle). Bottom left (b): superposition of the QRS complex of the experimental ECG signal without the base line (EXP in blue), the van der Pol fundamental signal (X1 in red), the first harmonic signal (X2 in green) and the reconstructed fundamental + first harmonic signal (X1 + X2 in violet). Bottom right (c): residual signal equal to EXP-(X1 + X2) (Colour figure online).

3.2   The Detection of the Loss of the Sinus Respiratory Arrhythmia

The cardiac instantaneous period (*i.e.*, the lapse of time between two cardiac beats) is anti-correlated with the time in the inspiration the actual cardiac cycle occurs (Fig. 4), due to a coupling (in the bulb) between the two (respiratory and cardiac) pacemakers.

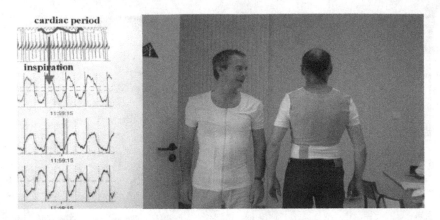

Fig. 4. Left: the sinus physiologic respiratory arrhythmia characterized by a decrease of the cardiac period during the inspiration. Right: the recording device giving the respiratory and cardiac rhythm from a smart tee-shirt containing a conductor whose impedance varies with chest expansion.

We consider that these pacemakers can be modelled by two van der Pol oscillators, classical examples of regulons (the simplest regulation systems showing one positive and one negative loop inside the graph having their Jacobian matrix as incidence matrix). Indeed, for the sake of simplicity, by neglecting the peripheral Aschow-Tawara node, the cardiac control system is made of two groups of excitable cells, one located in the bulb, composed of neurons and called the cardio-moderator centre CM with electric activity x, which inhibits the sinus node S located in the heart septum, whose activity is denoted by the variable y and results from an autocatalytic loop moderated by CM.

Reciprocally, S activates CM. Then, the van der Pol system representing the rhythmic cardiac activity reads:

$$\mathrm{d}x/\mathrm{d}t = y, \ \mathrm{d}y/\mathrm{d}t = -\omega x + \mu(1 - x^2/b^2)y, \tag{2}$$

where μ represents the anharmonic parameter of the oscillator. Because the generator of the heart rate is well modeled by the van der Pol equation, the QRS ECG waveform is well approximated by a sum of solutions of this equation, having as period sub-multiple of the fundamental period. Early detection of neurodegenerative diseases such as Alzheimer's or Parkinson's disease, is then made possible by looking at the gradual disappearance of the inspiratory cardiac acceleration, which serves as an alarm, triggering the consultation in a hospital department of neurology.

4 Actigram Emulation

To emulate persistent behaviors linked to the Alzheimer's disease in residential care settings, we first start from stable behaviors deriving from basic scenarios encountered in everyday life in the home environment [14]. Based on the fact that we all possess basic needs and patterns (*e.g.*, circadian or nycthemeral activity rhythms [23]), no matter the living conditions and the geographical location, we assumed that these scenarios would remain essentially identical in centers for Alzheimer's. In other words, we basically model the Alzheimer's conditions of life in a healthcare setting putting forward the hypothesis that patients still tend to follow a regular life rhythm based on 24 h (circadian or nycthemeral), such as in familiar environment at-home. Then, we slightly modify these scenarios to reveal persistent behaviors at the spatial-temporal level setting abnormal prolonged periods staying in a room or performing a daily routine.

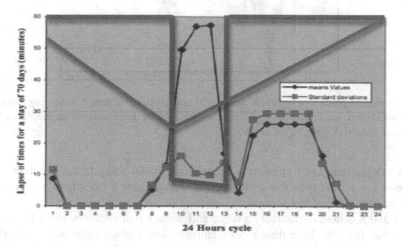

Fig. 5. Expectation (in blue), standard deviation (in pink) and variation coefficient (physiologic in green and pathologic in red) of the lapse of times passed in the kitchen at different hours of the nychthemeron, calculated after 70 days of observation (Colour figure online).

4.1 Data Modeling

To model usual scenarios of daily living progressing toward persistent behaviors, we have used homogeneous Markov chain model, which is a sequential method quite adapted to describe resident's successive room occupancies (or activities) in a home or by extension in a healthcare facility. After 70 days of observation in such a residency for elderly people, we get the statistics given on Fig. 5 for staying in the different rooms of the observed smart flat in which different sensors record the activity of the dependent early person. These statistics allow to calculate different temporal or histogram profiles assigning the observed person in different clusters corresponding to a normal or pathologic behavior [23, 24]. Alarms are triggered when passing from a normal type of nycthemeral activity to a pathologic one. For example, we model the phenomenon of persistence in an activity by setting atypical extended occupancy periods in a room.

4.2 Modeling Persistent Behaviors with Memory Parameters

Modeling persistence with memory effects consists in taking into account the time elapsed in a state before to determine the outcome of the next trial. In other words, trials

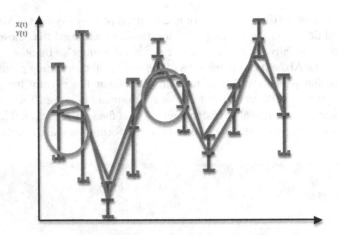

Fig. 6. Temporal profiles of signals X and Y (red and green) over time t, indicating monotonic segments between successive averages, each average being the center of an empirical 95 % confidence interval (Colour figure online).

are not independent. Let's consider a Polya's urn model using first a negative law of parameter $\alpha = 1$. This provokes an increasing waiting time Y (to stay in a state) as the trials go along without any success.

If W and B denote respectively a white and a black ball numbers, and k the number of successes (*i.e.*, we have drawn consecutively $k + 1$ black balls before drawing a white ball), then (3) gives the probability to stay in the same state (a room or an activity):

$$
\begin{aligned}
P(Y = k+1) &= \left(\frac{B}{B+W}\right) \times \left(\frac{B+1}{B+1+W}\right) \cdots \left(\frac{B+k}{B+k+W}\right)\left(\frac{W}{B+k+1+W}\right) \\
&= \left(\frac{(B+k)!(B)}{(B-1)!} \times \frac{W}{(B+k+1+W)!}\right)
\end{aligned}
$$

$$(3)$$

The reverse effect (the more we stay in the room, the more we have some chance to leave it) can be thus obtained using a negative law of parameter $\alpha < 0$ (2) whose expectancy $E(Y)$ is given by (4) and by (6) using Stirling approximation (5) for large factorials:

$$
E(Y) = \sum_{k=0}^{\infty} k\left(\frac{B}{B+W}\right) \cdots \left(\frac{B+k\alpha}{B+k\alpha+W}\right)\left(\frac{W}{B+(k+1)\alpha+W}\right) \qquad (4)
$$

$$
\text{If } K = -[-k\alpha] \text{ and } M! \approx \frac{M^M\sqrt{2\pi M}}{e^M} \qquad (5)
$$

$$E(Y) \approx \sum\nolimits_{k=0,\infty} \frac{k(B+W-1)^{B+W-1}\sqrt{2\pi(B+W-1)}e^{B+K+W}W(B+K)!}{e^{B+W-1}(B+K+W)^{B+K+W}\sqrt{2\pi(B+K+W)}(B+K+\alpha+W)(B-1)!}$$

$$(6)$$

Considering $B \gg W$, permits to simplify (6) in (7):

$$E(Y) \approx \sum\nolimits_{k=0,\infty} k(1-(k+1)\alpha/B)W/B \qquad (7)$$

4.3   Alarm Triggering of Persistence or Perseveration

We focus here on persistent behaviors causing an excessive occupancy periods in the same state (i.e., a room or possibly a well identified daily activity), or corresponding to the persevering repetition such as often opening and closing the doors or checking the contents of the refrigerator without necessity. These abnormal behaviors can be detected when room occupancy curves (Fig. 5) show a profile significantly different from classical temporal profiles of activity corresponding to the profiles cluster to which the patient belongs. A way to compare different temporal evolutions of the room occupancies is to test if the signature of monotony of a temporal profile (i.e., the succession of signs + for an increasing interval and – for a decreasing one) is significantly different from a reference profile (Fig. 6). We can compare the signatures of two signals X (observed) and Y (reference) and test the similarity of their signatures, against a random choice of signs, using the probability P_ to decrease from x to y (Fig. 7):

$$\text{if } D_2 \geq \delta, \ P\_ = \int_{\sup(0,D1)}^{\inf(\delta,D2)} (x-D_1)dx/\delta D = \int_{\sup(0,D1)}^{\inf(\delta,D2)} f(x)F(x)dx, \qquad (8)$$

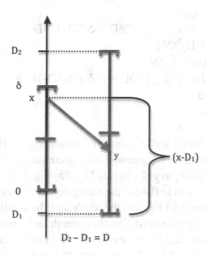

Fig. 7. Calculation of the probability P_ of negative monotony.

If $D_2 < \delta$, $P_- = 1 - P_+ = 1 - \int_{\sup(0,D1)}^{\inf(\delta,D2)} dx/\delta D$, where f (resp. F) is the uniform density function (resp. cumulative distribution function).

If the law of errors is Gaussian, (8) becomes:

$$P_- = \int_{-\infty}^{+\infty} f_1(x)F_2(ax + b)dx \tag{9}$$

where f_1 (resp. F_2) is the density function (resp. cumulative distribution function) of the first (resp. second) error on x, *i.e.*, of the Gaussian law $N(\mu_1,\sigma_1)$ (resp. $N(\mu_2,\sigma_2)$), where $a = \sigma_1/\sigma_2$ and $b = (\mu_1-\mu_2)/\sigma_2$. Because the cumulative distribution functions of uniform law on $[-2\sigma, 2\sigma]$ and Gaussian law $N(0,\sigma)$ are very close, results concerning calculation of P_- are similar (Fig. 8).

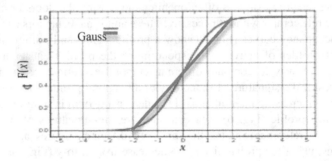

Fig. 8. Cumulative distribution function of the uniform (blue) and Gaussian (red) laws (Colour figure online)

There are 6 different cases:

There are 6 different cases:
1) $D_1 < 0 \leq \delta \leq D_2$ $P_- = [(\delta - D_1)^2 - D_1^2]/2\delta D = \delta/2D - D_1/D$ I
2) $D_1 < 0 \leq D_2 < \delta$ $P_- = 1 - D_2^2/2\delta D$ II
3) $D_2 \geq \delta \geq D_1 \geq 0$ $P_- = (\delta - D_1)^2/2\delta D$ III
4) $0 \leq D_1 \leq D_2 < \delta$ $P_- = 1 - (D_2^2 - D_1^2)/2\delta D = (2\delta - (D_2 + D_1))/2\delta$ IV
5) $D_1 > \delta$ $P_- = 0$ V
6) $D_2 < 0$ $P_- = 1$ VI

The first confidence interval for the observed signal equals $[0, \delta]$. The second to be compared to the first for deciding if there will be a decrease equals $[D_1,D_2]$. P_- is just the probability to go from x in $[0, \delta]$ to $y \leq x$ in $[D_1,D_2]$. On Fig. 6, the probability of decay of the observed signal X(t) is equal to 0.4 for the first interval of monotony, 1 for the second and the fifth (circled in orange in Fig. 6), the sixth and the ninth, and the probability of growth of X(t) is equal to 0 for the third, fourth, seventh and eighth. The values of X(t) at different time points are assumed to be stochastically independent. Let denote by **P** the probability of having at most 1.4 difference into the signs of monotony between the observed signal X(t) and the reference signal Y(t) like in Fig. 6. Suppose that the event $(+, -, +, +, -, -, +, +, -)$ is obtained by pure chance (0.5) of having the allowed sign at any monotony interval. Then the probability **P** in this hypothesis H0 is equal to:

$$0.4 \, C_9^2/2^9 + C_9^1/2^9 + C_9^0/2^9 = 24.4/2^9 \approx 4.8\,\% \qquad (10)$$

We can therefore consider that the probability of rejecting falsely the hypothesis of similarity of monotony due to chance, except one interval at most, is less than 5 %, and say that the similarity of monotony observed between X and Y is not due to a uniform random tossing of signs of monotony, and this with an error less than 5 %. This test is less powerful than a correlation test, but is sufficient in the case of a low number of longitudinal observations in which the amplitude of the signal is not pertinent compared to the signal monotony, for which the variance of the empirical correlation is important. The test requires that reference Y(t) and observed X(t) signals are known at same instants and that the values of X(t) at various time are stochastically independent.

5 Conclusion and Perspectives

Perspectives consider two complementary aspects of the actimetric and physiologic supervision of the person at-home: (i) the ability to record noninvasively different physiological parameters should allow, in the future, documenting automatically after a suitable filter (because the data volume is very large) the personalized medical record of the person followed at-home, which would greatly facilitate its updating, so enhance its pertinence, (ii) the rehabilitation programs in nutrition, locomotion and perception using the serious games allow, thanks to the bio-feedback inherent in these games, to integrate many individual data sources of customization and alarms. Eventually, through their ability of patient empowerment and the virtuous circle that can be installed between the person and the e-educator, these e-learning programs might be the best informational framework to improve the "health trail" during the lifetime of a person.

References

1. World Population Ageing 2009. Department of economical and social affairs report, United Nations publication, New York (2010)
2. Jamison, D.T., Breman, J.G., Measham, A.R., Alleyne, G., Claeson, M., Evans, D.B., Jha, P., Mills, A., Musgrove, P.: Disease Control Priorities in Developing Countries. World Bank, Washington (2006)
3. Demongeot, J., Virone, G., Duchêne, F., Benchetrit, G., Hervé, T., Noury, N., Rialle, V.: Multi-sensors acquisition, data fusion, knowledge mining and triggering in health smart homes for elderly people. C.R. Biol. **325**, 673–682 (2002)
4. Virone, G., Noury, N., Demongeot, J.: A system for automatic measurement of circadian activity deviation in telemedicine. IEEE Trans. Biomed. Eng. **49**, 1463–1469 (2002)
5. Abdulrazak, B., Mokhtari, M., Feki, M.A., Ghorbel, M.: Integration of home networking in a smart environment dedicated to people with disabilities. In: ICTTA'04, pp. 125–126. IEEE, Piscataway (2004)

6. Benneyan, J.C.: An introduction to using computer simulation in healthcare: patient wait case study. J. Soc. Health Syst. **5**, 1–15 (1997)

7. Lowery, J.C.: Introduction to simulation in healthcare. In: WSC'96 28th Conference on Winter simulation, pp. 78–84. IEEE Press, Piscataway (1996)

8. O'Connor, C.M., Smith, R., Nott, M.T., Lorang, C., Mathews, R.M.: Using video simulated presence to reduce resistance to care and increase participation of adults with dementia. Am. J. Alzeimer's Dis. Other Dementias **26**, 317–325 (2011)

9. Lowery, J.C., Martin, J.B.: Design and validation of a critical care simulation model. J. Soc. Health Syst. **3**, 15–36 (1992)

10. Gibson, B., Weir, C.: Development and preliminary evaluation of a simulation-based diabetes education module. AMIA Annu. Symp. Proc. **2010**, 246–250 (2010)

11. Berg, D.R., Carlson, A., Durfee, W.K., Sweet, R.M., Reihsen, T.: Low-cost, take-home, beating heart simulator for health-care education. Stud. Health Technol. Inf. **163**, 57–59 (2011)

12. Wong, P., Graves, M.J., Lomas, D.J.: Integrated physiological flow simulator and pulse sequence monitoring system for MRI. Med. Biol. Eng. Comput. **46**, 399–406 (2008)

13. Mahmoud, S.M., Akhlaghinia, M.J., Lotfi, A., Langensiepen, C.: Trend modelling of elderly lifestyle within an occupancy simulator. In: UKSim'11 International Conference on Computer Modelling and Simulation, Cambridge, pp. 156–161. IEEE Press, Piscataway (2011)

14. Virone, G., Lefebvre, B., Noury, N., Demongeot, J.: Modeling and computer simulation of physiological rhythms and behaviors at home for data fusion programs in a telecare system. In: HealthCom'03, pp. 118–127. IEEE Press, Piscataway (2003)

15. Nabih, K., Gomaa, M.M., Osman, H.S., Aly, G.M.: Modeling, simulation, and control of smart homes using petri nets. Int. J. Smart Home **5**, 1 (2011)

16. Cardinaux, F., Brownsell, S., Hawley, M.S., Bradley, D.: A home daily activity simulation model for the evaluation of lifestyle monitoring systems. Comput. Biol. Med. **43**, 1428–1436 (2013)

17. Lazovik, A., Kaldeli, E., Lazovik, E., Aiello, M.: Planning in a smart home: visualization and simulation. In: ICAPS'09, pp. 13–16. AAAI Press, Menlo Park (2009)

18. Poland, M.P., Nugent, C.D., Wang, H., Chen, L.: Development of a smart home simulator for use as a heuristic tool for management of sensor distribution. Techn. Health Care **17**, 171–182 (2009)

19. Virone, G., Istrate, D.: Integration of an environmental sound module to an existing in-home activity simulator. In: 29th IEEE-EMBS Engineering in Medicine and Biology Society) Microtechnologies in Medicine & Biology, pp. 3810–3813. IEEE, Piscataway (2007)

20. Istrate, D., Castelli, E.: Information extraction from sound for medical telemonitoring. IEEE Trans. Inf Technol. Biomed. **10**, 264–274 (2006)

21. Albæripæ, W.: Tractatus Numerorum a ternario usque ad duodenarium, ad Thomam monachum. Manu- scrit incunable, Médiathèque de Troyes, manuscript 969, l° 195 (vers 1180)

22. Demongeot, J., Françoise, J.P.: Approximation for limit cycles. C. R. Biol. **329**, 967–970 (2006)

23. Virone, G., Vuillerme, N., Mokhtari, M., Demongeot, J.: Persistent behaviour in healthcare facilities: from actimetric tele-surveillance to therapy education. In: Mellouk, A., Fowler, S., Hoceini, S., Daachi, B. (eds.) WWIC 2014. LNCS, vol. 8458, pp. 297–311. Springer, Heidelberg (2014)

24. Franco, C., Fleury, A., Guméry, P.Y., Diot, B., Demongeot, J., Vuillerme, N.: iBalance-ABF: a smartphone-based audio-biofeedback balance system. IEEE Tr. Biomed. Eng **60**, 211–215 (2013)

Monitoring Patient Recovery Using Wireless Physiotherapy Devices

Nirmalya Roy[1]($\boxtimes$) and Brooks Reed Kindle[2]

[1] Department of Information Systems,
University of Maryland Baltimore County, Baltimore, USA
nroy@umbc.edu
[2] School of Electrical Engineering and Computer Science,
Washington State University, Pullman, USA
brooks.kindle@email.wsu.edu

Abstract. We aim to improve physiotherapy patients' recovery time by monitoring various prescribed tasks and displaying a score associated with how well the patient has performed said task. This kind of feedback would be desirable in situations where physical proximity between the physiotherapist and his patient is not always convenient or achievable. Having a way to remotely perform and receive feedback on prescribed tasks remedies that problem. We used a wireless device that contains accelerometer (acceleration) and gyroscope (angular velocity) sensors to collect motion information from the patient. After this information has been collected, it is processed in order to provide a more accurate representation of the performed task. The processed data is then broken up into micro-exercises, parts that make up the specified exercise, to evaluate qualitatively how accurately the exercise was performed and quantitatively how many times the task was performed. Finally, a task score is provided to the user that is based on the Functional Ability Scale and a weighted linear algorithm of the sum of the micro-exercise scores. This allows a patient to receive instant feedback on a performed task without the need to physically interact with a physiotherapist.

1 Introduction

In a day and age where mobile technology is ubiquitous, there still are not that many medical applications that take advantage of such a technology. Medical technology that incorporates smart phone technology for use in their program stand to gain ease of use and compatibility, since so many people already own the platform required. Our goal is to create a mobile app that tracks the recovery progress of physiotherapy patients with motor deficits - such as stroke patients - by collecting real time data from wireless sensors about various prescribed exercises and then providing both qualitative and quantitative feedback to the patient without the need for the physiotherapist to be present [1,2].

As a remedy to the possible schedule conflicts or difficulty in transporting patients with motor deficits, physiotherapists often prescribe exercise regiments in order to help the patient regain his or her motor ability that was lost.

© Springer International Publishing Switzerland 2015
C. Bodine et al. (Eds.): ICOST 2014, LNCS 8456, pp. 71–79, 2015.
DOI: 10.1007/978-3-319-14424-5_8

Oftentimes however, these regimens are either followed incorrectly or not as often as prescribed, as the only way of verifying if a regimen is being followed is through patient self-reporting - the accuracy of which cannot be guaranteed.

Our app would remedy this problem. By using a mobile phone to analyze the exercise data sent by the SHIMMER sensor [4], the patient would be able to receive qualitative and quantitative feedback on the regimen exercise he or she performed, thus helping he or she determine how to best remedy the problem. Qualitative feedback would be based on the Functional Ability Scale, FAS [3], while quantitative feedback would display the number of times the patient performed the exercise.

The SHIMMER sensor monitors real-time accelerometer (acceleration) and gyroscope (orientation) data and sends it over a Bluetooth connection. On the receiving end, raw accelerometer and gyrometer data is exported to a comma separated value file (.csv) for storage. As shown in Fig. 1, not everything in the file is accelerometer or gyrometer data. In order to begin processing the raw sensor data, we removed the SensorID, DataType, SeqNo, and TimeStamp values from the file. After that is completed, we process the data. This provides two benefits: the first being that the size of the dataset is reduced, which allows for a faster classification time later on, and second, it allows for a more accurate classification of the data.

	A	B	C	D	E	F	G	H	I	J
1	SensorID	DataType	SeqNo	TimeStamp	AccX	AccY	AccZ	GyroX	GyroY	GyroZ
2	0	255	50	42077	1885	1990	2774	1845	1847	1797
3	0	255	51	42237	1875	1998	2786	1845	1845	1797
4	0	255	52	42397	1885	1979	2782	1845	1848	1796
5	0	255	53	42557	1875	1993	2804	1844	1849	1799
6	0	255	55	42877	1866	2005	2778	1843	1849	1798
7	0	255	56	43037	1886	1961	2790	1843	1850	1796
8	0	255	57	43197	1886	2005	2770	1842	1850	1797
9	0	255	58	43357	1880	1964	2775	1843	1850	1797
10	0	255	59	43517	1901	1987	2787	1843	1850	1797
11	0	255	60	43677	1879	1982	2784	1845	1849	1797
12	0	255	61	43837	1890	1997	2773	1847	1850	1797
13	0	255	62	43997	1880	1989	2776	1848	1848	1796
14	0	255	63	44157	1888	1992	2777	1848	1849	1795

Fig. 1. A portion of the raw data exported to a comma separated value file

2   Related Work

The proliferation of pervasive and ubiquitous computing has accelerated the emergence of a new era of primary healthcare that has the potential to change the way healthcare is delivered and health is assessed. The American Medical Association (AMA) recently passed a resolution stating that insurers should reimburse for email consultations. In the resolution, there is also an encouragement for the reimbursement of other forms of virtual care including remote monitoring services. Recent advancement has helped to monitor the activities of daily living of seniors living alone using a combination of low-cost sensors, advanced mesh networking technologies and profile-based anomaly detection engines [12]. Individuals can also be monitored for illness and early symptoms with the help of real time monitoring, analysis and extrapolation of physiological data such as blood pressure, blood glucose levels, motion data, body weight etc. [8].

Wireless sensor networks will continue to play an important role in next generation smart healthcare. The Fitbit [7], a fitness monitoring equipment based on inertial sensors tracks a user's daily activities and the calories that the user has burned. This same motion data can also be used to monitor patients' progress in rehabilitation programs and to design new regimen. The data collected from body-worn accelerometers, gyroscopes, magnetometers, and pedometers can be assessed for the detection and treatment of gait anomalies, Parkinson's disease, stroke, total knee replacement, fall detection and prevention, etc., even when the subject is located in the home environment. Thus our goal is to provide therapists the technology that will help them to get high-fidelity real time context of the patients without manual intervention. Such technological advances will help people with functional disabilities to live in their home environment and manage their diseases from day to day in the best possible ways.

Existing advanced physiotherapy rehabilitation systems mostly use optical motion systems with high speed cameras for kinematic data collection. These systems are expensive, require a large space, and cannot be used outside a laboratory environment [13]. Other relatively standard systems using magnetic and sonic technologies are difficult to be applied without the patient being in rehabilitation clinic. These and other available industry products such as KinTools RT [9], OrthoTrak [10], and Phoenix Technologies Inc [11] do not possess the diversity of sensing systems necessary to monitor a patient's entire physiotherapy conditions, e.g., they lack an EMG sensor based system to measure muscle stiffness. A wearable sensor system with low cost that is easy to deploy and has a robust supporting software infrastructure will be an effective solution in this immersive physiotherapy domain [14]. Such systems can provide additional features to support tele-physiotherapy services and replace the intensive manpower needed for existing in-place physiotherapy approaches. A pervasive computing based physiotherapy approach will also extend the capabilities of monitoring to more varied settings, thereby making it simpler for therapists to examine new exercise regimen and interventions that might improve the patients' overall conditions.

Most of the above system target a specific healthcare problem instead of being adaptive to general purpose physiotherapy. The existing systems are often complex, closed-loop, expensive and proprietary. But recent advancement of pervasive computing and communications encourage us to go beyond the existing systems and visualize an open platform that can support a variety of healthcare services with a little modification on top of the single general-purpose underlying platform for situated health monitoring and maintenance. In relation to physiotherapy, this open platform will enable patients to avail themselves of physiotherapy treatment independent of their location and available clinical resources.

In the more general sense, this enables better awareness of general health and possible interventions that take advantage of a person's everyday environment. Motivated by these challenges and shortcomings we perform preliminary studies to attest the promise of remotely monitoring patient recovery using wireless physiotherapy devices.

3   Methodologies

In order to record exercise data, we used a SHIMMER (Sensing Health with Intelligence, Modularity, Mobility, and Experimental Reusability) wireless sensor [4]. The datasets have been collected from three subjects in a controlled environment using this SHIMMER sensor. Each of the subjects have been asked to perform 10 sets of the three exercises. We then combined the data for each set together to generate the training datasets. Figure 2 shows a flowchart of our data being collected and then segmented into micro and macro exercises in order to determine a qualitative and quantitative result [6]. We collected data that fell into two categories, micro exercise data and macro exercise data. More accurately, we collected macro exercise data and then segmented the exercise into sub exercises known as micro exercises. We then collected data for each individual micro exercise for classification. In total, we collected data about three

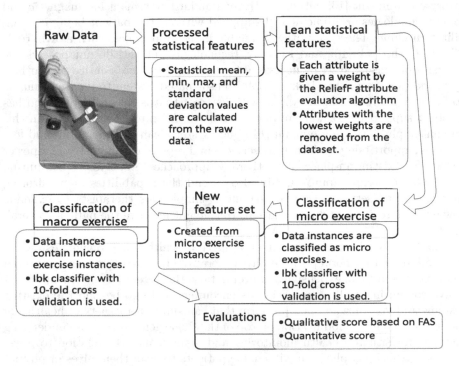

Fig. 2. An overview of the qualitative and quantitative evaluation procedure of micro and macro exercises

macro exercises and their eleven micro exercises that the macro exercises were segmented into. The three macro exercises we collected were named *armPump*, *armPlank*, and *armToTableCurl*. Each macro exercise was segmented into two, three, or four micro exercises.

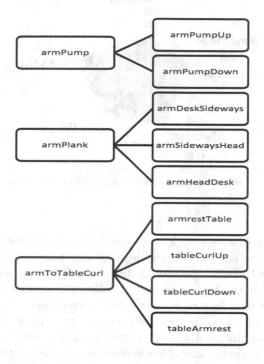

Fig. 3. Macro to micro exercise mapping

Figure 3 shows our macro exercises and which micro exercises they were segmented into. When classifying macro exercises, we chose to include the set of all eleven micro exercises, even though not all eleven micro exercises were used in a single macro exercise. In order to classify the macro exercises, we first needed to process the micro exercises that the macro exercises were segmented into. From the raw sensor data, we calculated the statistical mean, min, max, and standard deviation of the acceleration and orientation data with a window size of five. With our statistical data, we tested five algorithms implemented in WEKA [5], a program that contains a collection of machine learning algorithms for use in solving data mining problems, to determine which algorithm would provide us with the maximum accuracy in correctly classifying micro exercises. The Fig. 4 shows our results - the micro classification accuracies of each of the five algorithms.

Using WEKA's Ibk classifier gave us the highest percentage of correctly classified micro instances, so we decided to use that. In addition to that, we also used WEKAs implementation of the ReliefF attribute selection algorithm to

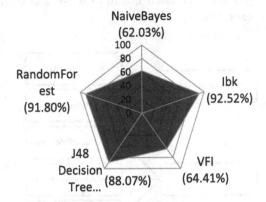

Fig. 4. Comparisons of micro exercise classification accuracies using various classification algorithms

determine which attributes were least important in classifying. Through experimentation, we determined that removing the five least important attributes, determined by the ReliefF algorithm, before classifying our data with the Ibk algorithm resulted in the highest correct classification accuracy.

The same steps used to classify segmented micro exercises were also used to classify the macro exercises. As with the process for the micro exercises, the raw acceleration and orientation data is extracted from the initial comma separated value file and then a window size of five is used to calculate statistical mean, min, max, and standard deviation values of the data. The same five least important attributes that were removed from the micro exercise instances are again removed from the macro exercise instances. However, instead of simply attempting to classify a macro exercise at this stage, we again use the Ibk classifier, but this time we also use the micro exercise classification file as a training set to classify each macro exercise instance. This classifies instances of a macro exercise as one of the micro exercise instances in our training set. From there, we further process the segmented macro exercise by taking a count of the micro exercises classified within a window size of five. While this additional step reduces the macro exercise classification accuracy by around one percent, it has the added benefit of being able to use a vastly reduced sample size, thereby requiring less processing power to compute.

Figures 5 and 6 show the confusion matrices of the two methods of processing macro exercises. Our method is to classify a macro stretch according to the micro exercise count within a window size of five, rather than just the processed statistical data.

```
=== Confusion Matrix ===

   a    b    c    <-- classified as
4082    0   25 |    a = armPlank
   0 2392    0 |    b = armPump
  24    5 4112 |    c = armToTableCurl
```

Fig. 5. Confusion matrix of macro exercise classification using statistical instances

```
=== Confusion Matrix ===

  a    b    c    <-- classified as
810    0   11 |    a = armPlank
  2  475    1 |    b = armPump
 17    2  809 |    c = armToTableCurl
```

Fig. 6. Confusion matrix of macro exercise classification using micro instance counts

4 Evaluation Results

We found that classifying our macro exercises using just the statistical data yielded a higher percentage classification than our method of classifying macro exercises using the counts of micro exercise instances. Figure 7 details the accuracy comparison between the two methods aforementioned. The difference in accuracies of the two methods is close to one percent, which at 99.49 % and 98.45 % respectively is still fairly reasonable accuracies.

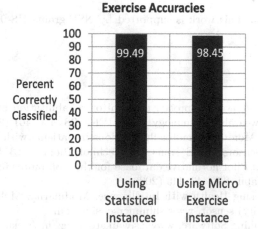

Fig. 7. Comparison in accuracies of the two methods, statistical and micro instance counts

In addition to being able to classify over 98 % of our macro exercises correctly, we have also developed prototype software that enables us to count the number of *armToTableCurl* macro stretches that a user has performed.

5   Discussion and Conclusion

Our decision to classify macro exercises based on the number of micro exercise instances rather than just the statistical mean, min, max, and standard deviation values of the raw data was based on the hope that our method would provide higher exercise classification accuracy over the other method. However, our classification method was not quite as accurate as simply classifying based on statistical values. Our method, however, does provide a couple of obvious benefits over the other method. The first being that the size of the data required to classify is much less. In our case, since we chose to count the micro exercise instances in a window size of five, our data set was five times smaller than the other method. The second benefit is that because the dataset is smaller, the time required to classify macro exercises is greatly reduced. Since our goal was to create a mobile app, having a faster classification time is a benefit when dealing with a smaller, mobile processor.

Future work for this project would include providing a more exhaustive qualitative feedback score based on the Functional Ability Scale (FAS) [3], as well as an improved method of determining the quantitative feedback. In addition to these, we would also need to refine our algorithm to be more lightweight in order for our application to be viable for use in a mobile phone as well as collect data from a more diverse set of micro and macro exercises.

Acknowledgement. This work is supported by NSF-grants IIS-0647705 and CNS-1344990.

References

1. Patel, S., et al.: A novel approach to monitor rehabilitation outcomes in stroke survivors using wearable technology. Proc. IEEE **98**, 450–461 (2010)
2. Patel, S., et al.: Monitoring motor fluctuations in patients with Parkinson disease using wearable sensors. IEEE Trans. Inf. Technol. Biomed. **13**, 864–873 (2009)
3. Wolf, S.L., et al.: Pilot normative database for the wolf motor function test. Arch. Phys. Med. Rehabil. **87**, 443–445 (2006)
4. SHIMMER (Sensing Health with Intelligence, Modularity, Mobility, and Experimental Reusability) sensor. www.shimmersensing.com
5. WEKA Data Mining Software. www.cs.waikato.ac.nz/ml/weka
6. Yan, Z., Chakraborty, D., Misra, A., Jeung, H., Aberer, K.: SAMMPLE: detecting semantic indoor activities in practical settings using locomotive signatures. In: International Symposium on Wearable Computers (ISWC) (2012)
7. Fitbit. http://www.fitbit.com

8. Hayes, T.L., Pavel, P., Larimer, N., Tsay, I.A., Nutt, J., Dami, A.G.: Distributed healthcare: simultaneous assessment of multiple individuals. IEEE Perv. Comput. **6**(1), 36–43 (2007)
9. KinTools RT. http://www.motionanalysis.com/html/movement/kinetics.html
10. OrthoTrak. http://www.motionanalysis.com/html/movement/orthotrak.html
11. Phoenix Technologies Inc. http://www.ptiphoenix.com/
12. Reanex Technologies. http://www.reanex.com
13. Simi Reality Motion Systems. www.simi.de
14. Varshney, U.: Pervasive healthcare and wireless health monitoring. Mobile Netw. Appl. **12**(2–3), 113–127 (2007)

Cognitive Technology

Comparison of Two Prompting Methods in Guiding People with Traumatic Brain Injury in Cooking Tasks

Jing Wang, Harshal Mahajan, Pamela Toto, Ashlee McKeon,
Michael McCue, and Dan Ding[(✉)]

Department of Rehabilitation Science and Technology, School of Health
and Rehabilitation Sciences, University of Pittsburgh, Pittsburgh, PA, USA
{jiw78,mhp3,pet3,amckeon,mmccue,dad5}@pitt.edu

Abstract. This study aims to examine the effectiveness of two prompting methods (i.e., a paper-based method vs a step-by-step user-controlled method on an iPad mini) in guiding individuals with traumatic brain injury (TBI) through the cooking tasks. Eight individuals with traumatic brain injury participated in this study. They were asked to prepare two meals in their home kitchens following the guidance of the two methods, respectively. Their performance were evaluated using the Performance Assessment of Self-Care Skills (PASS) tool. The perceived ease-of-use, usefulness, and cognitive loads of the two prompting methods were assessed using a custom questionnaire. In addition, problems of participants in completing the cooking tasks with both prompting methods were categorized. Results showed that four participants completed cooking tasks more independently with the user-controlled prompting method and most participants preferred the user-controlled method to paper-based prompting. Recommendations for future development of prompting methods were also discussed.

Keywords: Prompting method · Traumatic brain injury · Cooking tasks

1 Introduction

Each year, approximately 1.7 million people in the United States sustain a traumatic brain injury (TBI) [1]. Survivors of TBI usually suffer from various cognitive deficits such as problems with memory, attention, planning and executive functions [2]. These cognitive deficits often limit these individuals from completing activities of daily living (ADLs) independently. Among ADLs, cooking tasks are cognitively demanding and have been identified essential for living independently and important for an individual's health, accomplishment in social roles, self-esteem, and sense of control [3–6].

Many strategies have been recommended to compensate for cognitive deficits. External aids often termed as Assistive Technology for Cognition (ATC) [7], provide users with a tool or device that either limits the cognitive demands of a task or transforms the task or environment to match users' abilities [7, 8]. A variety of prompting methods are being used in ATC. Some low-tech ATC, like paper-based tools (e.g. paper calendars, and paper recipes), are most widely recommended for interventions,

© Springer International Publishing Switzerland 2015
C. Bodine et al. (Eds.): ICOST 2014, LNCS 8456, pp. 83–92, 2015.
DOI: 10.1007/978-3-319-14424-5_9

especially for cooking tasks [9–12]. High-tech ATC, such as applications (Apps) on smart phones and computers, use a step-by-step user-controlled prompting method to assist individuals in completing multi-step tasks [13, 14]. With the growing use of smart mobile devices and the increasing number of Apps, it would be useful to observe how individuals with TBI interact with the devices/apps and whether the user-controlled prompting method afforded by such apps can better assist these individuals. Most ATC studies focus on evaluating scheduling services, and evidence about the effectiveness of prompting methods in guiding multistep tasks is relatively scarce [7, 15–17].

The objective of this study is to observe how individuals with TBI interact with a paper-based recipe versus a step-by-step user-controlled recipe on an iPad mini in completing typical cooking tasks in their home kitchens. We will compare user performance and their perceived ease-of-use, usefulness, and cognitive loads with the two prompting methods. We are also interested in communicating the nature of problems faced by people with TBI when performing activities in the kitchen with current available prompting methods, and gathering design recommendations to inform the design of future advanced assistive devices for cognition.

2   Methods

The study was approved by the University of Pittsburgh Institutional Review Board and was conducted in each participant's residence.

2.1   Participants

Participants were recruited from the local TBI support groups and rehabilitation institutes. Inclusion criteria consisted of (1) over the age of 18; (2) having a self-reported diagnosis of TBI; (3) capable of understanding the objectives, risks, voluntary nature, and procedures of this study. Eight individuals with TBI participated in this study so far.

2.2   Settings

Two types of prompting methods were used in this study: a paper-based method and a step-by-step user-controlled prompting App on an iPad Mini. To minimize the learning effect, two different recipes (i.e., pancake and French toast) with same number of sub-steps and similar complexity were made available for each prompting method. Two online recipes (i.e., one for pancake and one for French toast) were converted to paper-based and iPad-based recipes, respectively. The iPad-based recipes were programmed with a commercial available App, Visual Impact Pro [18]. The interface of the iPad recipe is shown in Fig. 1, where participants could navigate the prompts for each step by pressing "Back" and "Next" buttons on the screen. No verbal prompts were provided by this App.

Fig. 1. The interface of the step-by-step user-controlled prompting method

2.3 Protocol

Researchers paid one visit to each participant's residence. After the consent process, participants filled a questionnaire including questions on demographics, injury related information, and experience with assistive technology (AT). A short interview followed to obtain more information about the participant and his/her recovery process. A brief orientation session was then followed where an investigator demonstrated how to use the paper recipe and the step-by-step recipe on iPad, and made sure participants were able to use both recipes based on a usability checklist. The checklist mainly included whether participants were able to see the text/images clearly, to understand the sentences/phases, and to press the buttons to navigate the recipe on the iPad.

Participants were then asked to complete two cooking tasks using different prompting methods. The sequence of prompting methods was counterbalanced. All ingredients and utensils needed for these two tasks were brought with investigators in case a household did not have them. During the cooking tasks, participants' performance were evaluated by an investigator using the Performance Assessment of Self-Care Skills (PASS) tool [19]. Up to nine levels of assistance can be provided by the investigator, including verbal supportive, verbal non-directive, verbal directive, gestures, task or environment rearrangement, demonstration, physical guidance, physical support, and total assist. Only necessary assistance at minimal level was provided by the investigator. The steps of a task were marked if assistance was provided or unsafe/inadequacy behaviors were observed. After each task, a custom questionnaire was administered in a semi-structured interview to assess perceived ease-of-use and usefulness of the two prompting methods, as well as obtain qualitative feedback from the participants.

2.4 Data Collection

The PASS provides scores for three areas of performance including independence, adequacy, and safety. Independence score was rated for each step and then summarized as the mean score of all steps for the whole task on an ordinal scale from 0–3 (0 = most negative and 3 = most positive). The full score 3 indicated no external assistance was needed. The adequacy and safety were rated similarly from 0–3 but for the whole task, based on how many inadequate and safety-threatening activities were observed and a score of 3 indicates no such activities happened.

The custom questionnaire assessed user perceived ease-of-use and usefulness of the two methods based on the adaption of Technology Acceptance Model (TAM) [20] using 7-point Likert scale responses (1 = strongly disagree and 7 = strongly agree). There were 10 statements for perceived usefulness and 7 statements for ease-of-use. The total score for perceived usefulness was calculated by adding the user response for each statement and ranged from 10 to 70, while the total score for perceived ease-of-use was ranged from 7 to 49. Both scores were then scaled between 0 and 1(0 = most negative, 1 = most positive). Participants' stress level was evaluated using a 5-point Likert scale (1 = not at all stressful and 5 = extremely stressful). The overall satisfaction was evaluated using a 7-point Likert scale (1 = completely dissatisfied and 7 = completely satisfied).

2.5   Data Analysis

Descriptive statistics was used to analyze the data obtained from the demographic and custom evaluation questionnaires. Content analysis was conducted to extract common themes from the observation and interview.

3   Results

3.1   Participants

Eight adults with TBI participated in this study (Table 1). The average age was 40.6 ± 8.5 years old and the duration post brain injury was 15.8 ± 10.9 years. Seven participants lived in community and one participant (P8) lived in the group home of a local rehabilitation institute. All participants were able to walk without using any mobility assistive technology. Five participants (P2, P4, P5, P6, and P8) had ATC in use and all of them used calendar applications on smart phone or iPad. In addition, P5 also used Timex datalink watch and P6 used pillbox and paper calendars.

3.2   Performance Evaluation

Participants' PASS scores in terms of independence, safety, and adequacy are shown in Table 2.

3.3   User Feedback

Ratings of perceived usefulness, ease-of-use, stress, and satisfaction with the two prompting methods are shown in Table 3.

Qualitative feedback during the interview was summarized as follows. All participants had experience of using paper-based method prior to the study. Recipe books and online recipes were the main sources. P1 emphasized that she was so used to paper recipes that this method is much easier to follow. Three participants indicated that separate list of ingredients in paper recipe was very helpful. Regarding disadvantages of this method, four participants commented that keeping track of steps and self-checking

Table 1. Demographic information of participants

Demographic variables		Mean ± SD
Age		40.6 ± 8.5
Duration of TBI (yrs.)		15.8 ± 10.9
Sex	Female	4
	Male	4
Ethnicity	African-American	2
	Caucasian	5
	Hispanic	1
ATC in use	Yes	5
	No	3

Table 2. Performance evaluation using PASS

Participants	No. of Assistance		Independence		Safety		Adequacy	
	P*	U*	P*	U*	P*	U*	P*	U*
P1	7	5	2.76	2.88	3	2	1	2
P2	6	3	2.76	2.88	2	3	2	2
P3	15	26	2.65	2.24	2	2	1	2
P4	1	2	2.94	2.94	3	3	2	2
P5	2	0	2.88	3.00	2	3	3	3
P6	18	6	2.47	2.76	2	3	2	3
P7	0	4	3.00	2.76	3	2	2	2
P8	0	4	3.00	2.88	3	2	2	1

P*: paper-based prompting method, U*: step-by-step user-controlled prompting method.

Table 3. Perceived Usefulness, Ease-of-Use, Stress, and Satisfaction

Participants	Usefulness		Ease-of-use		Stress		Satisfaction	
	P*	U*	P*	U*	P*	U*	P*	U*
P1	0.70	0.00	0.95	0.36	2	3	7	3
P2	0.85	1.00	1.00	1.00	1	1	7	7
P3	0.57	0.95	0.57	0.79	2	3	6	7
P4	0.05	1.00	0.38	1.00	4	1	5	7
P5	0.80	0.97	0.67	0.81	3	1	5	6
P6	0.85	1.00	0.71	0.98	2	1	5	7
P7	0.57	0.93	0.60	0.90	3	2	5	7
P8	0.28	0.82	0.52	0.95	2	1	3	7

P*: paper-based prompting method, U*: step-by-step user-controlled prompting method.

on completion of steps consumed significant mental effort and created stress. P7 commented "I have to constantly go back to look at it (paper recipe). I lost my direction when I look back on it". P5 and P6 commented that text instructions on the paper were very difficult to use for individuals' with injured reading abilities as sequela of TBI. P5 shared that it took her many years to regain the ability to read more than one word at a time after the injury.

Regarding the user-controlled prompting method, none of the participants had previous experience. However, seven participants showed greater satisfaction with this method and especially favored picture prompts and step-by-step instructions. Five participants also liked that they can navigate steps on their own pace easily. Limitations of this method were also identified by participants. First, users may forget to press the button to get further prompts after distracted. P5 commented "There is nothing to say 'come back to me (the user-controlled App)' for the next step". Second, two participants expressed that pressing "Next" button for each step was distracting and not convenient, especially when their hands were busy with cooking. P8 would prefer to control the pace of prompts by voice. Third, the content and sequence of steps need to be improved. P8 commented that instructions should be less discrete and inform both specific goals and actions within one step. For example, two steps "Measure 1 TBSP butter" and "Melt the butter in the pan" should be combined as one step. Participants also suggested that the sequence of steps can be reorganized to enable multi-tasking and increase cooking efficiency. P4 and P5 thought cleaning up parts should also be added to the steps.

3.4   Problems Encountered During the Cooking Tasks

Abnormal behaviors of participants during completing cooking tasks with two different prompting methods were identified based on observation and categorized in Table 4. These incidents were classified into three main themes.

Problems related to cooking experience. The absence of adequate cooking common sense and techniques led to participants' problems in completing tasks efficiently with both prompting methods. Most participants had problems determining the timing to flip food and whether the food was fully-cooked. Use of wrong utensils led participants to spend excessive amount of time on a task and ended up with failure or low adequacy.

Difficulties with following the instructions of the recipes. For both prompting methods, participants encountered similar difficulties with efficiency and safety during cooking tasks. Two participants constantly asked for confirmations from investigators. However, more problems happened with the paper-based recipe in keeping track of steps, kitchen storage, and utensils, and failure to follow instructions.

Cognitive/emotion difficulties. With the user-controlled method, participants had fewer incidents from distraction and impulsively flipping food. However, three participants acted before pressing "Next" button for following steps which required investigators' assistance to prevent mistakes that participants were going to make. When using the paper-based prompting method, participants showed more non-verbal behaviors of dysfunction and self-deprecating comments during the cooking tasks.

Table 4. Problems observed during cooking tasks

Category of problems*	Paper-based prompting method	User-controlled prompting method
Problems related to cooking experiences		
Inadequate common sense on cooking	Did not know to adjust heat level to improve efficiency (2, 2)	Did not know to adjust heat level to improve efficiency (3, 3)
		Had difficulties in identifying status of food (e.g. whether burned) (1, 1)
Inadequate techniques for kitchen tasks	Had difficulties in understanding markings of measuring tools (3, 3)	Used inappropriate utensils in tasks (2, 2)
	Used inappropriate utensils in tasks (1, 3)	Did not know to use a utensil to improve efficiency (1, 1)
	Used utensils with inadequate technique (1, 1)	
Difficulties with following the instructions of recipes		
Difficulties in follow steps of recipes	Lost track of steps (1, 1)	Ignored text instructions (1, 1)
	Lost track of kitchen storage/utensils (2, 2)	Misunderstood pictures (2, 2)
	Misunderstood instructions (2, 2)	Kept asking for confirmations during tasks (2, 10)
	Failure to follow instructions after coming back from distractions (1, 1)	
	Kept asking for confirmations during tasks (2, 9)	
Safety threats activities	Left pan on hot burner after cooking (3, 3)	Left pan on hot burner after cooking (3, 3)
	Put paper recipe and ingredients on stove (1, 1)	Turned on a wrong burner (1, 1)
Inefficiency	Spent excessive amounts of time on specific parts of tasks (e.g. measuring ingredients and mixing) (1, 3)	Spent excessive amounts of time on specific parts of task (e.g. measuring ingredients and mixing) (1, 2)
Cognitive/emotion difficulties		
Distraction	Distracted by environment (2, 9)	Distracted by environment (2, 5)
Impulsiveness	Flipped food before right timing (4, 13)	Flipped food before right timing (3, 3)
		Acted before seeing instructions (3, 4)
Non-verbal behavior	Performed non-verbal behavior (e.g. jaw clenching, picks or scratches skin, rocking, rubbing, moaning or other self-stimulating behavior) (6, 18)	Performed non-verbal behavior (e.g. jaw clenching, picks or scratches skin, rocking, rubbing, moaning or other self-stimulating behavior) (5, 11)
Verbal behavior	Sub-vocalization (i.e. talking or mumbling under breath) (5, 25)	Sub-vocalization (i.e. talking or mumbling under breath) (6, 32)
	Self-deprecating comments (4, 10)	
Resistance	Refused to accept advice prompted by investigators (2, 2)	Refused to accept advice prompted by investigators (1, 3)

* For each bullet of categorized incidents (N1, N2), N1 indicates the number of participants encountered the difficulties, and N2 indicates the number of total incidents among participants.

4 Discussion

Despite the small number of subjects we have tested so far, we observed that four participants were able to complete more steps of a cooking task independently and required less assistance with the step-by-step user-controlled prompting method. Participants showed comparable performance in safety and adequacy dimensions for both methods. However, user-controlled method showed advantage in helping with tracking steps, decreasing mental effort and stress. Thus, most participants preferred this method to paper-based prompting.

Nevertheless, participants still needed external assistance to complete tasks with the user-controlled prompting method. The open-loop fashion of this method required users' self-monitoring and pressing a button for further prompts. No additional prompts can be provided after users made mistakes or were distracted. Participants still faced different categories of problems with this method and better solutions are in need to address these limitations.

Future development of step-by-step prompting devices may consider adding some sensing components to help users monitor their actions, thus enhancing safety and reducing stress from self-prompting and self-monitoring. The authors proposed specific types of incidents that may need to be detected or inferred by sensing components, and possible prompts to be generated to prevent or recover from the problems (Table 5).

The main strength of this study was that it was conducted in each participant's home kitchen. The familiar environment and kitchen set-up minimized the influence of other factors on participants' performance and allowed investigators to observe their natural behaviors when interacting with the prompting methods. One limitation of the

Table 5. Proposed sensing and prompting solutions for problems observed

Category of problems*	Sensor Inference	Future Prompts
Problems with cooking experiences		
Inadequate common sense and techniques on cooking tasks	Power/gas consumptions of the appliances	Provide prompts for appropriate utensils, how to use, and recommended food status through images or short video clips
	Cooking temperature of the appliances	
	Cooking time	
	Object recognition for utensils	
Difficulties with following the instructions of the recipes		
Difficulties in following the steps of the recipes	Infer what kind of task is being carried on	Make sure text instructions in big font with high contrast background
	Infer correct completion of a sub-task	Provide verbal instructions
		Allow users/family members to adapt pictures in prompting devices
		Provide check boxes for users
		Provide confirmations by sensor inference

(Continued)

Table 5. (*Continued*)

Category of problems*	Sensor Inference	Future Prompts
Safety threats activities	Locations of pans/pots and active burners	Include explicit prompts to prevent possible safety threats
	Consumption of power, gas, and water	Inform caregivers or family members when safety threats detected
	"On/off" status	Direct control by the system (e.g. cut off power of the stove)
	"On" duration of appliances	
	Location of the user	
Inefficiency	Amount of time spent on a specific task	Inform time spent on the task
		Remind goal of the task
Cognitive/Emotion difficulties		
Distraction & Impulsiveness	Infer what kind of task is being carried on	Prompt to draw attention to the task
	Location of the user	Inform time spent on the task
	Action of the user	Remind criteria for actions (e.g. flip the toast when the underside is brown)
	Amount of time spent on a specific task	Give automatic following prompts after the sensor inference of completion

study is the small sample size. As the study is still ongoing, we hope to conduct more comprehensive analysis when more participants are tested, and more importantly, to develop design guidelines for ATC that aim to assist individuals with cognitive impairments in completing multi-step tasks.

Acknowledgements. This research was funded through the National Science Foundation, Quality of Life Technology Engineering Research Center (grant #EEC 0540865). No commercial party having a direct financial interest in the results of the research supporting this article has or will confer a benefit on the authors or on any organization with which the authors are associated.

References

1. Faul, M., et al.: Traumatic brain injury in the United States: Emergency department visits, hospitalizations and deaths 2002–2006. Centers for Disease Control and Prevention, National Center for Injury Prevention and Control, Atlanta, GA (2010)
2. Sohlberg, M.K.M., Mateer, C.A.: Cognitive Rehabilitation: An Integrative Neuropsychological Approach. Guilford Press, New York (2001)
3. Graves, T.B., et al.: Using video prompting to teach cooking skills to secondary students with moderate disabilities. Educ. Train. Dev. Disabil. **40**(1), 34–46 (2005)

4. Horsfall, D., Maggs, A.: Cooking skills instruction with severely multiply handicapped adolescents. J. Intellect. Dev. Disabil. **12**(3), 177–186 (1986)
5. Mechling, L.C.: High tech cooking: a literature review of evolving technologies for teaching a functional skill. Educ. Train. Dev. Disabil. **43**(4), 474 (2008)
6. Schuster, J.W.: Cooking instruction with persons labeled mentally retarded: a review of literature. Educ. Train. Ment. Retard. **23**, 43–50 (1988)
7. LoPresti, E.F., Mihailidis, A., Kirsch, N.: Assistive technology for cognitive rehabilitation: state of the art. Neuropsychol. Rehabil. **14**(1–2), 5–39 (2004)
8. Sohlberg, M., et al.: Evidence-based practice for the use of external aids as a memory compensation technique. J. Med. Speech Lang. Pathol. **15**(1), xv (2007)
9. Constantinidou, F., Thomas, R., Best, P.: Principles of cognitive rehabilitation after traumatic brain injury: an integrative approach. Trauma. Brain Inj. Rehabil. **2**, 338–365 (2004)
10. DePompei, R., Tyler, J.: Learning and Cognitive Communicative Challenges: Developing Educational Programs for Students with Brain Injuries. Lash & Associates Pub./Training Incorporated, Wake Forest (2004)
11. Parente, R., DiCesare, A.: Retraining memory: theory, evaluation, and applications. In: Kreutzer, J., Wehman, P. (eds.) Cognitive Rehabilitation for Persons with Traumatic Brain Injury: A Functional Approach, pp. 147–162. Paul H. Brookes, Baltimore (1991)
12. Ylvisaker, M., Szekeres, S.F., Haarbauer-Krupa, J.: Cognitive rehabilitation: organization, memory and language. In: YlVisaker, M. (ed.) Traumatic Brain Injury Rehabilitation: Children and Adolescents, pp. 181–220. Butterworth-Heinemann, Boston (1998)
13. Ramdoss, S., et al.: Use of computer-based interventions to promote daily living skills in individuals with intellectual disabilities: a systematic review. J. Dev. Phys. Disabil. **24**(2), 197–215 (2012)
14. Tsui, K.M., Yanco, H.A.: Prompting devices: a survey of memory aids for task sequencing. In: QoLT International Symposium: Intelligent Systems for Better Living, held in conjunction with RESNA (2010)
15. Gottfried, B.: Behaviour monitoring and interpretation. In: Mertsching, B., Hund, M., Aziz, Z. (eds.) KI 2009. LNCS, vol. 5803, pp. 572–580. Springer, Heidelberg (2009)
16. Van Tassel, M., Bouchard, J., Bouchard, B., Bouzouane, A.: Guidelines for increasing prompt efficiency in smart homes according to the resident's profile and task characteristics. In: Abdulrazak, B., Giroux, S., Bouchard, B., Pigot, H., Mokhtari, M. (eds.) ICOST 2011. LNCS, vol. 6719, pp. 112–120. Springer, Heidelberg (2011)
17. Wherton, J.P., Monk, A.F.: Technological opportunities for supporting people with dementia who are living at home. Int. J. Hum. Comput. Stud. **66**(8), 571–586 (2008)
18. AbleLink Technologies, I., Visual Impact Pro. (2012). http://www.ablelinktech.com/index.php?id=130
19. Holm, M.B., Rogers, J., Hemphill-Pearson, B.: The performance assessment of self-care skills (PASS). In: Hemphill-Pearson, B. (ed.) Assessments in Occupational Therapy Mental Health, 2nd edn., pp. 101–110. SLACK, Thorofare (2008)
20. Sauro, J.: Measuring Usefulness: The Technology Acceptance Model (TAM) (2011)

A Collaborative Patient-Carer Interface for Generating Home Based Rules for Self-Management

Mark Beattie[1], Josef Hallberg[2], Chris Nugent[1], Kare Synnes[2],
Ian Cleland[1(✉)], and Sungyoung Lee[3]

[1] Computer Science Research Institute and School of Computing
and Mathematics, University of Ulster, BT37 0QB Newtownabbey,
Co. Antrim, Northern Ireland, UK
{mp.beattie,cd.nugent,i.cleland}@ulster.ac.uk
[2] Department of Computer Science, Electrical and Space Engineering,
Luleå University of Technology, 971 87 Luleå, Sweden
{Josef.Hallberg,Kare.Sunnes}@ltu.se
[3] Ubiquitous Computing Laboratory, Kyung Hee University,
Seocheon-dong, Giheung-gu, South Korea
sylee@oslab.khu.ac.kr

Abstract. The wide spread prevalence of mobile devices, the decreasing costs of sensor technologies and increased levels of computational power have all lead to a new era in assistive technologies to support persons with Alzheimer's disease. There is, however, still a requirement to improve the manner in which the technology is integrated into current approaches of care management. One of the key issues relating to this challenge is in providing solutions which can be managed by non-technically orientated healthcare professionals. Within the current work efforts have been made to develop and evaluate new tools with the ability to specify, in a non-technical manner, how the technology within the home environment should be monitored and under which conditions an alarm should be raised. The work has been conducted within the remit of a collaborative patient-carer system to support self-management for dementia. A visual interface has been developed and tested with 10 healthcare professionals. Results following a post evaluation of system usability have been presented and discussed.

Keywords: Self-management · Visual interface · Dementia · Home based monitoring

1 Introduction

Supporting self-management of chronic conditions is viewed as one way of alleviating the social and economic issues associated with an ageing population [1]. Indeed, one of the most common demands from a patient's perspective is the ability to live independently at home for a long as possible. This facilitates less time spent in the hospital and institutionalised settings, thus reducing health and social care costs. Recently, much consideration has been directed towards the use of home or community based

© Springer International Publishing Switzerland 2015
C. Bodine et al. (Eds.): ICOST 2014, LNCS 8456, pp. 93–102, 2015.
DOI: 10.1007/978-3-319-14424-5_10

technology solutions that may be developed in order to assist in the self-management process [2, 3]. Remaining at home, may, however, require a degree of informal care from a family member or spouse. This may subsequently cause burden to the carer, placing further strain on their physical and mental health and wellbeing in addition to causing financial and social implications.

Cognitive impairments represent a significant challenge to older people. Difficulties can revolve around task completion or even commencing the task at all. For conditions such as dementia, the notion of self-management is a relatively new concept [4]. Traditionally, learning new tasks, such as remembering to take medications or remembering to schedule healthcare appointments, was perceived as beyond the ability of persons with dementia. Nevertheless, this represents a narrow view of self-management. A more contemporary view of self-management for dementia is considered as being a collaborative process between the person with dementia and their carer, which extends beyond traditional tasks and aims to improve personal resilience, quality of life, and increase levels of activity [4]. Technology has the potential to help individuals overcome the barriers associated with cognitive impairment in terms of performing activities of daily living and therefore help to maintain independence and enhance quality of life [5]. In particular, home based care, supported through a sensorized smart environment is considered as one way of supporting people with dementia and their carers [6]. The success of such an environment, however, relies on its ability to be customised and personalised to suit the needs of the user and the environment [7]. Many of the specific details required for the personalisation of the smart environment relating to the behaviours of the person with dementia are known only by the carer, who themselves may be older and not fully skilled in using technology. This poses a challenge given that a considerable part of the behaviour in smart environments relies on event-driven and rule specification [8]. The expressiveness of the rules available to users is usually either limited or the available rule editing interfaces are not designed for end-users with low skills in programming [8].

This paper presents HomeCI, a collaborative visual interface for the generation of machine interpretable rules to support self-management in dementia through remote monitoring of activities within a smart home environment. The ability to collaboratively generate rules through a simple visual interface allows the person with dementia and their carer to take a greater role in the provision and management of their own care. Specifically, this paper focuses on the process of designing, specifying and tailoring rules[1] to the individual through an easy to use visual editor. The aim of the research was to provide a solution which could involve those with the domain knowledge and the actual user in the process of creating the rules for home monitoring. Furthermore, a solution was desired which could generate rules that could be easily shared and reused by others and made available in the general research community through an online repository.

---

[1] A rule in this context is a set of guidelines on how data collected from sensors either on the person or within the environment should be interpreted and what feedback, if any should be provided by the environment itself. Rules define the sequence of sensor events that are expected for a certain activity, expected or desired behavior.

2   Background

Context can be described as the interrelated conditions in which something exists or occurs. From a computer science perspective, context awareness refers to the ability to sense and react to the environment. In this case sensors may gather information about the circumstances and based on rules or an intelligent response, react accordingly. In summary rule based languages preserve the natural essence of context aware applications "when something happens, if some facts are present then do something" [8]. Recently, visual methods of rapid programming, which require less technical knowledge, are becoming more popular. Graphical programming interfaces such as, Labview [9], BioMOBIUS [10] and MIT's app inventor [11], allow users, with only a basic knowledge of the underlying system functionality, to effectively program complex systems. A growing number of visual methods for defining rules within a smart environment have also been presented within the literature.

SiteView, created by Beckmann and Dey [12], allows end-users to create and view automation control rules through an intuitive interaction method. The system relies on a small scale representation of the environment in which the user interacts with tangible objects. These objects represent rule conditions and may also have real-world counterparts (e.g., a thermostat or light bulb). The system was subsequently evaluated by generating a variety of rules using a combination of up to three conditions to produce predefined state changes in the environment. The interface was, however, limited to one environment (research lab) and as such the scalability and flexibility of the approach was not fully validated.

It has been said that users should be allowed to specify the behaviour of their own environment. When considering end-users, who may have little programming experience, the process of rule creation must be as simple and as intuitive as possible. iCAP [13], is a visual tool to facilitate the design of rules by end users with little programming knowledge. The iCAP interface comprised two main components. The first was a tabbed repository area which stored the user defined inputs, outputs and rules. These components could then be dragged onto the main canvas area where they were subsequently constructed into conditional rule statements. More recently, Bonino et al. [14] described a drag and drop visual interface that specifically targeted non-skilled or low technology skilled users. The system relied upon a rule format based on an IF-THEN structure with optional When and OR-IF blocks for expression of conditions and rule alternatives. Within this study, emphasis was placed on providing strong visual cues and suggestions to facilitate incremental rule construction by end-users.

HomeCI extends these works through the representation of objects in a simulated 3D environment. This allows for a more intuitive user interface in order to select objects for inclusion within rules. Furthermore, HomeCI represents a key component within an end to end system to support the creation, representation and storage of data and rules generated within a smart environment. Therefore, HomeCI relies heavily on established and open formats for storing and sharing data and rules. HomeCI is a companion to XML storage formats such as homeML and homeRuleML in addition to providing an intuitive interface [15]. The usability and usefulness of this interface is further validated within this paper.

3 Overview of HomeCI

The concept of a visual editor to support the capture of rule design within Smart Home environments was previously developed by the authors [16]. The solution was largely of a prototype nature and initial evaluations provided positive feedback. In the current study a fully functional version of the system has been designed and developed which produces, as an output, a set of rules conforming to homeRuleML [17]. This support the long term storage and exchange of the system's output. The following Sections describe the structure of the visual interface.

3.1 The Visual Interface

HomeCI is comprised of three separate main screens, each screen providing a sophisticated although user friendly interface. This interface supports users without prior experience or training to quickly and efficiently create complex rules. The first screen provides the user with an overview of the house (Fig. 1). From this screen the user can select a room in which they would like to create a rule. Users can also select objects for use in the creation of a global rule. This screen is highly extensible, allowing for the addition of further rooms if required, therefore expanding the scope of this interface. A number of development languages including jQuery, PHP and HTML were used throughout the development of the HomeCI platform. This included libraries such as jsPlumb and MapHighlight. jQuery is a JavaScript library used to simplify the client side scripting of HTML and as such was used for the main content of each separate page.

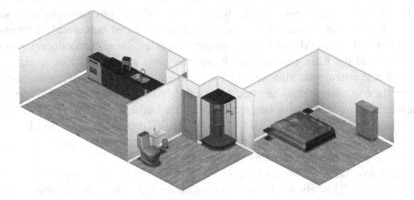

Fig. 1. Initial screen of the homeCI interface providing the user with the option to select a room within which rules can be specified for.

The level of detail provided is increased as the user progresses through the system. Within the room view, objects relevant to each specific room selected are presented to the user. Users can select objects they wish to include in either a local (single room) or global (multiple room) rules. For example the activity of morning routine could be considered a global rule if the rule takes place in the bathroom for grooming and then the bedroom for dressing. During rule creation users are required to provide a "Rule Name" along with a "Rule ID". Users are also asked to set the "Rule Type" via a drop down menu (Fig. 2). Rule Type selection specifies how the inference engine interprets the sensor data recorded. Two types of rules can be selected "Activity Rule" and "Intervention Rule". An activity monitoring rule selection instructs the system to trigger when a series of events have taken place based on the rule created. An intervention rule detects anomalies occurring within an expected flow of events, leading to a required intervention. Users are also expected to set the outcome, i.e. what should happen when a specific activity has been detected or completed. These are again set via a drop down menu offering the user two choices, "Activity Detected" or "Warning". In the case of an intervention rule, the outcome could be "warning" or something specific relating to the particular rule, such as "Breakfast Activity has been interrupted". Activity Rules would have a notification indication that the user has completed the task, such as "Breakfast Completed".

Fig. 2. Room view within the HomeCI interface. Details of each rule can be added on the left hand side of the interface.

When a user hovers over a selectable object, it is highlighted with a red outline. Users can proceed to select this object for use. No upper limit exists on the number of objects that can be used in each rule. Within this screen users also have the option to use activities. Activities are displayed on the right hand side of the room view and can be used in a similar manner as an object. Activities are pre-defined rules that can be reused. Activities can consist of a number of events, and even other activities. An example of such as activity could be that of "making a cup of tea", this activity could be integrated within a rule to "Make Breakfast". When users have selected all objects required they may create a rule immediately utilizing the objects selected by clicking "Create Rules". They can also use the selected events as part of a global rule by selecting "Create Global Rule". At this point, the user will be redirected back to the home view. Users can then navigate through other rooms selecting events until they are ready to create such a global rule.

The visual interface for creating rules relies heavily on established formats for storing and sharing data and rules, in addition to an intuitive interface that is easily accessed and easy to use. In previous work we have already investigated and established a format for storing and sharing data [18]. This format, referred to as homeML, is based on XML and supports data generated from a home or from mobile and carried devices.

We have also developed a format for storing and sharing rules [17] which is based on the homeML format and is extensible to support a great variety of different rules.

3.2   The Workspace

The workspace is used to display to the user the objects and their inter-connections (Fig. 3). This screen allows the user to combine the previously selected items in such a manner that a rule will be generated. The workspace allows users to drag and drop the objects and activities in any order. A distinguishing feature of HomeCI is the ability to include conditional expressions. When generating a rule, it is possible to specify that an activity should take "Less than 20 min" to complete or that a number of activities combined should not exceed a preset time limit. The use of such conditional expressions ensures users can easily connect the objects in an intelligent manner while retaining the user-friendly interface.

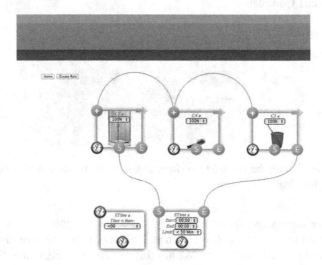

Fig. 3. Example of workspace and how objects selected from room view may be connected together.

4   Evaluation: Results and Discussion

The evaluation was undertaken with 10 Nurses (Male n = 2) recruited from Lulea Technical University. All participants were over the aged 45 and over. All users were experienced in working in the domain of elderly care and had good appreciation of the needs of technological solutions to be deployed in the home environment to support independent living. Participants were asked to complete two tasks. The first task requested the participant to create a rule from two pre-defined narrative for the activities of Grooming and taking medication. Participants were asked to use the homeCI interface and the visual notations to select the necessary objects and rooms from the home view to build the necessary set of rules to monitor if a person had correctly undertaken the activities.

The average time for the 10 participants to complete the tasks was 118 s for grooming and 97 s for taking medication. Full results are presented in Table 1. Further testing is required to gain a deeper insight into exactly how much time is spent creating the rules; however, all participants were able to correctly define the rules in a reasonable period of time.

Table 1. Table showing task completion time for creating rules to represent grooming and taking medication for each participant.

Participant No.	Grooming	Taking medication
1	103	112
2	102	87
3	59	98
4	210	70
5	54	55
6	84	90
7	105	92
8	242	186
9	125	100
10	92	98
Mean	117.6	97.3
Std	61.4	36.4

The second task required the user to interpret rule and create the narrative. Participants were presented with a rule for the activity of preparing a drink (Fig. 4) and were asked to provide their interpretation. All participants were able to correctly interpret the rules.

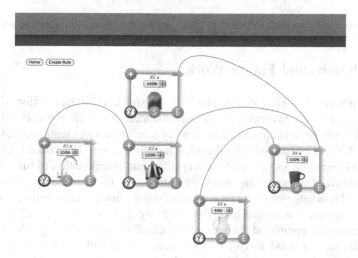

Fig. 4. Rule created for the activity of preparing a drink. This rule was shown to participants to interpret.

At the end of the both tasks each participant was asked to complete a post-evaluation questionnaire to gather feedback on their experience of using the system. Data was anonymized, with no identifiable information collected and participants were provided with the opportunity to complete the questionnaires in private. Questions were rated on a 10 point Likert scale (1- poor, 10 – excellent). Plots of responses by each participant, including the mean, for each question are presented in Fig. 5.

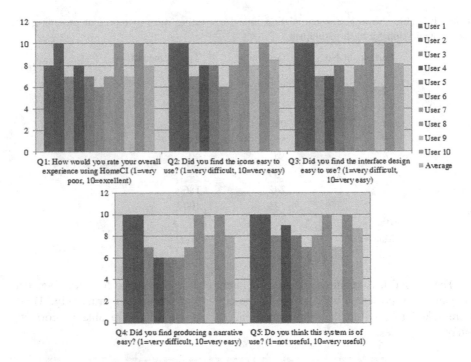

Fig. 5. Participant responses to questions investigating the system usability and usefulness.

5   Conclusions and Future Work

This paper presented an evaluation of HomeCI, a visual tool for the creation of machine visible rules for smart environments. It is envisioned that such a tool could be used within a self-management context by facilitating a collaborative creation of rules by the knowledge holders i.e. person with dementia and their carer. The visual interface was chosen as it is intuitive and allows for the creation and interpretation of rules with little technical knowledge. To test this theory, the interface was evaluated by 10 nurses who have a good knowledge of the requirements of older persons with chronic conditions. Over all the system was ranked highly on usability and usefulness by all participants and all participants completed the required tasks effectively. Although the healthcare professionals have a good insight into the needs of an older cohort, they may not necessarily have the same cognitive or technology ability as an older cohort with dementia. Future work will therefore investigate the usability and utility of HomeCI to facilitate the collaborative creation of rules between persons with dementia and their careers as part of a self-management programme.

It is important that tools that allow for personalisation of rules are used within smart homes and that these rules are created in open formats that allow integration with other systems. Further work will seek to evaluate HomeCI with the dyad, including a person with dementia and their informal carer i.e. most likely the next of kin/spouse. Further validation of such tools will allow for the creation of a black-box inference engine which will facilitate adoption of this advanced technology by the general public.

Acknowledgments. Invest Northern Ireland is acknowledged for supporting this project under the R and D grant RD0513844.

References

1. Jonsdottir, H.: Self-management programmes for people living with chronic obstructive pulmonary disease: a call for a reconceptualisation. J. Clin. Nurs. **22**, 621–637 (2013)
2. McCullagh, P., et al.: Promoting behavior change in long term conditions using a self-management platform. In: Langdon, P.M., Clarkson, P.J., Robinson, P. (eds.) Designing Inclusive Interactions, pp. 229–238. Springer, London (2010)
3. Zheng, H., et al.: Smart self-management: assistive technology to support people with chronic disease. J. Telemed. Telecare **16**, 224–227 (2010)
4. Martin, F., et al.: Conceptualisation of self-management intervention for people with early stage dementia. Eur. J. Ageing **10**, 75–87 (2013)
5. Mason, S., et al.: Electronic reminding technology for cognitive impairment. Br. J. Nurs. **21** (14), 855 (2012)
6. Morris, M.E., et al.: Smart-home technologies to assist older people to live well at home. J. Aging Sci. 1. 101 (2013)
7. Chang, A.Y., Han-Chen, H., Dwen-Ren, T.: Development of practical smart house scenario control system. Przegląd Elektrotechniczny **89**, 159–161 (2013)
8. Catala, A., et al.: A meta-model for dataflow-based rules in smart environments: Evaluating user comprehension and performance. Sci. Comput. Programm. **78**(10), 1930–1950 (2013)
9. National Instruments: Labview. http://www.ni.com/labview/
10. McGrath, M.J., Terrance, J.D.: A common personal health research platform. Intel Technol. J. **13**(3), 122–147 (2009)
11. Wolber, D., et al.: App Inventor. O'Reilly Media Inc, Sebastopol (2011)
12. Beckmann, C., Anind, D.: Siteview: Tangibly programming active environments with predictive visualization. In: Adjunct Proceedings of UbiComp (2003)
13. Sohn, T., Anind, D.: iCAP: an informal tool for interactive prototyping of context-aware applications. In: CHI'03 Extended Abstracts on Human Factors in Computing Systems. ACM (2003)
14. Bonino, D., Corno, F., De Russis, L.: A user-friendly interface for rules composition in intelligent environments. In: Novais, P., Preuveneers, D., Corchado, J.M. (eds.) ISAmI 2011. AISC, vol. 92, pp. 213–217. Springer, Heidelberg (2011)
15. Hong, X., et al.: Open Home: approaches to constructing sharable datasets within Smart Homes. In: CHI 2009 workshop on developing shared home behavior datasets to advance HCI and ubiquitous computing, 4 April 2009

16. Nugent, C.D., et al.: HomeCI-A visual editor for healthcare professionals in the design of home based care. In: 29th Annual International Conference of the IEEE Engineering in Medicine and Biology Society, EMBS 2007. IEEE (2007)

17. McDonald, H.A., Nugent, C.D., Hallberg, J., Finlay, D.D., Moore, G.: homeRuleML version 2.1: A revised and extended version of the homeRuleML concept. In: Roa Romero, L.M. (ed.) XIII Mediterranean Conference on Medical and Biological Engineering and Computing 2013. IFMBE Proceedings, vol. 42, pp. 1243–1246. Springer, Heidelberg (2014)

18. Nugent, C.D., Finlay, D.D., Davies, R.J., Wang, H.Y., Zheng, H., Hallberg, J., Synnes, K., Mulvenna, M.D.: homeML – An open standard for the exchange of data within smart environments. In: Okadome, T., Yamazaki, T., Makhtari, M. (eds.) ICOST. LNCS, vol. 4541, pp. 121–129. Springer, Heidelberg (2007)

Measuring the Impact of ICTs on the Quality of Life of Ageing People with Mild Dementia

Mounir Mokhtari[1,2,3(✉)], Romain Endelin[1,3], Hamdi Aloulou[1,3],
and Thibaut Tiberghien[1,2]

[1] Institut Mines Telecom, Paris, France
{Mounir.Mokhtari,Romain.Endelin,Hamdi.Aloulou,
Thibaut.Tiberghien}@Mines-Telecom.fr
[2] CNRS IPAL (UMI 2955), Singapore, Singapore
[3] CNRS LIRMM (UMR 5506), Montpellier, France

Abstract. The growing of ageing population worldwide and the need to focus research efforts on a specific target group motivate our research to focus on frail ageing people with chronic disease and physical/cognitive deficiencies. The primary goal is to enable the frail and dependant persons, through reliable assistive technologies, to maximize their physical and mental functions, and to continue to engage them in social networks, so that he can continue to lead an independent and purposeful life. Our target is to analyze the users' habits at home through an extensive survey performed in France recently, and to design a suitable assistive system, which is mainly composed of devices available in the market. This research activity led to the deployment of a simplified hardware infrastructure (gateway, sensors, actuators) in the home of end-users with a limited number of wireless sensors, and to the outsourcing of all the software for data analysis in a framework running on a distant server. The research focuses on the quality of life of ageing people having cognitive and functional limitations, and on recent achievements realised in France and Singapore through several European and national projects, and through Quality of Life Chair (QoL) directed by Mounir Mokhtari and supported by two major health insurance companies in France, namely la Mutuelle Generale and REUNICA.

Keywords: Ageing people · Ambient Assisted Living (AAL) · Activities of Daily Living (ADL)

1 Introduction

Today, providing assistive services for frail and dependant people could be done following two ways: the first option consists in looking for a reliable industrial solution to be deployed in the user's living space, which may not fit exactly with the users' specific requirements and usually imposes to modify extensively the living environment itself. The second option is to design a specific application, which meets exactly the needs of the end-users, but developers will be confronted with a wide spread of technologies and APIs which impose a huge amount of human-efforts and associated cost. This second option may require a long time (several years) to build a reliable running prototype. Consequently, in both options, the development cost is high, and

© Springer International Publishing Switzerland 2015
C. Bodine et al. (Eds.): ICOST 2014, LNCS 8456, pp. 103–109, 2015.
DOI: 10.1007/978-3-319-14424-5_11

this is also the reason why most smart home projects are still at a laboratory prototype level worldwide [1]. There are efforts trying to transfer these prototypes into homes or hospitals [2], but migrating systems from a well controlled research lab environment into a much more complex real-world environment introduces tremendous challenges in terms of correctness, reliability and fault-tolerance of the system.

Ageing is a highly individualized, irreversible and inevitable process by which a person becomes more vulnerable and dependent on others [3]. It proceeds at different rates and within different functions depending on people. Changes, that can occur in cognitive, physiological and social conditions, are not necessarily related to a disease since they are, in a certain magnitude, a normal part of the ageing process.

Cognitive changes related to normal ageing span across several aspects of the mind [4]. *Sensory memory* is the ability for each of the five senses to hold a large amount of sensory information for a very short period of time, and is independent of the attention to the stimulus. It suffers no major influence of ageing. *Short term memory* is a 20 to 30 seconds memory used to hold information for processing. It is a working memory that can hold 7 elements for direct manipulation. It is highly involved in Activities of Daily Living (ADL) as it enables multi-tasking and manipulation of information. The capacity to hold 7 elements is not affected by age, but the manipulation of this memory becomes difficult as elders have a limited capacity to divide their attention between two related tasks or inhibit unimportant information. *Long term memory* is a series of memory modules each responsible for holding different sorts of information. It is subject to three mechanisms (encoding, storage, retrieval) that are not affected by age in the same way. Encoding is usually subject to a less spontaneous organization of information, so elders might need support on this.

Conducting a survey that involves aged people and their associated caregivers will help to understand the needs of this portion of the society and to provide solutions that Respond to their requirements. Our ultimate goal is to maintain the quality of life of aged people in their own home as long as possible by the integration of ICTs in an acceptable way for both the end-users and the stakeholders [5]. This means that eco-nomical and social impacts are key issues in our approach.

2 Methods

To properly define and address this issue, our methodology consisted on performing 2 parallel activities, in one hand a survey investigating the need of 123 frail aged people living in their own homes, and on the other hand designing and developing a suitable system for the provision of assistive services.

2.1 Survey - The Lifestyle of the Elders

In order to observe the lifestyle of the elders within their home, we have sent a questionnaire to elderly people, in collaboration with a national association of retired people.[1] The same questions have been asked to both the elders and their family

---

[1] Association Nationale des Retraités de La Poste et de France Télécom (ANR).

caregivers, so that we can observe the bias in their perception. We have gathered 246 questionnaires, making up a total of 35,178 questions answered. After investigating the population of the elders and the caregivers, this survey gives insights on the elders' activities at home and outdoor, as well as the healthcare services they receive. From this survey, we aim to determine the most critical needs of elderly people in their daily lives.

In the Fig. 1 below, we observe the causes of insecurity, as felt by the elders as well as their caregivers. We observe that, many of the elders have developed a fear of other people (20 %). But only 14 % are concerned by their own condition and the risk of having an accident. On the other hand, from the caregivers' point of view, 23 % have fear because the house is not suited for the patient (e.g. presence of stairs). In total, 50 % are worried for the health of the patient, dispatched between an unsafe house, cognitive problems, autonomy problem, and the risk of accident.

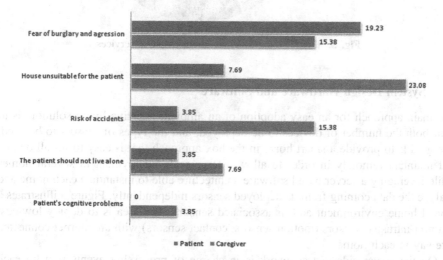

Fig. 1. Causes of patient's insecurity within the house

From this study, we observe a strong divergence in opinion between the patient and the caregiver. The caregivers tend to be more worried about the elders' condition, whereas the elders themselves may deny it, and develop social complications.

Figure 2 shows the caregivers' opinions about healthcare services for elderly people. As we can see, 1 % of them are concerned about health monitoring, while 29 % want to support the elderly people for living independently, and 29 % mention the improvements in the patient's quality of life. 18 % of the caregivers acknowledge that these services maintain a social connection for the elders (Fig. 1 has shown the importance of it, as patients may have social inabilities). Finally, 21 % of the family caregivers say that assistive services are also a support for the family, giving a glimpse of the difficult condition of the family caregivers who support the patients in their daily life.

As we can see from Fig. 2, the caregivers tend to be far more concerned by the quality of life and the autonomy of the elderly people, rather than by their medical condition.

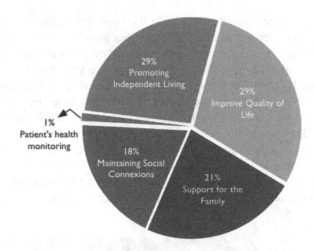

Fig. 2. Families' expectations about assistive services

2.2   System Design Hardware and Software

Our main approach for an easy adoption of an ambient assistive living solution, is to limit both the number of devices to be deployed, and the types of sensors to be used. The goal is to provide a smart home in the box approach that is easy to install on site and maintain remotely in order to allow a large-scale deployment in several homes while leveraging a server based software architecture able to instantiate each home and analyze the data coming from its deployed sensors independently. Figure 3 illustrates a typical home environment and its associated sensors. The idea is to deploy low-cost and non-intrusive sensors (motion sensors, contact sensors) with an internet connected gateway in each home.

On the server side, a framework is in charge of processing events sent by each home gateway and providing assistive services [6]. Our software framework is based on the OSGi (Open Service Gateway initiative) modular principle. This allows decomposing the platform into several modules, having each its specific functionality, and all communicating with each others. These modules are responsible of sensors' events reception, reasoning, taking decisions about users' situations, and providing the assistive services. A semantic model is used by the platform to represent the environment and the end-user profile.

The platform's OSGi modules are identical for each deployed house and the abstract semantic model is instantiated with information concerning each new house. Therefore, on the server side, a new instance of our framework is created and launched after the deployment of our system (sensors and gateway) in a new house and the semantic model is instantiated with the new user profile (name, address, disease, etc.), as well as the description of the house and the deployed sensors characteristics (type, code, possible events, localization, etc.). Figure 4 represents the architecture of the framework developed on the server side.

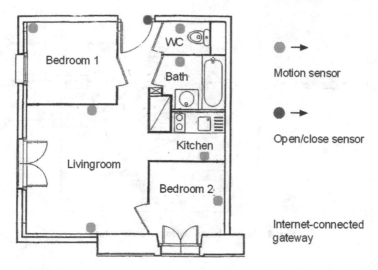

Fig. 3. Smart home is a box setup for activities recognition

The gateway (BeagleBone Black[2]) of each house sends events received from the sensors deployed to the central server (hosted by CNRS LIRMM Lab. in Montpellier city in France). The CGI (Common Gateway Interface) on the server receives these events and routes them to the appropriate OSGi instance. After reasoning and making decisions, assistive services are provided to the end-users (patients or caregivers) on different interaction devices using the D3.js (Data-Driven Documents) library.

3 Results

The goal of this experimentation was to confirm the feasibility of reasoning in an AAL solution based on a stripped-down hardware deployment. This means that we must demonstrate that valuable knowledge can be extracted about an elderly person's life-style from coarse sensor data. Moreover, we must verify that the scalability of the incurred processing remains within an economical level, where an economy of scale is possible with one server providing enough processing power to cater for hundreds of houses.

Multiple assistive services can be provided for the end-users. These services are based on the patients' locations and activities inferred by our platform deployed on the centralized server. Figure 5 represents a Real-time visualization of a patient's activities during the day.

Relying on our conducted survey, we have identified several assistive services which are requested by the end-users and that can be provided based on the inferred information from our platform. Table 1 illustrates some of the assistive services that can be provided.

---

[2] beagleboard.org/Products/BeagleBone+Black.

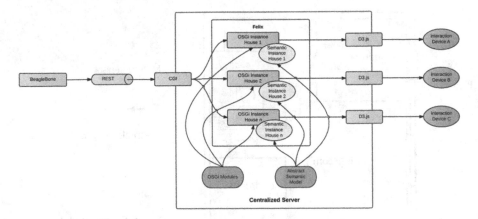

Fig. 4. Server based software architecture

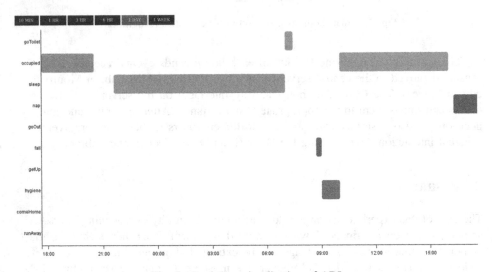

Fig. 5. Real time visualization of ADL

Table 1. Assistive services deduced from the conducted survey

End users expectations	Assistive services
Improve quality of life	Serious games for memory stimulation
	Wandering at night alert
Promoting independent living	Meals time reminders
	Medication agenda
Support for the family	Elderly ADL visualization
	Emergency calls in critical situations
Maintaining social connexions	Video conferences with families and friends

4   Discussion

Several technical issues have emerged from deploying technological systems in real living spaces. To perform the validation, these issues had to be dealt with, which is often considered as a "waste of time" by researchers and engineers developing systems in their lab. However, this experience allowed us to learn a lot about the targeted users and stakeholders in general, and it provides us with essential and extremely valuable knowledge related to bringing value out of our research work and making an impact in society. This knowledge, collected through an extensive survey, is mainly related to the feedback received from the stakeholders, the acceptance of the solutions, their ease of deployment and maintenance, usage issues, etc. Even though such deployments felt like a burden at some point in time, we can only recommend to researchers in our field to get out of the lab, deploy their solutions, and include stakeholders early in the research work.

After deploying in four bedrooms in a nursing home in Singapore [7] and three individual homes in France [8], we have improved the system along two aspects, on one hand, to simplify the hardware architecture by limiting drastically the number of devices; and on the other hand, to design a server-based framework able to instantiate each deployed site independently in a scalable manner. Experimentation within living labs in Grenoble (France) and Starhome (Singapore) provided promising results. Our next target is to deploy 10 individual homes and one nursing home in France within the Quality of Life Chair.

Acknowledgements. This project is funded under Quality of Life Chair of Institut Mines Telecom and supported by Mutuelle Generale and REUNICA.

References

1. Orwat, C., Graefe, A., Faulwasser, T.: Towards pervasive computing in health care–a literature review. BMC Med. Inform. Decis. Mak. J. **8**, 26 (2008). (Biomedcentral)
2. Bardram, J.E., Hansen, T.R., Mogensen, M., Soegaard, M.: Experiences from real-world deployment of context-aware technologies in a hospital environment. In: Dourish, P., Friday, A. (eds.) UbiComp 2006. LNCS, vol. 4206, pp. 369–386. Springer, Heidelberg (2006)
3. Routhier, S.: Aging health and aging need. In: ICOST 2011 Summer School Talks (2011)
4. Kausler, D.H.: Learning and Memory in Normal Aging. Academic Press, New York (1994)
5. Mokhtari, M., Aloulou, H., Tiberghien, T., Biswas, J., Racoceanu, D., Yap, P.: New trends to support independence in persons with mild dementia - a mini-review. Gerontology **58**(6), 554–563 (2012). (Karger)
6. Aloulou, H., Mokhtari, M., Tiberghien, T., Biswas, J., Yap, P.: An adaptable and flexible framework for assistive living of cognitively impaired people. IEEE J. Biomed. Health Inform. (J-BHI) **18**(1), 353–360 (2014). (IEEE)
7. Aloulou, H., Mokhtari, M., Tiberghien, T., Biswas, J., Phua, C., Lin, J.H.K., Yap, P.: Deployment of assistive living technology in a nursing home environment: methods and lessons learned. BMC Med. Inform. Decis. Mak. J. **13**(1), 42 (2013). (Biomedcentral)
8. Tiberghien, T., Strategies for context reasoning in assistive livings for the elderly. Ph.D. thesis, Institut SudParis (2013)

VA SmartHome for Veterans with TBI: Implementation in Community Settings

Kristina M. Martinez[1](✉), Karen M. Mann[2,3],
Christina Dillahunt-Aspillaga[4], Jan M. Jasiewicz[2], Deborah Rugs[2],
Yorick Wilks[5], and Steven G. Scott[2]

[1] Defense and Veterans Brain Injury Center (DVBIC),
James A. Haley Veterans' Hospital, Tampa, FL, USA
kristina.martinezl@va.gov
[2] HSR&D/RR&D Center of Innovation on Disability Rehabilitation Research
(CINDRR), James A. Haley Veterans' Hospital, Tampa, FL, USA
[3] Ubisense Inc., Denver, CO, USA
[4] University of South Florida (USF), Tampa, FL, USA
[5] Florida Institute for Human and Machine Cognition (IHMC), Ocala, FL, USA

Abstract. Individuals with traumatic brain injury (TBI) are at risk for reduced
levels of independence, safety issues, falls, and institutionalization. VA
SmartHome (SH) technology, developed for Veterans with TBI, uses an accurate indoor tracking technology capable of following numerous individuals
simultaneously and resolving their location to approximately 15 cm in an open
environment. In addition, SH technologies provide time- and location-dependent
prompts to promote independence of the participant by providing reminders for
the management of daily activities such as medication, meal planning, and other
necessary tasks. SH tech-nology was initially developed for clinical rehabilitation settings, however, was recently expanded to private homes of Veterans with
TBI. Current features available in the SH and the process of implementation are
presented.

Keywords: SmartHome · Traumatic brain injury · Veterans · Smart technology ·
Rehabilitation · Smart home · RFID tracking

1 Introduction

VA SmartHome (SH) technology delivers a home-based cognitive prosthetic on the
foundation of an advanced indoor tracking system to monitor the activities of participants with traumatic brain injury (TBI). The SH technology was first deployed in 2010
at the James A. Haley VA Polytrauma Transitional Rehabilitation Program (PTRP) in
Tampa, Florida [1]. With funding from the Department of Veterans Affairs, the SH was
developed as a clinical demonstration project to monitor and provide location-based
prompts to patients with polytrauma, including traumatic brain injury. Polytrauma is
defined as "concurrent injury to the brain and several body areas or organ systems that
results in physical, cognitive, and psychosocial impairments [2]."

© Springer International Publishing Switzerland 2015
C. Bodine et al. (Eds.): ICOST 2014, LNCS 8456, pp. 110–118, 2015.
DOI: 10.1007/978-3-319-14424-5_12

Recently, the SH has been expanded to include individual homes in the community. This technology was developed to (a) improve patient safety and (b) address inadequate timing and repetition of prompts used to address the myriad of TBI related cognitive and memory deficits.

Generally, smart homes reported in the literature monitor residents' behaviors and provide assistance for various physical and neurological disabilities [3]. The SH discussed in this paper includes a highly supportive environment to facilitate rehabilitation of participants with TBI by analyzing and extracting data from the continuous identification of the movements and locations of users [1]. This location-based information permits intelligent software to deliver customized prompts and information to the users via numerous interactive multimedia panels located on walls throughout the home. These location- and time-based prompts promote independence of the participant by providing reminders for the management of daily activities such as medication, meal planning and other necessary tasks. In addition, Veterans and caregivers have access to a web application that provides information pertaining to activity levels, movement trends, task lists, social interaction, interactive task sequencing as well as exercise, medication, and ingress/egress logs. The SH technology is a powerful tool which provides precise customized therapeutic information that can be utilized by the participants with TBI, their caregivers, and clinicians.

1.1 Traumatic Brain Injury

TBI is one of the leading causes of death and disability in the US. Approximately 1.7 million individuals sustain a TBI each year and over 3.2 million people are living with the long-term effects of this injury [4, 5]. It has been suggested that these numbers maybe under-reported due to those with mild TBI not seeking medical attention [6]. In addition, these numbers do not account for brain injuries treated in military treatment facilities, during deployment and in Veterans Affairs hospitals. Further, TBI is referred to as the "signature injury" of Operation Enduring Freedom (OEF), Operation Iraqi Freedom (OIF), and Operation New Dawn (OND) conflicts due to the types of explosives used and the improved survivability of those injured in combat [2]. Individuals with TBI are at risk for reduced levels of independence, safety issues, falls, and institutionalization.

Costs associated with medical treatment, rehabilitation and lost earnings due to a TBI are estimated to be over $76 billion in the US [7, 8] and this type of injury often affects young adults in their economically productive years [9, 10]. Costs associated with TBI in OEF/OIF/OND Veterans are not well known and there is "little information about the long-term healthcare needs of Veterans with TBI" [11].

Individuals with TBI encounter many challenges including functional deficits, such as physical, cognitive, and psychosocial limitations, which may result in dynamic short- and long-term consequences that affect one's ability to reintegrate into the home and community [12–14]. Common impairments associated with brain injury include memory and attention deficits, organizational and problem-solving deficits, as well as difficulty with social skills. These impairments greatly affect an individual's ability to perform daily activities. Memory impairment is one of the biggest barriers to successful reintegration and independence [15].

1.2   Technology and Traumatic Brain Injury

There is a differentiation among smart home projects where the majority incorporate various assistive technologies including electronic control units (ECUs), but don't always consider continuing patient care beyond the institution [16]. Assistive technology (AT) can be a vital component for individuals who wish to remain independent in their homes [17, 18], however, there is a recognized need for homes to be intelligent and assist their inhabitants [19]. Use of technology for TBI is becoming more prevalent, particularly to address memory impairments [20–22]. Memory deficits hinder functional performance in daily tasks such as medication management, task sequencing, managing appointments, organization, planning, problem solving and concentration [21]. In addition to increasing independence, smart technology is touted as a way to keep persons with TBI safe in their own homes and while navigating their communities [19, 23, 24].

1.3   VA SmartHome and Traumatic Brain Injury

The SH is designed to improve patient safety, maximize functional independence, reduce caregiver burden and prevent institutionalization. SH technology uses advanced indoor tracking technology to monitor the physical activity of Veterans with polytrauma including TBI. In addition, SH technology provides prompts for activities of daily living (ADLs), including medication and appointment reminders based upon the location of the Veteran in the home. Veterans and caregivers are provided an RFID tag worn on their person. The ultra-wideband (UWB) Real-time Location System (RTLS) assigns a unique identifier to each user. Prompts are provided on a panel or specially designed smart watch that also contains the RFID transmitter. The advantage of the smart watch is that prompts are delivered based on time and location – thus maximizing the probability of complying with the desired behavior [25].

2   VA SmartHome Technology

2.1   Current VA SmartHome Architecture

The SH technology has been deployed in six locations comprised of the PTRP containing five two-bedroom units as well as five private homes. By end of fall 2014 five additional homes will be installed and operational with a rate of expansion averaging five homes per year.

A secure remote database stores all raw, extracted and analyzed data. There is a separate instance of the database for each installation, which is subsequently integrated on the central server as shown in Fig. 1. The local server contains all of the tracking software and intelligent decisions with regard to sending out prompts (Fig. 2). Data include interactions, prompt acknowledgements, appliance use, tracking, etc. The architecture allows remote monitoring of each SH and reports errors, bugs and equipment failure in real-time, as well as allows for remote updating and configuration of each SH. In addition, there is a SH web application, which allows users to access specific de-identified data and information. The layout and design of the web application's features are based on the patient and caregiver workflow.

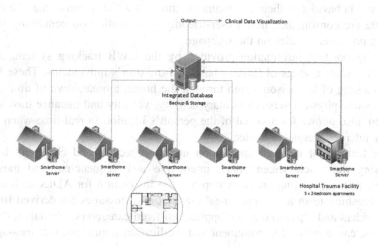

Fig. 1. VA SmartHome integrated database

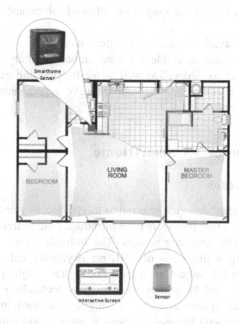

Fig. 2. Floor plan of a VA SmartHome including examples of interactive panels and sensors.

2.2 VA SmartHome Features

Tracking the activity of individuals is only one aspect of the SH in the development of a truly pervasive smart environment deeming the system an electronic caregiver. A powerful component of the SH is the precision of customized therapeutic information that is available for participants [1]. Since 2011, many new features are available in the SH. Current SH technology continuously and objectively monitors and documents participants' behaviors in their environments through which patterns may be derived. These data are consolidated into a user-friendly web application containing features, which are presented as tiles on the webpage.

Utilizing position information provided by the UWB tracking system, data are extracted to create a series of features based on the user's movements. These features include tracking of the person's path through the home, a breakdown of time spent in specific rooms, physical versus sedentary activity, velocity and distance traveled. The SH system also allows for a visual of the person's location in real-time when viewed from any internet-accessible device.

Other features of the web application include check-in and check-out from the home using the touch screen panel, interactive task sequencing, and messaging. Interactive task sequencing provides step-by-step instruction for ADLs such as doing laundry, brushing teeth and simple meal preparation. Messages are derived from personal calendars and input to the web application from caregivers. Messages, delivered as prompts, can consist of appointment and medication reminders, text messages and events.

An integrated GPS application on the user's Android smartphone can detect their coordinates to track outdoor movement. The web application provides access for users and displays their location on the map. Consolidated tables and maps help the user understand the data.

A weekly report is available to chart progress over time; a day, week, or month. Within the report, data are available for compliance of daily tasks assigned and completed, messages acknowledged, as well as medication and exercise logs.

The SH provides a comprehensive and intuitive representation of the Veteran within their environment.

3 Implementation of VA SmartHome

3.1 Participant Selection

At this time, potential candidates are referred to the project by either current healthcare providers or their peers. Once providers have introduced the individual to the SH team, they undergo an in-depth screening process. The individual must meet specific eligibility criteria including a diagnosis of TBI, no psychological disorder that would impede participation in the project, own their home, have high-speed internet for the duration of the project, and be willing to learn new technology. Additional criteria include a good support system at home, willingness to participate in ongoing and frequent communication with the team, as well as interest and enthusiasm in being an early adopter of the program.

3.2 Clinical Interview/Needs Assessment

An occupational therapist and a rehabilitation counselor perform the clinical interview in the participant's home. One purpose of this interview is to observe the potential participant in their home environment. During the initial in-home interview information is obtained regarding prior medical history, current and ongoing medical needs, functional performance levels, rehabilitation goals, support systems, and current interest and familiarity with technology. The needs assessment evaluates the participant's current level of performance as it relates to ADLs, their rehabilitation and personal goals, along with the level of burden reported by the caregiver. Participants and their families also complete a 'features checklist' in which they identify features of the SH they are most interested in to meet their needs. At this time the operations engineer conducts a survey of the home.

3.3 Installation and Equipment

The installation process typically spans two to three days and involves physically installing the sensors, panels/tablets, wiring for the sensors and panels, switches and a laptop. These devices drive and control the system and its features.

Sensors in the SH are mounted to provide optimal tracking coverage with maximum accuracy through a user-donned UWB-emitting tag or smart watch. In an open environment, Ubisense technology permits the SH to track numerous individuals to within an accuracy of 15 cm, in 3 dimensions, 95 % of the time [26]. This level of accuracy is advantageous because it can distinguish whether an individual stands in front of a refrigerator or a microwave, although not all areas require such accuracy. Touch sensitive panels strategically placed within the homes [1] provide text-based and auditory prompts to the users. Members of the SH team along with a certified electrician are responsible for the installation process which is provided to the Veteran at no cost.

Users have input on where sensors are placed determined by where they choose to be monitored. After installation, spatial regions are named and set to monitor specific activities. For example, the couch, exercise area, or stove within the family room, gym, or kitchen, respectively.

3.4 Training

After installation in the Veteran's home, a training program is implemented. The training program is tailored to each individual, with specific emphasis on learning patterns that may require additional time and modified instruction for those with cognitive deficits. In general, the training program consists of one to three sessions per week with instruction time lasting anywhere between 30 and 45 min. Information manuals with step-by-step instructions are provided for the users to follow-up with the training after the session has ended. Initial training includes education regarding wearing of the tag, basic use of the panels and accessing the web application. It is requested that users wear their tag during all waking hours, although, they have the ability to remove the tag if tracking is not desired. Further in-depth training involves the input of the user's calendar, selection of interactive task sequencing and reminders, and use of the data and reports. It is critical that the participants have a good understanding of the use and functionality of the system in order to promote engagement and enhance the level of assistance provided by the SH technology.

3.5   Participant Involvement

To increase the adoption and utilization of the SH technology all participants are strongly encouraged to attend monthly user meetings, which are facilitated by the participants themselves. This is an open forum in which they have the opportunity to discuss what is working well, what isn't working well, what they like about the SH and overall system improvements. Information is relayed to staff members as necessary. This also provides a peer support group in which they can participate in typical social interaction.

As discussed in [27], the acceptability and usability of smart technologies are frequently not assessed. User's expectations, beliefs and perceptions are taken into consideration through participant-led meetings and follow-up assessments, for the continued development of the project. Follow-up assessments occur one month post-installation and after completed training and then reoccur every three months. As early adopters of the system, participants feel that they truly are a part of the development team and continue to pave the way forward.

4   Future Directions

The expansion of the SH project will allow the technology to become available to a wider range of Veterans, including those with dementia, multiple sclerosis (MS), and spinal cord injuries, as well as other disadvantaged or vulnerable populations. In addition, specific funding opportunities within the Department of Veterans Affairs allows for the project to reach underserved and rural Veterans in their homes.

The future development of the SH is to integrate a *companion* dialogue system, in which the SH becomes knowledgeable of its user. This system is called Calonis, which is conceptually similar to Siri but has the ability to learn the user's habits and routines [28]. Calonis is a way to more effectively engage the Veteran and provide verbal prompting to achieve greater levels of independence. Initial results have been very promising with viability testing of Calonis as a means to increase participant engagement.

The long-term development plan is to create an electronic caregiver that incorporates machine learning and AI algorithms. Initial testing will begin on fall detection capabilities and an alert system for caregivers and clinicians. Future research will include evaluation of the efficacy of the SH system using outcome measures from participant assessments and feedback.

The views, opinions, and/or findings contained in this article are those of the authors and should not be construed as an official position, policy or decision of the Departments of Defense or Veterans Affairs unless so designated by other official documentation.

Acknowledgements. This work is supported by grants from the U.S. Department of Veterans Affairs, Ubisense PLC and Defense and Veterans Brain Injury Center (DVBIC) through the US Army Medical Research and Materiel Command under General Dynamics Information Technology (GDIT) (Award Ref: W91YTZ-13-C-0015).

References

1. Jasiewicz, J., Kearns, W., Craighead, J., Fozard, J.L., Scott, S., McCarthy, J.: Smart rehabilitation for the 21st century: the Tampa Smart Home for veterans with traumatic brain injury. J. Rehabil. Res. Dev. **48**(8), xii–xvii (2011)
2. Lew, H.L., Poole, J., Vanderploeg, R.D., Goodrich, G.L., Dekelboum, S., Guillory, S.B., Sigford, B., Cifu, D.X.: Program development and defining characteristics of returning military in a VA polytrauma network site. J. Rehabil. Res. Dev. **44**(7), 1027–1034 (2007)
3. Chan, M., Estève, D., Escriba, C., Campo, E.: A review of Smart homes—present state and future challenges. Comp. Methods Programs Biomed. **91**(1), 55–81 (2008)
4. Centers for Disease Control and Prevention: Surveillance for traumatic brain injury-related deaths-United States, 1997–2007. Morbid. Mort. W. Rep. **60**(5), 1–32 (2011)
5. Corrigan, J., Selassie, A., Langlois-Orman, J.: The epidemiology of traumatic brain injury. J. Head Trau. Rehabil. **25**(2), 72–80 (2012)
6. Ruff, R.L., Riechers II, R.G., Wang, X.-F., Piero, T., Ruff, S.S.: A case-control study examining whether neurological deficits and PTSD in combat veterans are related to episodes of mild TBI. BMJ Open **2**, e000312 (2012)
7. Coronado, V., McGuire, M., Faul, M., Sugerman, D., Pearson, W.: The Epidemiology and Prevention of TBI (2012)
8. Faul, M., Xu, L., Wald, M.M., Coronado, V.: Traumatic Brain Injury in the United States: Emergency Department Visits, Hospitalizations and Deaths, 2002–2006. Centers for Disease Control and Prevention, National Center for Injury Prevention and Control, Atlanta, GA (2010). http://www.cdc.gov/traumaticbraininjury/pdf/blue_book.pdf
9. Hart, T., Dijkers, M., Whyte, J., Braden, C., Trott, C.T., Fraser, R.: Vocational interventions and supports following job placement for persons with traumatic brain injury. J. Voc. Rehabil. **32**(3), 135–150 (2010)
10. Kissinger, D.B.: Traumatic brain injury and employment outcomes: integration of the working alliance model. Work **31**(3), 309–317 (2008)
11. Sayer, N.: Polytrauma and Blast-Related Injuries QUERI Strategic Plan (2012). http://www.queri.research.va.gov/about/strategic_plans/ptbri.pdf. Accessed March 2014
12. Andelic, N., Stevens, L., Sigurdardottir, S., Arango-Lasprilla, J., Roe, C.: Associations between disability and employment one year after traumatic brain injury in a working age population. Brain Inj. **26**(3), 261–269 (2012)
13. Corrigan, J., Hammond, F.: Traumatic brain injury as a chronic health condition. Ach. Phys. Med. Rehabil. **94**, 1199–1201 (2013)
14. Hammond, F., Malec, J.: Rethinking Brain Injury. Brain Inj. Prof. **10**(1), 8–10 (2013)
15. DePompei, R., Gillette, Y., Goetz, E., Xenopoulos-Oddsson, A., Bryen, D., Dowds, M.: Practical applications for use of PDAs and Smartphones with children and adolescents who have traumatic brain injury. Neur. Rehabil. **23**(6), 487–499 (2008)
16. Rialle, V., Duchêne, F., Noury, N., Bajolle, L., Demongeot, J.: Health 'smart' home: information technology for patients at home. Telemed. J. E-Health **8**, 395–409 (2002)

17. Lancioni, G.E., Perilli, V., O'Reilly, F., Singh, N.N., Sigafoos, J., Bosco, A., Caffo, A.O., Picucci, L., Cassano, G., Groeneweg, J.: technology-based orientation programs to support indoor travel by persons with moderate Alzheimer's disease: impact assessment and social validation. Res. Dev. Disabil. **34**, 286–293 (2013)
18. Gorman, A.: LifeLine Project (2003). http://www.cs.colorado.edu/~l3d/clever/projects/lifeline.html
19. Symonds, J., Parry, D., Briggs, J.: An RFID-based system for assisted living: challenges and solutions. Stud. Hea. Tech. Inform. **127**, 127–138 (2007)
20. Dry, A., Colantonio, A., Cameron, J., Mihailidis, A.: Technology in the lives of women who live with memory impairment as a result of a traumatic brain injury. Assistive Technol. J. RESNA. **18**(2), 170–180 (2006)
21. Gentry, T., Wallace, J., Kvarfordt, C., Lynch, K.B.: Personal digital assistants as cognitive aids for individuals with severe traumatic brain injury: a community-based trial. Brain Inj. **22**(1), 19–24 (2009)
22. Oddy, M., Ramos, S.: Cost effective ways of facilitating home based rehabilitation and support. Neuro. Rehabil. **32**, 781–790 (2013)
23. Sohlberg, M.M., Fickas, S., Hung, P.F., Fortier, A.: A comparison of four prompt modes for route findings for community travelers with severe cognitive impairments. Brain Inj. **21**(5), 531–538 (2007)
24. Stock, S.E., Davies, D.K., Wehmeyer, M.L., Lachapelle, Y.: Emerging new practices in technology to support independent community access for people with intellectual and cognitive disabilities. Neuro. Rehabil. **28**, 261–269 (2011)
25. Kearns, W., Jasiewicz, J.M., Fozard, J., Webster, P., Scott, S., Craighead, J., Bowen, M.E., McCarthy, J.: Temporo-spatial prompting for persons with cognitive impairment using a smart wrist-worn interface. J. Rehabil. Res. Dev. **50**(10), vii–xiii (2013)
26. Steggles, P., Gschwind, S.: The Ubisense smart space platform. In: Adjunct Proceedings of the Third International Conference on Pervasive Computing, vol. 191, pp. 73–76 (2005)
27. Faucounau, V., Riguet, M., Orvoen, G., Lacombe, A., Rialle, V., Extra, J., Rigaud, A.S.: Electronic tracking system and wandering in Alzheimer's disease: a case study. Ann. Phys. Rehabil. Med. **52**, 579–587 (2009)
28. Wilks, Y., Jasiewicz, J.: Calonis: an artificial companion for the care of cognitively impaired patients. In: The Society for the Study of Artificial Intelligence and Simulation of Behaviour (AISB). Machine Ethics in the Context of Medical and Care Agents (MEMCA), Goldsmiths College, University of London, United Kingdom, 1–4 April 2014. http://doc.gold.ac.uk/aisb50/AISB50-S17/AISB50-S17-Wilks-Paper.pdf

Activity Recognition

Regression Analysis for Gesture Recognition Using RFID Technology

Kevin Bouchard$^{(\boxtimes)}$, Bruno Bouchard, and Abdenour Bouzouane

Université Du Québec à Chicoutimi (UQAC), 555 Boul. Université, Saguenay,
QC G7H 2B1, Canada
{Kevin.Bouchard, Bruno.Bouchard,
Abdenour.Bouzouane}@uqac.ca

Abstract. The recognition of gestures performed by humans always attracted researchers that applied such algorithms in a broad range of disciplines. In particular, it was exploited on pervasive environments to enable simple communication with automation systems. In this paper, we present a novel gesture recognition algorithm that works under uncertainty. The algorithm is based on the tracking of passive RFID tags installed on everyday life objects. The method is able to perform the difficult task of segmentation and recognize basic directions within noisy dataset of positions. A set of tests was conducted in a realistic environment, and the results obtained are encouraging.

Keywords: Regression · Smart home · Gesture recognition · Passive RFID

1 Introduction

Many researchers are working to implement technological solutions, such as smart environments, to assist the cognitively impaired or the semi autonomous elders. However, many difficulties must be first overcome (opportunistic networking, security, etc.). In particular, extensive research has been conducted on context modeling and Activity Recognition (AR) [1], but the challenges remain important. Many researchers think that the raw information extracted from the sensors need to be exploited more intelligently. For example, Jakkula and Cook [2] exploited the temporal relationships between events created by the sensors. Gesture recognition could enable better context modeling and help in AR. This field has particularly attracted researchers on Human-Computer Interfaces (HCI) and many algorithms are currently used for natural and efficient design in video games, software engineering and even in smart homes [3] where cameras are usually the privileged sensors [4]. Accelerometers can also be exploited for gesture recognition [5]. Nevertheless, it is hard to ensure the resident always wears the equipment in a smart home context.

One of the most promising technologies for smart home is the Radio-Frequency IDentification (RFID). This technology possesses the advantages of being cheap, but also non intrusive. Passive tags can basically be placed on any object of a smart home due to their small size. This technology has been ignored for gesture recognition, until recently [6], because of its inherent imprecision. In this paper, we propose to exploit the recent advances in passive RFID tracking [7, 8] to recognize ongoing gestures.

© Springer International Publishing Switzerland 2015
C. Bodine et al. (Eds.): ICOST 2014, LNCS 8456, pp. 121–128, 2015.
DOI: 10.1007/978-3-319-14424-5_13

2 Related Work

Gesture recognition is a well-established field of research that traditionally focuses on HCI [9]. A gesture is widely described and recognized as an expressive and meaningful body motion (hand, face, arms, etc.) that conveys a message or more generally, embeds important information of spatio-temporal nature. The usual steps to perform gesture recognition from spatio-temporal data series are: 1. Segmentation, 2. Filtering of the data, 3. Limiting directions and 4. Matching. In many cases, however, the segmentation step is ignored because it is assumed that it is known. A difficult challenge of segmentation is the support of gestures of varying length interleaved with small to big *idle* time. The filtering is a straightforward step consisting in standardizing and compensating the data (time, format, etc.). The step of the limitation of directions is used to limit the entropy of the inference. Finally, the research have always focused on the matching step which consist of using the basic extracted directions and matches them in a knowledge base of gestures.

2.1 Main Gesture Recognition Models

Many gesture recognition approaches are based on statistical modeling such as the Hidden Markov Machine (HMMs), the Kalman filtering or other particles filtering. For instance, Samaria and Young [10] exploited HMMs to extract efficiently facial expressions from a single camera. The reasoning corresponds to the process of finding the HMM with the highest probability of explaining that set of observations. Methods exploiting particle filters are also very popular. For instance, Shan et al. [11] combined the technique with Mean shift to perform real time hand tracking. Finally, a large number of gesture recognition approaches effectively exploited Finite State Machines (FSMs). For instance, Hong et al. [12] exploited spatial clustering to learn a set of FSMs corresponding to gestures. They tested their approach using four sample gestures performed in front of a video camera. They achieved a hundred percent recognition rate, but admitted that with a very noisy data sample, the recognition would fail. The team of Wang et al. [13] used body sensor networks to recognize gestures and complex activities. Their approach achieves an accuracy of 82.87 %. The main issue is the requirement for the user to wear the equipment at all time.

The main problem with the models of the literature for our specific context is with the assumptions that are made. First of all, it is often assumed that obtaining the basic directions of the movement is straightforward. It is not the case with passive RFID tracking. Secondly, it is assumed that the amount of noise is not a problem. Thirdly, segmentation is often known within an HCI context; therefore, few models address this issue. Finally, the user is assumed as cooperative; an intended recognition context while in our case, the recognition is done unbeknownst to the user (more difficult).

2.2 Gesture Recognition Using RFID

Many researchers, including our team, believe that passive RFID technology is the best option in the context of smart home. For gesture recognition, we could put passive tags on any objects and track their movement. A lot of research has been conducted on the tracking of RFID tags. Despite this, the team of Asadzadeh et al. [6] is, to the best of our knowledge, the only one that investigated the gesture recognition with this technology. With three antennas on a desk, they monitored an 80 cm by 80 cm area, which was divided into 64 equally sized square cells (10 cm by 10 cm) and localized using reference tags. Their system is based on few important assumptions. First, it is fast enough to never miss any cell in a sequence; that is, the tracked object cannot move farther than one cell away in between two readings. Second, only forward local moves are possible. Their algorithm cannot recognize two consecutive gestures (no segmentation) but works well (93 %) on a dictionary of twelve gestures. Their work showed that there is potential for gesture recognition with passive RFID.

3 Gesture Recognition

In this section, we present a new gesture recognition method that takes as input the coordinates of tagged objects, every 20 ms, extracted from a localization algorithm such as [7, 8]. The method depends directly on the accuracy of the localization algorithm and takes it as a parameter. That is, a valid direction cannot be less than the average error (ε). This is the limitation of the granularity of our gestures. The main contribution of this new method is on the step of identification of the basic directions that are generally assumed as known in the literature and on the segmentation of these directions which is particularly arduous with passive RFID technology. The Fig. 1 depicts the overall method.

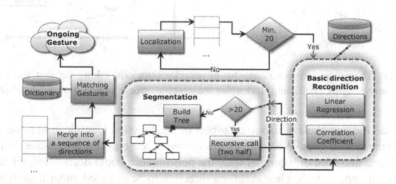

Fig. 1. The overall gesture recognition method.

3.1 Basic Direction Recognition

The most important thing to first discuss is how to convert the set of positions that we obtain to basic direction information. There are three essential elements to this step. First of all, the possible directions have to come in a limited set in order to recognize high level gestures. Since our data is noisy, we think that a limit to eight qualitative directions is a good tradeoff between precision and accuracy (Fig. 2a). Moreover, we found that there is not a significant increase in accuracy under eight basic directions. In that qualitative model, a quantitative direction is converted by using its angle with the abscissa axis. For example, between $-22.5°$ and $22.5°$ the direction is E (for east). The second part of this step is to infer the said direction from the set of positions gathered. To do so, we perform linear regressions. At this step of the process, we suppose that the set of data correspond only to one of the qualitative direction. Later in this paper, we explain how to perform the important but difficult step of segmentation. From a set of positions, the linear regression gives a linear function of the form $y = ax + b$ using Eq. 1.

$$a = \frac{\left(n\left(\sum_{i=0}^{n} x_i y_i\right) - \left(\sum_{i=0}^{n} x_i\right)\left(\sum_{i=0}^{n} y_i\right)\right)}{\left(n\left(\sum_{i=0}^{n} x_i^2\right) - \left(\sum_{i=0}^{n} x_i\right)^2\right)} \qquad b = \frac{\left(\sum_{i=0}^{n} y_i\right)}{n} - a\frac{\left(\sum_{i=0}^{n} x_i\right)}{n} \qquad (1)$$

From the resulting equation, we can compute directly the angle from the x-axis by doing the *arctan*($|a|$) of the slope. The result of this operation leads to two opposite possible directions (from the qualitative framework). We chose between both direction simply by doing an average of the starting points and comparing it with the average of the ending points. To be clear, the set is divided in two equal part (if possible) and the both average are computed. We cannot simply compare the first and the last point because it could mislead us in unlucky situations (Fig. 2b).

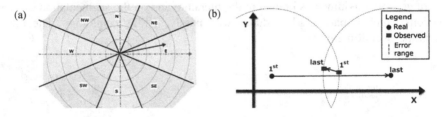

Fig. 2. (a). The qualitative directions. (b). In unlucky situations, taking the first and the last position can be highly misleading. It doubles the average error obtained from the localization.

The last but nonetheless, important aspect of the direction identification is the speed at which the system goes. We could let the system execute as fast as possible, but with many objects and a lot of incoming data, the performance could decrease significantly. Moreover, it appears to be clear that for a direction to be detected under uncertainty, a minimum of half a second of data is needed. Additionally, humans usually do not perform gestures shorter than few seconds. For those reasons, the recognition is only executed every 200 ms and when we have at least 20 positions.

3.2   Segmentation

Being able to identify the current direction is not the only challenge toward gesture recognition with RFID. Another very difficult part is to be able to understand where the individual directions are ending or if the object is actually moving or not. This part of our new algorithm is based on the correlation coefficient which can be computed using Eq. 2.

$$\varphi = \frac{\left(n\left(\sum_{i=0}^{n} x_i y_i\right) - \left(\sum_{i=0}^{n} x_i\right)\left(\sum_{i=0}^{n} y_i\right)\right)}{\sqrt{n\left(\sum_{i=0}^{n} x_i^2\right) - \left(\sum_{i=0}^{n} x_i\right)^2} * \sqrt{n\left(\sum_{i=0}^{n} y_i^2\right) - \left(\sum_{i=0}^{n} y_i\right)^2}} \tag{2}$$

From that equation, we always obtain a value of φ comprised between -1 and 1. If the value is far from 0, the correlation is high between the data points. Our first hypothesis was that this information could be exploited to distinguish between an idle object (with high localization error) and a moving one. Knowing that, we recorded the values of several subsets of data during when an object was idle to learn the correct threshold of the correlation coefficient to exploit in our model. We found out that on average, when the object was idle, $\varphi < 0.4$. However, assuming that an idle object is moving when it is not can be very damaging for the algorithms using the data (keeps in mind that we work on gesture recognition in the goal of exploiting the knowledge for assistive smart homes). Consequently, we used a slightly higher value (0.5) in our implementation to decide whether the object is idle over the period evaluated or moving in a certain direction.

To perform the segmentation, we exploit this knowledge with a divide and conquer method. The idea is simply to divide the data in half and redo the previous steps until stop conditions are met. The stop conditions are either when we have 20 positions or less or when the correlation coefficient drop under idle while resulting in the same direction. The idea is that by doing that, it should be possible to identify that a data sequence, is, in fact, composed of multiple different directions. The Fig. 3 shows an example of such a situation (the coefficients are given as an example) where the data is the result of two atomic directions.

Decision process. The previous step gives a tree structure where each level corresponds to a potential sequence of directions. To choose the sequence of direction (0 to n), we need to merge the tree hypothesis by comparing the various correlation coefficients at each level. There are three possible situations. If two leafs have the same direction, they are merged to the superior level. If one of the two leafs is idle but not the other, the algorithm takes the decision in function of the value of φ. If the direction of the lower-level leaf has a higher coefficient value, the conclusion is that the sequence is comprised of those two leafs. If it is lower, the leafs are deleted and the higher level is considered correct. The last possibility is that the two leafs are of different direction (but not idle). In that situation, to decide if they are kept, the algorithm computes the average value of both coefficient and compares it with the superior level. The Fig. 4 depicts an example tree structure that could be created during the step of segmentation.

In that case, the conclusion would be that the first half of the data was NorthEast with a very high correlation (0.9). The second half would be composed of a short idle time with an East direction.

Limiting the data. Alongside the segmentation, it is important to limit the growth of the dataset if we do not want the computation time to explode. To do so, we designed a simple solution that exploit the growing certainty of our conclusions over time. That is, we only reevaluate the data points of the two last direction excluding the idle time in between. For example, it supposes that the first three recognition iterations give respectively: {(1; N), (2; NE, E), (3; N, NE, E)}. Then, for the fourth recognition iteration, the first direction (N) will be locked, and the data associated with it will no more be evaluated. The data associated is the set of positions that was used to infer that direction (in the tree structure).

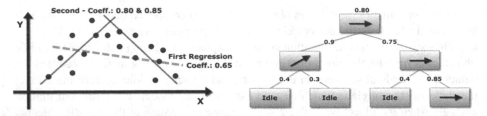

Fig. 3. Segmentation with the coefficients.   **Fig. 4.** An example of resulting tree.

3.3 Matching the Gestures

The final part of our method consists of matching the list of identified directions to the gestures in the dictionary. For this part, the literature proposes a variety of methods developed through years of research [9]. Our gesture dictionary is a set of finite state machines representing each gesture. The selected ongoing gesture is the state machine that matches the sequence of atomic directions identified. However, the matching module is not strict. If a sequence comprising of small idle moment does not match any gesture, they are progressively eliminated until either the sequence match or until no more remain. Contrary to most work in the literature, we do not assume that a gesture was intended. That is because in our context the user is a normal resident or a resident with a cognitive deficit that does not purposely intend to perform a gesture with the objects he moves. Finally, note that for our experiments, each FSM was directly designed by us since they are fairly small. However, they could certainly be learned automatically with knowledge discovery techniques.

4 Experiments

To validate the potential of our new method, we implemented it in a smart home laboratory. Our smart home infrastructure is composed of eight RFID antennas and a large number of various sensors and effectors. The antennas we are currently using are A-PATCH-0025 working on the 860–960 MHz band and are circularly polarized for a better indoor GSM coverage. The localization is based on trilateration and exploits four antennas that cover approximately 9 m^2 (the kitchen). The RFID system is set at high sensitivity, and the emission rate is set at each 20 ms. Each object of the smart home has 2 to 4 class 3 RFID tags attached to it. It limits the bad angle of arrival. Another point worth mentioning is that cabinets are shielded (partially) in order for the objects inside to remain mostly invisible to the antennas. The RFID system can support a lot of objects before the localization accuracy significantly decreases, but further experiments would be needed to determine exactly how many.

4.1   Generation of Random Gestures

As a preliminary set of experiment, we implemented a simulator that generated gestures to be recognized by our new method. The simulator enabled us to do an extensive amount of tests in a short time interval that the complex protocol needed with human subjects would never allow us to do. The generator works by randomly selecting a gesture's FSM in the dictionary and computing the next position using the parameters. The average error is used to generate noise. Our algorithm is able to detect gestures composed of any sequence of basic directions. However, the experimental setting Asadzadeh et al. [6] was reproduced for comparison purposes. They used only four basic directions and, on average, their gestures lasted 4.5 s at 20 cm/s with ±10 cm of localization error. The length of the gestures was on average approximately 40 cm per basic directions (−10 to +20 cm). We also added the *idle* gesture since in a realistic context, objects are often idle (see Fig. 5).

Fig. 5. Example gestures used for the experiments. The last on the picture is *Idle*.

We let our generator work for about 2000 gestures generated randomly, and we obtained 86 % success. Most of the errors were due to the process of segmentation. It means that with the same assumption of the team of Asadzadeh et al. [6] our new method would have performed better.

4.2   Experiments with a Human Subject

For the second set of experiments, a human was asked to perform each gesture ten times. The human was using a standard cup of coffee with four RFID tags that was tracked in real-time. As shown on the Table 1, the results are slightly worse than those obtained with the generator. There are two explanations to this. First, the noise in the data obtained from the RFID system is not random. It means that often, when the data begin to be inaccurate, it moves in a distinguishable direction. Secondly, in a realistic environment, there are unpredictable interferences that lead to recognize directions that never happened. For example, if the human is hiding one or many antennas for a certain time, this might lead to a significant modification of the estimated position and thus to identify a movement that is not real.

Table 1. The results from the set of gestures simulated by a human subject.

R	L	F	B	FR	BL	FL	BR	RF	LB	LF	RB	Idle	Total
9	8	7	9	7	8	8	7	7	8	7	7	9	77%

5 Conclusion

In this paper, we presented our first attempt to address the problem of gesture recognition from passive RFID technology in smart environments. In particular, we proposed a new algorithm based on linear regressions and correlation coefficients to address the difficult challenge of recognizing and segmenting basic directions. The recognition of gesture could enhance context modeling and help with AR toward the assistive smart home vision. In future work, we aim to pursue that objective by designing a complete set of experiments with a more realistic gestures' dictionary. Finally, we are working to obtain an approval certificate from the ethical committee in order to conduct larger experiments with normal and cognitively impaired subjects.

References

1. Ramos, C., Augusto, J.C., Shapiro, D.: Ambient intelligence: the next step for artificial intelligence. IEEE Intell. Syst. **23**, 15–18 (2008)
2. Jakkula, V., Cook, D.J.: Mining sensor data in smart environment for temporal activity prediction. In: KDD'07. ACM (2010)
3. Westeyn, T., Brashear, H., Atrash, A., Starner, T.: Georgia tech gesture toolkit: supporting experiments in gesture recognition. In: Proceedings of the 5th International Conference on Multimodal Interfaces, pp. 85–92. ACM (2003)
4. Mäkelä, K., Belt, S., Greenblatt, D., Häkkilä, J.: Mobile interaction with visual and RFID tags: a field study on user perceptions. In: Proceedings of the SIGCHI Conference on Human Factors in Computing Systems, pp. 991–994. ACM, San Jose, California, USA (2007)
5. Liu, J., Zhong, L., Wickramasuriya, J., Vasudevan, V.: uWave: accelerometer-based personalized gesture recognition and its applications. Pervasive Mob. Comput. **5**, 657–675 (2009)
6. Asadzadeh, P., Kulik, L., Tanin, E.: Gesture recognition using RFID technology. Pers. Ubiquit. Comput. **16**, 225–234 (2012)
7. Fortin-Simard, D., Bouchard, K., Gaboury, S., Bouchard, B., Bouzouane, A.: Accurate passive RFID localization system for smart homes. In: 3th IEEE International Conference on Networked Embedded Systems for Every Application. Liverpool, UK (2012)
8. Chen, C.Y., Yang, J.P., Tseng, G.J., Wu, Y.H., Hwang, R.C.: An Indoor positioning technique based on fuzzy logic. In: MultiConference of Engineers and Computer Scientists (IMECS) (2014)
9. Mitra, S., Acharya, T.: Gesture recognition: A Survey IEEE Transactions on Systems, Man, and Cybernetics, Part C: Applications and Reviews, vol. 37, pp. 311–324 (2007)
10. Samaria, F., Young, S.: HMM-based architecture for face identification. Image Vis. Comput. **12**, 537–543 (1994)
11. Shan, C., Wei, Y., Tan, T., Ojardias, F.: Real time hand tracking by combining particle filtering and mean shift. In: Proceedings of the Sixth IEEE International Conference on Automatic Face and Gesture Recognition, pp. 669–674 (2004)
12. Hong, P., Turk, M., Huang, T.S.: Gesture modeling and recognition using finite state machines. In: Proceedings Fourth IEEE International Conference on Automatic Face and Gesture Recognition, pp. 410–415 (2000)
13. Wang, L., Gu, T., Tao, X., Lu, J.: A hierarchical approach to real-time activity recognition in body sensor networks. Pervasive Mob. Comput. **8**, 115–130 (2012)

Improving Activity Recognition in Smart Environments with Ontological Modeling

Zachary Wemlinger$^{(\boxtimes)}$ and Lawrence Holder

School of Electrical Engineering and Computer Science,
Washington State University, Box 642752, Pullman, WA 99164, USA
{zewemli,holder}@wsu.edu

Abstract. The problem of activity recognition in smart environments has produced multiple divergent paths of research in an attempt to improve the usability and usefulness of smart environments. In this paper we merge these research paths by defining a method for mapping smart environment sensor activities into an ontologically defined semantic feature space. We show that by using this approach we are able to improve activity recognition by between 5–20 %.

Keywords: Activity recognition · Ontological modeling · Ontologies · Semantic Web

1 Introduction

Recent advances in pervasive computing technologies have enabled the exploration of intelligent environments as a means of providing daily activity monitoring and cognitive support for aging populations. In order to meet this potential the environment must be able to efficiently and accurately recognize the state of the resident and in what activity, or activities, the resident is engaged.

Unfortunately, activity recognition in a real-world smart environment is a challenging task, partly due to the sparsity of the available data and its highly skewed class distribution. Also, variability between individuals and environments can amplify the difficulty and expense of collecting and annotating data required to learn in a new environment. While some researchers have proposed expert systems based on semantic modeling as a method to avoid dependence on machine learning algorithms, these approaches carry expectations related to sensor utility and activity structure which often do not transfer well to the real-world.

The main contribution of this paper is a process for integrating semantic knowledge into the process of learning activity recognition models. We model five existing smart environments using Semantic Web technologies and existing ontologies related to smart environments and demonstrate that activity recognition can be reliably improved by 5–20 %, depending on what measure is used.

© Springer International Publishing Switzerland 2015
C. Bodine et al. (Eds.): ICOST 2014, LNCS 8456, pp. 129–137, 2015.
DOI: 10.1007/978-3-319-14424-5_14

2   Ontological Models of Smart Environments

Several researchers have defined ontologies for smart environments, each with a slightly different focus. Of these ontologies, DogOnt[1] [1] and COSE[2] [16] are both publicly available. To the best of our knowledge the ontologies in [2,15] are not generally available.

DogOnt provides a rich ontology for smart homes with an emphasis on facilitating device interoperability. As such it provides many concepts related to device capabilities, functionality and commands providing an API for smart environments. This focus makes DogOnt a good ontology for use by intelligent agents when controlling and communicating with devices in a smart environment. COSE, on the other hand, is a smaller ontology focused on modeling objects and sensors within a smart environment. In [16], the authors make clear that one of their design goals was to integrate COSE with a top level ontology, namely OpenCyc [10]. The authors argue that mapping into an upper-level ontology provides extra portability for models utilizing COSE and enables more integration with the wider Semantic Web.

For this work, we have chosen to use COSE due to its richer model of objects in the environment. It is worth noting that, given the structure of the Semantic Web, using one ontology in no way prohibits the use of a different ontology when the need to express different concepts arises. Thus, applications in smart environments can easily reference concepts from both COSE and DogOnt whenever needed.

3   Smart Environments

In this section we discuss the details of the environments which we have modeled for this paper. For a more general discussion of smart environments, refer to [4].

We have modeled five environments using the COSE ontology. One, named Kyoto, is a testbed for smart home research and is used in seven out of the eleven datasets in this study. The other four environments are homes which have been instrumented with sensors in order to gather longitudinal data on activities, the names for these environments are Aruba, Cairo, Milan, and Tulum. Table 1 provides details about these environments.

Figure 1 shows the locations of sensors in the Kyoto environment. This environment is a three-bedroom apartment with two levels. The upper level contains the bedrooms and a bathroom, while the lower floor contains the living room, kitchen and dining area. Controlled experiments in this environment were conducted on the lower level of this apartment. Those experiments account for five of the seven datasets gathered in Kyoto.

---

[1] http://elite.polito.it/ontologies/dogont.owl.
[2] http://casas.wsu.edu/owl/cose.owl.

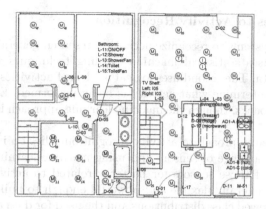

Fig. 1. Sensor layout for the Kyoto Smart Environment. This environment contains: 52 Motion sensors; 17 Light-switch sensors; 15 Door sensors; 12 Object contact sensors; 2 Temperature sensors; 2 Water flow sensors; 1 Home energy usage sensor; 1 Range burner sensor

Table 1. Environments used in this study

Name	Aruba	Cairo	Milan	Tulum	Kyoto
Sensors	39	32	33	18	102
Sensor Events	1,709,866	724,738	432,416	1,085,026	5,078,005
Sensor Types	Door, Motion, Temperature	Motion, Temperature	Door, Motion, Temperature	Motion	Door, Motion, Object, Power Usage, Temperature, Water Flow
Number annotated activities	9	9	7	13	118
Relevant Publications	[3]		[6]	[3]	[6,7,12,14]

4 Activity Recognition

Activity recognition is the task of recognizing when a person is performing a certain task. The set of possible tasks is unbounded, so smart home researchers generally consider a small number of tasks know as the Activities of Daily Living, or ADLs [9], which are of particular interest in elder care applications. These activities include: Grooming, Eating, Toileting, Bathing, and Personal Hygiene. The authors of [11] also suggest Instrumental Activities of Daily Living, or IADLs, which include: Using a Telephone, Shopping, Cooking, Housekeeping, Laundry, Taking Medications and Handling Finances.

These activities are the baseline around which much of the research, particularly health-care related smart environment research, has focused. Research groups tend to instrument an environment, observe research participants performing these activities, develop recognition algorithms, and then use the data to assess algorithm effectiveness.

4.1   Approaches to Activity Recognition

When designing systems to recognize activities, research generally falls into two areas. The first uses statistical machine learning techniques to learn models given observed data. The second uses logical models of activities defined *a priori* to build rules to determine what activity is being performed. Each method has benefits and drawbacks, though the machine learning approach is generally more popular.

The data-driven approach to activity recognition relies on instrumenting an environment with a range of sensors and using machine learning algorithms to mine the output of those sensors for patterns related to activities of interest. This approach is generally flexible and powerful enough to build useful activity models, though skewed class distributions and the need for data annotation make learning in new environments difficult.

In contrast, a "knowledge-based" approach is based on expert systems which contain activity models as a set of logical constraints. These models are used by inferencing engines to determine what activity is being performed. In [2], the authors propose such a system using Semantic Web technologies and a novel decision algorithm based on lattice-theory. The challenges when applying this approach are that getting data out of an environment which is clean enough to fit into a rule-based system is difficult. Also, building and extending these systems is difficult and costly.

In this work we demonstrate a hybrid approach which combines the best of both worlds in order to minimize the drawbacks of each while capitalizing on their strengths.

5   Learning with Semantics

The proposal is simple: Map sensor data into an ontologically defined feature-space for use by machine learning algorithms. This allows learned models to be applied in any environment where these mappings are defined, and if needed, integrate semantic rules into the activity recognition process.

5.1   Defining Semantic Space

Statistical machine learning algorithms necessarily learn by example. Given a dataset, the attributes for each example are considered to be the "feature space" of that dataset. When we say a "semantic feature space" we mean a feature space which is defined by concepts in an ontology. The challenge is to choose which concepts to use in our feature space.

To do this, we have taken inspiration from natural language processing techniques and have adopted an n-gram approach. With this approach, we define the feature space to be a set of n-grams built up from the concepts in COSE. In this approach each sensor is mapped to one or more n-grams based on the following.

First, let S be the set of concepts in COSE which are directly instantiable in a smart environment. This excludes abstract concepts such as *Sensor*, but does include concepts such as MotionDetector. Next, for each sensor e of type t we find the set of concepts $C \subset S$ to which e has a relationship. Further, let $\mathcal{B}$ be a set of predefined base concepts around which n-grams will be built. Consider $\mathcal{P}$ to be a partitioning of C into $|\mathcal{B}| + 1$ sets such that all concepts in set i are a specialization of the concept B_i. The last set in $\mathcal{P}$ contains all concepts in C which have no parent in $\mathcal{B}$. The features in semantic space to which e maps are its type t and the set of features in the cross product of the sets in $\mathcal{P}$.

As an example, sensor M014 is a motion detector which is situated above the table in the dining room in the Kyoto smart environment. For this work we let $\mathcal{B}$ be $\{Sensor, SpaceInAHOC\}$[3]. Thus, M014 is mapped to features that are the cross-product of the sets $\{MotionDetector\}$, $\{DiningRoom\}$ and $\{Table\}$. These features can be expressed with statements such as "Motion in the dining room" and "Motion in the dining room above the table".

5.2   Creating Feature Vectors

When creating feature vectors from streaming events we maintain the state of the environment as a vector V. We allow sensor events to change this vector and every g time units we shift this vector onto a stack of state vectors which extend back for a limited amount of time; we call this H or the history matrix. Given a list of window sizes W_s, we create a set of matrices W_m over H which define windows extending back a specific amount of time from the current moment. If we consider the state vectors to be the rows of the matrix, then the columns provide a history of each individual sensor.

The output feature vectors are, for each window, the mean of the columns plus the union of 1D FFTs run over each column. The real-valued inputs to the FFT mean that the result is symmetric and we only need to retain half of the FFT which helps to reduce excess noisy features. In order to map into semantic space, we observe that each ontological concept can be thought of as a sensor with a real value. The state of the sensor is simply the mean of the real sensors which map into the concept.

6   Experiments

In order to test our hypothesis that adding semantic models can improve activity recognition in smart environments, we have testing activity recognition algorithms over eleven datasets using three feature spaces.

6.1   Feature Spaces

The first feature space, which we refer to as sensor space, is a standard approach which directly takes features from sensor activities. In this space, each sensor produces two basic features for each time window: the sensor's mean activity and the dominant frequency of the sensor.

---

[3] SpaceInAHOC is short for Space In A Human Occupation Construct.

The second space is the COSE space, which is built by mapping sensor activities into semantic space using the procedure described in Sect. 5.1. The features in this space are the mean activity and dominant frequency of each n-gram.

Finally, we also have tested the union of these two spaces, which we refer to as the hybrid space.

6.2   Experimental Setup

Here we use window sizes of 3, 7, 14, 30 seconds and g is 0.5 seconds. As suggested in [3], we sample one feature vector every 10 seconds. All features are discretized using equal width binning with 5 bins then mapped to binary features. Feature vectors are labeled using the set of all labels observed on a sensor event during the 10 second window.

Activity recognition is inherently a multi-label classification problem and this is addressed here by training a single classifier for each activity in each dataset over each feature space and evaluating the performance of each model independently.

We have split each activity into n separate and temporally continuous sections. We train and test our models iteratively, such that on iteration i we train our model on the first i sections and test on the remaining $n - i$ sections. In our tests we have set $n = 10$.

Results are based on using Sofial-ML[4] which is a support vector machine implementation and which is partly described in [13]. This particular implementation allows calculating support vectors by stochastically selecting examples from both the positive and negative class. Doing this is necessary for our datasets due to the highly skewed class distribution where the median density of positive examples is only 2.8 %. Throughout these analyses, statistical significance is tested using student t-tests at the $p = 0.05$ level.

6.3   Results

In Fig. 2 we present performance using four metrics: accuracy, precision, recall, and RMSE. The RMSE is calculated on the error in the probabilities produced by our classifier. Due to the significant differences between precision and recall, we do not present the F-score directly. If the top ranked feature space has a statistically significantly improvement over other spaces it is marked with a diamond.

As the reader can observe, in 70 % of the cases, using a hybrid feature space provides a significant improvement over other feature spaces. In terms of performance relative to a standard sensor approach, using a hybrid space provides 5.1 % more accuracy, 20 % better precision, 5.6 % higher recall, and 9.7 % lower RMSE.

---

[4] Available at: https://code.google.com/p/sofia-ml/.

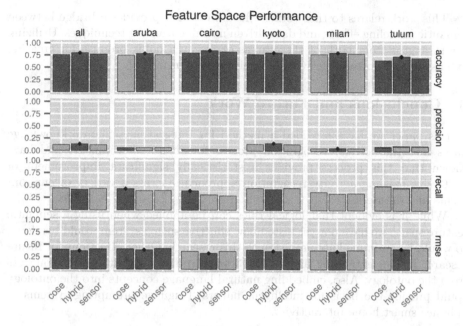

Fig. 2. Means for performance measurements given learning in the three feature spaces. Marked bars indicate the top ranked space with statistical significance. Significance is based on paired t-tests across all tests and activities in the environment. Note, RMSE is an error measure, so lower is better.

The sensor space used here is consistent with the feature spaces used in other data-driven approaches to activity recognition, e.g. [3,8]. Specifically, [3] evaluated performance of learning algorithms using several of the datasets utilized in this paper and reported an accuracy of 75 % using a hidden Markov model. The overall accuracy for the sensor space used here was 77 % and the accuracy for the hybrid space was 80 %.

7 Related Work

In Sect. 2 we discuss related ontological modeling efforts and in Sect. 4.1 we discuss ongoing research into activity recognition. In [3], Cook uses non-semantic method for mapping sensors into a common feature space with good effect. The authors of [5] provide an overview of transfer learning, which is highly related to this work. Transfer learning can avoid the need to create an ontology in order to map sensor events between environments, however in doing so also does not provide a method for integrating other semantic knowledge into the activity recognition process.

This work relates to these other efforts in that it provides a bridge between semantic modeling efforts and data-driven machine learning techniques. Utilizing the strengths from both of these areas of research holds promise for creating extensible and portable activity recognition systems.

8   Conclusions and Future Work

In this paper we have provided a method for integrating semantic knowledge bases into the activity recognition process for smart environments and have shown that this process provides a statistically significant improvement of 5–20 % to existing activity recognition approaches across a variety of environments and datasets.

While it is evident that logical rules can be applied when using a semantic feature space, we have not yet tested how effective such a system would be; doing so would be an immediate next step to this research. Other directions for future research include extending the work in [3] to learn novel activities using concepts from the ontology. Also, embedding natural language concepts into the ontology could provide the basis for intelligent natural language prompting systems to enhance smart home interactivity.

Acknowledgements. Thanks to the CASAS project at Washington State University for making the data used in this study available. This work is supported in part by National Science Foundation grant DGE-0900781.

References

1. Bonino, D., Corno, F.: DogOnt - ontology modeling for intelligent domotic environments. In: Sheth, A.P., Staab, S., Dean, M., Paolucci, M., Maynard, D., Finin, T., Thirunarayan, K. (eds.) ISWC 2008. LNCS, vol. 5318, pp. 790–803. Springer, Heidelberg (2008)
2. Chen, L., Nugent, C.: Ontology-based activity recognition in intelligent pervasive environments. Int. J. Web Inf. Syst. **5**(4), 410–430 (2009)
3. Cook, D.: Learning setting-generalized activity models for smart spaces. IEEE Intell. Syst. **27**(1), 32–38 (2010)
4. Cook, D., Das, S.: Smart Environments: Technology, Protocols and Applications, vol. 43. Wiley, New York (2004)
5. Cook, D., Feuz, K.D., Krishnan, N.C.: Transfer learning for activity recognition: A survey. Knowl. Inf. Syst. **36**(3), 537–556 (2013)
6. Cook, D.J., Schmitter-Edgecombe, M., et al.: Assessing the quality of activities in a smart environment. Methods Inf. Med. **48**(5), 480 (2009)
7. Dernbach, S., Das, B., Krishnan, N.C., Thomas, B.L., Cook, D.J.: Simple and complex activity recognition through smart phones. In: 2012 8th International Conference on Intelligent Environments (IE), pp. 214–221. IEEE (2012)
8. Krishnan, N.C., Cook, D.J.: Activity recognition on streaming sensor data. Pervasive Mob. Comput. **10**, 138–154 (2014)
9. Lawton, M.P., Brody, E.M.: Assessment of older people: self-maintaining and instrumental activities of daily living. The Gerontologist **9**(3), 179–186 (1969)

10. Matuszek, C., Cabral, J., Witbrock, M.J., DeOliveira, J.: An introduction to the syntax and content of Cyc. In: AAAI Spring Symposium: Formalizing and Compiling Background Knowledge and Its Applications to Knowledge Representation and Question Answering, pp. 44–49. Citeseer (2006)
11. Rashidi, P., Cook, D.J., Holder, L.B., Schmitter-Edgecombe, M.: Discovering activities to recognize and track in a smart environment. IEEE Trans. Knowl. Data Eng. **23**(4), 527–539 (2011)
12. Sahaf, Y.: Comparing Sensor Modalities for Activity Recognition. Master's thesis, Washington State University (2011)
13. Sculley, D.: Large scale learning to rank. In: NIPS 2009 Workshop on Advances in Ranking, pp. 1–6 (2009)
14. Szewcyzk, S., Minor, B., Swedlove, B., Cook, D.: Annotating smart environment sensor data for activity learning. Technol. Health Care **17**(3), 161–169 (2009)
15. Wang, X.H., Gu, T., Zhang, D.Q., Pung, H.K.: An ontology-based context model in intelligent environments. In: Proceedings of Communication Networks and Distributed Systems Modeling and Simulation Conference, vol. 2004, pp. 270–275 (2004)
16. Wemlinger, Z., Holder, L.: The COSE ontology: bringing the semantic web to smart environments. In: Abdulrazak, B., Giroux, S., Bouchard, B., Pigot, H., Mokhtari, M. (eds.) ICOST 2011. LNCS, vol. 6719, pp. 205–209. Springer, Heidelberg (2011)

Remote Monitoring Using Smartphone Based Plantar Pressure Sensors: Unimodal and Multimodal Activity Detection

Ferdaus Kawsar[1(✉)], Sheikh Ahamed[1], and Richard Love[2]

[1] Department of Mathematics, Statistics and Computer Science, Marquette University, 1313 W. Wisconsin Avenue, Milwaukee, WI, USA
{ferdaus.kawsar,sheikh.ahamed}@marquette.edu
[2] International Breast Cancer Research Foundation, Madison, WI, USA
richard@ibcrf.org

Abstract. Automatic activity detection is important for remote monitoring of elderly people or patients, for context-aware applications, or simply to measure one's activity level. Recent studies have started to use accelerometers of smart phones. Such systems require users to carry smart phones with them which limit the practical usability of these systems as people place their phones in various locations depending on situation, activity, location, culture and gender. We developed a prototype for shoe based activity detection system that uses pressure data of shoe and showed how this can be used for remote monitoring. We also developed a multimodal system where we used pressure sensor data from shoes along with accelerometers and gyroscope data from smart phones to make a robust system. We present the details of our novel activity detection system, its architecture, algorithm and evaluation.

Keywords: Algorithm · Measurement · Performance · Design · Remote monitoring

1 Introduction

Physical activity (PA) is bodily movement produced by skeletal muscles that results in energy expenditure [1]. Automatic detection and measurement of physical activity has applications in context sensitive systems [5], for remote monitoring the activity of patients and to track one's own activity level. It also has application in the area of monitoring elderly people while maintaining their independence. For people with impairments, due to disease or injury, an estimation of activity level reflects his/her wellbeing. Such system provides a tool to doctors by enabling them to remotely monitor activity level of patients.

The automatic physical activity detection systems mostly use accelerometer data collected from accelerometers placed on different locations in the body [2–4]. For example, Bao [2] used 5 accelerometers and placed them in five different parts of the body. Some of the systems use other sensor data along with accelerometer data [3]. Such systems suffer from some limitations. First, many of these studies primarily focused on the task of activity detection and ignored the usability part resulting in an

C. Bodine et al. (Eds.): ICOST 2014, LNCS 8456, pp. 138–146, 2015.
DOI: 10.1007/978-3-319-14424-5_15

obtrusive system. Second, some of the systems [4] perform well in a controlled laboratory environment but not so well in naturalistic environment.

We present a system that is wireless, requires no extra devices to wear and was designed to accommodate human phone behavior patterns. Recent activity detection systems are smart phone-based as they are unobtrusive, have built-in accelerometers and people carry them everywhere. The problem with such system is that it is based on the assumption that the smart phone will be 'worn' by the users (usually in the pocket) all the time. Such assumptions are not necessarily realistic as we have observed that people often put their phone on the table while working on desk. It is found that people's phone carrying habits varies a lot depending on gender, country, culture, the type of activity she/he is engaged in and some other factors. Cui et al. studied the phone carrying behavior of people in 11 cities in Europe, America, Africa, the Middle East, India and East Asia extensively and showed in their paper [12] that generally women used bags (61 % of women versus 10 % of men) and men use trouser pockets as the primary way to carry a phone. A significant percentage of men (~ 14 %) used belt cases to carry phones whereas the percentage of women using belt cases is insignificant. Culture also matters as 80 % women in Helsinki carry phones in their handbags while only 50 % do so in Delhi.

Consequently, people's behavior patterns limit the applicability of such systems although a smart phone based system is unobtrusive. Here, we present and discuss our novel activity detection system which overcomes this limitation. Also, at the same time as our system uses accelerometer and gyroscope data from smart phones and pressure data from pressure sensors placed in shoes, users will not be required to carry or wear any more devices they are not already carrying or wearing.

Our Contributions are manifold. First, we proposed a novel architecture for the unobtrusive detection of human physical activity using accelerometer and gyroscope data from smart phones as well as pressure data from shoes. Second, our architecture was designed to address unobtrusiveness as well as to ensure robustness against various human behavior patterns. Third, we built a prototype of the activity detection system using smart phones and plantar pressure sensors based on our proposed architecture that uses pressure data. Fourth, we developed the system so that activity can be monitored by someone remotely. Fifth, we analyzed data from 4 activities and based on our analysis we developed a fusion algorithm which uses accelerometer and gyroscope data from phone and pressure data from both shoes. We evaluated the performance of our fusion algorithm and observed very good accuracy.

The rest of the paper is organized as follows: Sect. 2 discusses related works, Sect. 3 describes the system architecture, Sect. 4 discusses the prototype system we built, Sect. 5 describes our multimodal system, and Sect. 6 is discussion, conclusion and future works.

2 Related Works

Phone-based accelerometers were used to perform human physical activity recognition by different researchers. Kwapisz and et al. [6] used labeled accelerometer data from Android phones where as Yang [7] used Nokia N95. Miluzzo et al. developed

CenceMe [8], using off-the-shelf, sensor-enabled mobile phones (Nokia N95) and exploited various sensors (such as a microphone, accelerometer, GPS, and camera) that are available for activity recognition. Sun Lin et al. [14] used accelerometer embedded cell phones to detect physical activities where the phone location is varying. In all of the above cases, the solution is phone based and the assumption is that the phone will be carried by the users all the time in their pockets.

Some studies tried using multiple sensors. Subramanya et al. in [9] built a model using data from a tri-axial accelerometer, two microphones, phototransistors, temperature and barometric pressure sensors, and GPS. Choudhury in [3] used multiple sensor devices consisting of seven different types of sensors to recognize activities. Cho et al. used a single tri-axial accelerometer, along with an embedded image sensor worn at the user's waist to identify nine activities [10]. Györbıró et al. [11] used "MotionBands" attached to the dominant wrist, hip, and ankle of each subject to distinguish between six different motion patterns. Each MotionBand contained a tri-axial accelerometer, magnetometer, and gyroscope and transmits the collected data wirelessly to a smart phone. The average recognition rate was 79.76 %.

3 Architecture

We propose an architecture where pressure sensors will be placed on the shoes and pressure data will be transmitted over Bluetooth to smart phone carried by the user. It does not matter where the phone is being carried as long as the phone is within the Bluetooth range of from the shoes. Our system works in two phases: Learning Phase and Activity Recognition Phase. In the learning phase, after the sensor data is collected and processed, the data is analyzed to develop an algorithm. In the activity recognition phase, the algorithm is implemented and the incoming sensor data is used by the algorithm to detect activities. Figure 1 shows this.

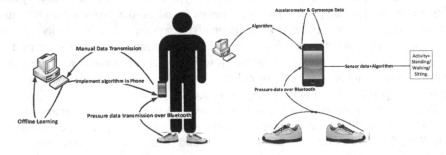

Fig. 1. **(a)** Architecture (Learning Stage) **(b)** Architecture (Activity Recognition Stage)

Our system has two principal components: the Data Collection System and the Activity Recognition System (AR). The Data Collection (DC) System is responsible for collecting sensor data. In our case, we are collecting pressure data from pressure sensors placed on the sole of both shoes, and accelerometer and gyroscope data from the cell phone and store them in four files. We used DC in two stages. First, the DC is used to collect the data and the collected data was later used to learn a classification algorithm. Second, the learnt algorithm detects activities from the incoming sensor data collected by DC during the activity recognition phase. The activity recognition system mainly consists of implementing the algorithm that was learnt in the learning phase. AR takes the sensor data as input continuously and detects the activities real-time and outputs the activity.

4 Prototype Remote Monitoring System

Based on the proposed architecture, we developed a prototype of activity recognition system. To reduce complexity, we only intended to detect sitting, standing, and walking. Also, instead of using data from all sensor systems, we only used pressure data from the left shoe. Development of the system consisted of five stages: data collection, data processing, learning algorithm, implementing recognition system and remote monitoring.

We decided to use an in-shoe plantar pressure sensor system based on a fabric sensor array. This system was developed by Lin Shu and others [13]. It has 8 pressure sensors in each shoe. There is also a Bluetooth interface to transfer the pressure data to an android phone.

Data Collection. We used the system for collecting pressure sensor data. We used data from only the left shoe. We collected data of sitting, standing and walking. While the data was being collected, the phone was in the user's hand. The collected data has 8 columns for data from 8 pressure sensors along with a time stamp.

Data Processing. We removed corrupted data from the beginning and the end as those data are likely contaminated by data collection process. There are about 37 samples of data for each second (sampling rate 37 Hz). First, we created a summery file where each row is a summary of 160 samples of raw data. Summary file for each of the three activities were generated. Each summary file contains 40 columns of data as we estimated mean, median, mode, standard deviation and summation of 160 samples for each of 8 pressure sensors of the left shoe. Then, we merged these three summary files and added another column at the end to indicate the activity class (sit/stand/walk).

Learning and Activity Recognition. We applied a decision tree based machine learning algorithm which generated a decision tree classifier. This classifier algorithm was able to classify correctly with 98.83 % accuracy. After we implemented this classifier in our recognition system, we found it took a long time to detect the activity.

According to our previous calculation, 160 samples should take 4.3 seconds at 37 Hz sampling rate. But it took much longer than that. To address this issue we reduced sample size to 60 from 160. As a result, the accuracy remained the same but it took less time to detect the activities than the prototype activity detection system. Whenever new data comes, the oldest data from buffer is discarded and features are calculated again. Then the algorithm is used to derive the activity.

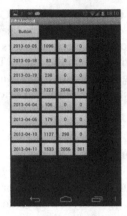

Fig. 2. Remote monitoring system screen shot

Remote Monitoring. Following figure (Fig. 2) shows a screen shot from our remote monitoring system. A user can login to view the summary of activities by date. After date column, first column is sitting time, followed by standing time and walking time in seconds.

5 Multimodal Approach

In the multimodal approach, we combined four classifiers obtained from analyzing data from gyroscope, accelerometer, right and left shoe. Each classifier was obtained following data collection, processing and learning. Four classifiers were combined and in the recognition phase, the combined classifier was used to detect activity.

System Description. We used three services on the android platform: 'TestService', 'GyroService' and 'DataReceiverService'. 'TestService' and GyroService, when started, collect data from the accelerometer and gyroscope in the cell phone respectively and stores it the SD card in two separate files. DataReceiverService' in similarly collects pressure data from the left and right shoes. In all cases, the time stamp is also recorded along with the data. Later during the preprocessing stage, we used the timestamp for synchronization so that data from all four sources start and end at the same time. While collecting data earlier for our prototype system, we only used pressure data from left shoe. Pressure data was transmitted over Bluetooth to the smart phone. As we were not collecting data from cell phones, the location of the phone was not important. But this time, we are collecting data simultaneously from the left shoe, the right shoe, the phone's accelerometer and the phone's gyroscope during different activities. The phone was kept in the right pocket of the trouser.

Data Collection. We collected data for four different activities: standing, sitting, walking and running. As we need to synchronize data from all four systems (gyroscope data collection system, accelerometer data collection system, left shoe data collection system, right shoe data collection system), we needed the timestamp. For each activity, we collected data three times (3 minutes each time).

Data Processing. Data preprocessing is very similar to what we did while developing our prototype. The extra step we did here is some extra preprocessing to ensure the synchronization of data from four different sources. We compile our data so that in each file we have the summary data for running, sitting, standing and walking. There are four such files for each of the four kinds of data: left shoe data, right shoe data, gyroscope data and accelerometer data (total 16files). Next we make a single file for each of the four sensor systems with an additional column indicating the activity.

Learning. Then, we applied decision tree algorithms to each file compiled to find a classifier. In each case, the decision tree algorithms gave us a classifier. Now we have four classifiers for each of four kinds of data from four sensor systems. The classifiers are mentioned below.

Classifier 1. This one classifies based on the accelerometer data. The accuracy is 99.5305 %.

Classifier 2. This classifier classifies based on the gyroscope data. The accuracy is 94.3662 %.

Classifier 3. This one classifies based on the pressure data from the left shoe. The accuracy is 99.061 %.

Classifier 4. This one classifies based on the pressure data from the right shoe. The accuracy is 98.8263 %.

Combined Algorithm for Activity Recognition. In this setting, we developed the following algorithm which basically is a fusion of four classifiers. Classifier 1 takes accelerometer data as input and outputs an activity. In the same way, classifier 2, 3, and 4 takes gyroscope data, pressure data from left shoe and pressure data from right respectively. All four classifiers output activity based on the decision tree they have learnt previously in the learning phase. After each classifier gives an activity as output, the algorithm decides the final activity based on the majority vote.

Activity Recognition and Evaluation. In this particular setting, we have 4 files each consisting of 426 rows of summary data. Each of these rows was created using a summary of 60 samples of pressure data (or 80 samples of accelerometer data from phone or 167 samples of gyroscope data from phone). Four separate classifiers were learnt (decision tree, in our case) based on four separate datasets in the learning phase. Now in the recognition phase, for a given input, each decision tree decides an activity using the corresponding classifier. Final activity is decided based on what the majority of classifiers has decided. In the case of a tie, the system fails to classify.

Here we discuss the results of this algorithm. Our results show that though each classifier individually shows errors, their combination results in a zero error system. For example, row 94 is classified as sitting by classifier 1, while classifier 2 decides it to be walking, classifier 3 and 4 both classifies it to be running. So the final activity will be decided as running (voted by majority classifiers). The following table summarizes different combination of sensor systems and corresponding number of errors (misclassification) by the arrangement.

Table 1. Relative performances

Structure	Number of errors
Classifier 1,2,3,4	0
Classifier 1,2,3	1
Classifier 1,2,4	1
Classifier 1,3,4	0
Classifier 2,3,4	0
Classifier 1,2	9
Classifier 1,3	1
Classifier 1,4	3
Classifier 2,3	9
Classifier 2,4	12
Classifier 3,4	3

As we can see, combined algorithm uses data from all four sensor system and using this algorithm for our data, there was zero error. Average number of errors in general decreases with the incorporation of more and more sensor system as can be seen in Fig. 3.

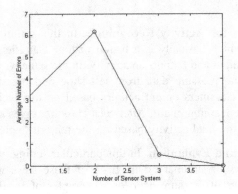

Fig. 3. Number of Sensor Systems vs Average Number of Errors

6   Discussion, Conclusions and Future Works

In Table 1, we want to emphasize the last row where we showed classifier 3 and 4 together made 3 errors. Classifier 3 and 4 were learnt based on pressure data collected from the left shoe and the right shoe. These two classifiers take pressure data as input during the recognition time. This means that classification based on only shoe data is possible with reasonable accuracy. As a result it is possible to detect activities in scenarios where people take their phone out of their pocket assuming they are keeping their shoes on. The advantage is that although people tend to use their phones in various ways, the phone is almost always within the Bluetooth range of them hence in range of their shoes. This shows that our architecture ensures robustness against various human behavior patterns.

Also, we plan to incorporate our fusion algorithm and use all four kinds of data in our future prototype. We are working on to deploy our current prototype to monitor patients remotely and evaluate its performance. We showed that a decision made from the data of multiple sensors is more accurate than decisions made from data of a single sensor system. The goal is to detect more activities, like climbing up and down stairs, driving and biking.

Acknowledgments. This work was partially supported by grant from IBCRF.

References

1. Caspersen, C.J., Powell, K.E., Christenson, G.M.: Physical activity, exercise and physical fitness: definitions and distinctions for health-related research. Public Health Rep. **110**, 126–131 (1985)
2. Bao, L., Intille, S.S.: Activity recognition from user-annotated acceleration data. In: Ferscha, A., Mattern, F. (eds.) PERVASIVE 2004. LNCS, vol. 3001, pp. 1–17. Springer, Heidelberg (2004)
3. Choudhury, T., Consolvo, S., Harrison, B., Hightower, J., LaMarca, A., LeGrand, L., Rahimi, A., Rea, A., Borriello, G., Hemingway, B., Klasnja, P., Koscher, K., Landay, J.A., Lester, J., Wyatt, D., Haehnel, D.: The Mobile Sensing Platform: an Embedded System for Capturing and Recognizing Human Activities, In IEEE Pervasive Computing Magazine. Spec, Issue on Activity-Based Computing, April-June (2008)
4. Foerster, F., Smeja, M., Fahrenberg, J.: Detection of posture and motion by accelerometry: a validation study in ambulatory monitoring. Comput. Hum. Beh. **15**(5), 571–583 (1999)
5. Randell, C., Muller, H.: Context awareness by analyzing accelerometer data. The Fourth Int'l Symposium on Wearable Computers, pp. 175–176. Atlanta, Georgia (2000)
6. Kwapisz, J.R., Weiss, G.M., Moore, S.A.: Activity recognition using cell phone accelerometers. In: Proceedings of the Fourth International Workshop on Knowledge Discovery from Sensor Data, pp. 10–18 (2010)
7. Yang, J.: Toward physical activity diary: Motion recognition using simple acceleration features with mobile phones. In: Proceedings First International Workshop on Interactive Multimedia for Consumer Electronics, pp. 1–10. ACM, New York (2009)
8. Miluzzo, E., Lane, N.D., Fodor, K., Peterson, R., Eisenman, S., Lu, H., Musolesi, M., Zheng, X., Campbell, A.: Sensing meets mobile social networks: the design, implementation and evaluation of the cenceme application. In: Proceedings of the 6th ACM Conference on Embedded Network Sensor Systems (SenSys '09), Raleigh, NC (2008)
9. Subramanya, A., Raj, A., Bilmes, J., Fox, D.: Recognizing activity and spatial context using wearable sensors. In: Proceedings of the Twenty-Second Conference Annual Conference on Uncertainty in Artificial Intelligence (UAI-06), pp. 494–502 (2006)
10. Cho, Y., Nam, Y., Choi, Y.-J., Cho, W.-D.: Smart-Buckle: human activity recognition using a 3-axis accelerometer and a wearable camera. In: Proceedings of the 2nd International Workshop on Systems and Networking Support for Healthcare and Assisted Living Environments (Healthnet '08) (2008)
11. Györbıró, N., Fábián, A.: An activity recognition system for mobile phones. Mob. Netw. Appl. **14**(1), 82–91 (2009)

12. Cui, Y., Chipchase, J., Ichikawa, F.: A Cross Culture Study on Phone Carrying and Physical Personalization. In: Aykin, N. (ed.) HCII 2007. LNCS, vol. 4559, pp. 483–492. Springer, Heidelberg (2007)
13. Shu, L., Hua, T., Wang, Y., Li, Q., Feng, D.D., Tao, X.: In-shoe plantar pressure measurement and analysis system based on fabric pressure sensing array. IEEE Trans. Inf Technol. Biomed. **14**(3), 767–775 (2010)
14. Sun, L., Zhang, D., Li, B.: Activity recognition on an accelerometer embedded mobile phone with varying positions and orientations. In: Aykin, Nuray (ed.) UIC 2010. LNCS, vol. 6406, pp. 548–562. Springer, Heidelberg (2010)

Mining for Patterns of Behaviour in Children with Autism Through Smartphone Technology

William Burns[1](✉), Mark Donnelly[1], and Nichola Booth[2]

[1] Computer Science Research Institute, University of Ulster,
Jordanstown BT37 0QB, UK
{wp.burns,mp.donnelly}@ulster.ac.uk
[2] PEAT NI, Parents' Education as Autism Therapists, Belfast, UK
nichola@peatni.org

Abstract. A requirement to maintain detailed recording of child behaviour is commonplace for families engaged in home-based autism intervention therapy. Periodically, a Behaviour Analyst reviews this data to formulate new behaviour change plans and as such, the quality and accuracy of data is paramount. We present a smartphone application that aims to streamline the traditional paper based approaches, which are prone to non-compliance and erroneous detail. In addition, we have applied association rule mining to the collected behaviour data to extract patterns in terms of behaviour causes and effects with a view to offer intelligent support to the Behaviour Analysts when formulating new interventions. The paper outlines the results of a small evaluation of the smartphone component before introducing the methodology used to mine that data to highlight behaviour rules and patterns. Consequently, based on an initial sample of child behaviours, the methodology is then compared to a Behaviour Analyst's assessment of corresponding paper based records.

Keywords: Smartphone · Behaviour monitoring · Autism spectrum disorders · Health records · Intelligent data analysis · Association rule mining

1 Introduction

The impact of autism on society and the associated cost to governmental health services is growing. Within the UK, for example, it is estimated that over 500,000 people have some form of autism, with recent studies estimating that this figure is rising [1]. Children with autism typically exhibit impairments in social imagination, communication and interaction. This often leads to difficulties in social and adaptive functioning, which can result in challenging behaviours that poses significant difficulties for parents and caregivers [2]. Consequently, enhanced support for parents and caregivers is needed in order to improve the quality of life for all of those involved in the care pathway. While there have been significant developments in assessment services, there still remains a need for information on effective interventions that could inform both users and providers in health and social services. Indeed, estimates within the UK indicate that only 8 % of autism research is currently concerned with intervention [3].

Applied Behaviour Analysis (ABA) is an evidence based intervention approach to help people with all forms of autism to achieve their full potential. ABA is the

© Springer International Publishing Switzerland 2015
C. Bodine et al. (Eds.): ICOST 2014, LNCS 8456, pp. 147–154, 2015.
DOI: 10.1007/978-3-319-14424-5_16

understanding of human behaviour and has emerged as one of the most effective approaches to interventions, based upon current research evidence [4, 5]. One of the cornerstones of an effective intervention programme is the meticulous collection of behaviour data. The proposed research aims to extend traditional paper based approaches, which have low compliance rates and are prone to errors. In this paper we present a smartphone application that aims to reduce the effort required to maintain behaviour records and increase compliance whilst also exploring the use of data mining approaches to intelligently correlate behaviour causes and effects.

In the following sections, we present related work in the area of behavioural data collection for autism, detail our system architecture, highlight how it differs from existing technologies and present our methodology and results.

2 Related Work

A number of studies have investigated technology-based interventions with children with autism. These technology solutions have targeted tactile/audio prompting, they employed video for behaviour modelling and investigated software for improving vocabulary, problem solving and communication amongst others [6]. Given the widespread uptake of smartphone application development, it is not surprising that several 'apps' already exist in the market place for monitoring behaviour, specifically facilitating the collection of *Antecedent*, *Behaviour* and *Consequence* (ABC) data [7–10]. Marcu et al. [11] presents a critique of several apps, however, in their findings they report that the data needs are unstandardised and complex. The demands of the 'job at hand' such as conducting the therapy session and engaging with the child appear to interfere with the ability to accurately collect in situ data. As such, in their view, existing technological solutions for data collection are inadequate.

In this paper we present a smartphone application called *BMAC* (Behaviour Monitoring for Autism in Children) that builds upon a standardised paper-based solution. In doing so, we attempt to supersede existing commercial offerings through the integration of data mining approaches. Specifically, we aim to employ Association Rule Modelling (ARM) to determine patterns in behaviour causes and effects, which will support Behaviour Analysts (BAs) assessment of home-based interventions. Furthermore, we aim to integrate these mining services to provide intelligent in-app decision support during data collection. This innovation will allow for patterns to be extracted that will inform the decisions of BAs and, as a result, aims to provide enhanced autism intervention. In this paper, we present the data mining of behaviour data and through a small user evaluation present the potential of our solution.

3 Prototype

Figure 1 presents the architecture of the proposed system. It consists of three main components: the *BMAC* application to facilitate the data collection both inside and outside of the home environment; a web portal to allow BAs and parents (caregivers) to review recorded data over time and for the BAs to implement interventions and; a data-mining component, used to extract patterns occurring within the recorded data. Within the *BMAC* application is a sub-component that acts as a decision support system (DSS) to inform and improve the process of home-based data collection. Figure 1 highlights the flow of information, from initial data collection (1) and transmission to the server (2), through to data-mining (3), the resulting intervention, the provision of DSS to parents and subsequent feedback from BAs (4).

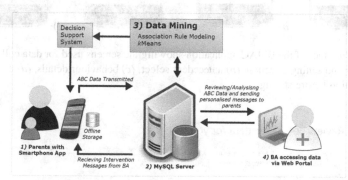

Fig. 1. High-level system architecture, detailing constituent components; (1) BMAC Application, (2) Server, (4) Web Portal and (3) Data-mining component.

Server and Database. All data collected via the *BMAC* application is securely stored on a central server that also holds responsibility for managing the data-mining algorithms. In addition to the storage of data, the server also contains any communication / feedback that the BA needs to send directly to the *BMAC* User.

BMAC Application. The *BMAC* application (Fig. 2) supports quick data collection of common behaviour *Antecedents*, *Behaviours* and *Consequences*, as specified in the clinically validated *SimpleSteps* Forced Choice ABC charts [12]. Consequently, these data can be reviewed and transmitted to the server. The users of the application can indicate the person recording the behaviour and the setting in which it occurs. They are then asked to select from a list of predefined *Antecedents*, *Behaviours* and *Consequences*, navigated with swipe gestures and presented within scrolling lists.

  If an *Antecedent*, *Behaviour* or *Consequence* is not available from the list the user has the ability to enter a free text entry. After selecting the events from the lists, contextual information is requested that includes: duration, intensity (scale of 1–5) and frequency of the behaviour. As it may not be possible for the user to record the event as and when it occurs the system allows the retrospective time stamping of collected data within the timeframe of 24 h.

Web Portal. The web portal is hosted from a secure (HTTPS) website. It allows BAs and parents to log in, review collected data, presented over time, and undertake analysis with the data-mining component. The data collected is visualized using charts and text, as presented in Fig. 3.

a)   b)   c)   d)

Fig. 2. User Interface of the BMAC application showing the screens used for data collection. *(a)* event recorder and setting selection, *(b)* antecedent select, *(c)* behaviour details, *(d)* confirmation of data collection before storing.

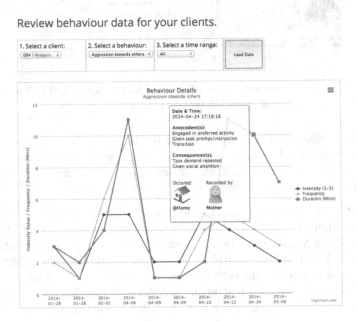

Fig. 3. Screenshot of the review interface of the web portal showing the Duration (Mins), Intensity (1–5) & Frequency of the selected behaviour (Aggression towards others). In addition to this information, details of the Antecedent(s) & Consequence(s) recorded are show along with the location of the behaviour and who recorded it.

The web portal is also used to support communication between BAs and parents via the *BMAC* application. As such, this component of the system endeavours to augment traditional and on-going face-to-face interactions between BAs, parents and children rather than serve to replace them.

Data-Mining Behaviour. At the center of the data-mining component is the requirement for accurate and annotated data, as collected by parents and BAs through the *BMAC* application. This component makes use of the collected data to mine for behaviour causes and effects patterns. Long term, it is envisaged that patterns extracted from the data would enable BAs to provide improved personalized interventions as well as enabling the parents to understand and rationalise troubling and reoccurring *Antecedents* or *Behaviours*. One example would be the identification that a particular *Antecedent* typically resulting in a particular inappropriate *Behaviour*, such as hitting. Providing the insight into which *Antecedent* is responsible could inform the parent of which situations to minimize in the environment in order to reduce /prevent the *Behaviour*.

The advantage of employing computer-based data-mining affords the opportunity to consider the interactions that may exist within the features describing the behaviours that are too complex for human comprehension. As such, mining approaches offer the potential to increase the likelihood of correctly characterising a behaviour. Specifically, the mining algorithms consider additional contextual features such as the environmental setting in which the behaviour event occurred, who the child was with at that time and other factors related to time of day etc.

4   Feedback from User Evaluations

The *BMAC* application was evaluated in a small study involving three children with autism and their family. Only caregivers (mother, father, grandparents) were eligible to engage with the application; children themselves were not allowed to record their own behaviour. Caregivers were asked to use the their existing paper based method for maintaining behaviour records for a five-day period, which was followed with a five-day period of using the *BMAC* application. Two of the participants participated over the full 10-day evaluation while the remaining participant recorded only two behaviour events during the *BMAC* usage phase. All participants completed a post-evaluation questionnaire that forms part of the results presented in this paper. Participant 1 (P1) recorded 12 paper-based events and 12 smartphone-based events. Participant 2 (P2) recorded 11 paper-based events and 9 smartphone-based events. Finally, Participant 3 (P3) recorded 14 paper-based events and 2 smartphone-based events. Although Participant 3 was able to record two events using the smartphone, they remarked in the questionnaire that they had difficulty using the application.

All three participants commented that they liked using the current paper-based methodology, with one remarking that it allowed them to add the 'specifics' of a behaviour (P2). Nevertheless, in general, reports indicate that paper-based collection poses challenges when outside of the home environment. When asked if they liked using the smartphone application for the collection of behaviour data, two of the participants responded favourably with one indicating that they thought the *BMAC* application definitely improved the reliability of their recordings (P1). P2 stated that they would possibly prefer the smartphone application over the paper based approach but noted the trade offs in the ability to enter specific data vs. the speedy general input. This additional requirement is easily added to the system. P3 had the most difficulty using the smartphone and the application. Nevertheless, they still stated that they would be happy to use the application again if they could "work it out sooner". All participants were given the opportunity to offer some additional feedback on what they thought could be improved about the application. Table 1 outlines some participant comments.

Table 1. Participant's additional feedback as written on the post-evaluation questionnaires.

Participant #	Additional feedback
1	"Selection of the 'Where did this occur' was limited as many behaviours took place at an activity such as swimming, leisure centre or even just in the car so probably would need an 'other' section for this also"
	"All in all a great app and look forward to using it for 'real'"
2	1. "For very straight forward events the app was useful. However if you needed to add additional info the process became slow and time-consuming"
	2. "I have 2 children with ASD and the app didn't allow me to identify which child was involved"
3	"Definitely think if the app was available on my own phone I would have been able to use it a lot better and more efficiently"

In general, the feedback reflects the findings discussed in the related worked section. In our system, however, we propose to enrich the recorded data by applying datamining to extract underlying patterns. All three participants responded favourably when asked if they would *"...find it useful to receive some 'suggestions' for A and C based on the behaviour observed?"*. Given the complexity of human behaviour, even when closely mapped to 'problem' behaviours, a sufficient pool of behaviour data is required to develop a valid data-mining tool. As such, the number of recordings collected during our trial serves more to direct future improvement of the usability and user experience than to progress the development of an automated data mining service. Consequently, a further experiment was undertaken.

5   Data Mining Experiment

As the data collected in the first evaluation phase was not sufficient to effectively apply the association rules, we used data collected previously by paper-based methods in order to assess the effectiveness of association rules on behaviour data. Clearly, this data does not provide contextual information and therefore we postulate that future results will be more valuable. Real life data was collected by observing a child with autism over a 14-day period. The data consisted of 55 recorded behaviour events, each listing at least one *Antecedent*, *Behaviour* or *Consequence*. For this experiment, a BA analysed the data independently of any computation framework and consequently, we compared the results. This data was manually entered into the *BMAC* database for analysis. Implementations of the *Apriori* [13], *PredictiveApriori* [14] and *Tertius* [15] algorithms, provided by Weka [16], were applied to generate rules. Of the three algorithms used, *PredictiveApriori* produced the most rules, (≥*0.9* accuracy), that are corroborated by the BA analysis. These rules are presented below:

```
1. Antecedents=[10] ==> Behaviours=[1] acc:(0.98049)
     Other ==> Aggression Towards Others
2. Antecedents=[0] ==> Behaviours=[2] acc:(0.92097)
     Given task Prompt/Instruction ==> Hitting
3. Antecedents=[7] ==> Behaviours=[3-4] acc:(0.92097)
     Transition ==> Kicking & Shouting
4. Antecedents=[9] ==> Behaviours=[5] acc:(0.92097)
     Alone ==> Crying
5. Antecedents=[9] ==> Behaviours=[4-5] acc:(0.92097)
     Alone ==> Shouting & Crying
6. Antecedents=[5]  ==> Behaviours=[1] acc:(0.92097)
     Preferred Activity Denied ==> Aggression Towards Others
7. Behaviours=[4] ==> Consequences=[0-4-5] acc:(0.92097)
     Shouting ==> Task Demand Repeated & Reprimanded & Given access to preferred
     Activity
```

A common trend that has appeared from this dataset is that if the child is 'denied their preferred activity' (*Antecedent*) it typically results in 'aggression towards others' (*Behaviour*). As a result, the parent usually 'reprimands' the child (*Consequence*). By looking at this trend a future intervention proposed by the BA would be to modify the *Consequence* element thereby offering an *intervention*. After identifying an intervention, further ABC recording would be recommended to ascertain if the occurrence of the behaviour is reduced. From the rules above, other behaviours have been documented that would require further analysis, most notable being that of 'crying' whilst alone which would suggest a self-stimulatory function of behaviour. An intervention is only suggested/reviewed whenever a clear pattern of the behaviour function emerges, as identified by the BA, and in future the data-mining component.

6 Conclusion

Based on the qualitative feedback from the participants of the evaluation, the use of a smartphone-based behaviour recording application is deemed beneficial and welcomed by end-users. The ability of this system to deliver real-time feedback as well as decision support with regards to possible *Antecedents* and *Consequences* has also been identified as beneficial to the target cohort. The user interface of the data collection application as well as the delivery form factor of a smartphone has been evaluated with positive feedback on the clarity and understanding of the user interface. All participants, to be expected, would prefer the application to be deployed on their own personal devices. By analysing historical data provided by qualified BAs, we have demonstrated that ARM can be used to extract recurring behaviours and identify their *Antecedents* and *Consequences*. The results of the ARM have been validated and verified by a BA and corroborated with their independent assessment. Future work involves improving the usability of the *BMAC* application. A longer evaluation is also planned (April 2014) that will last for a duration based on the number of the events collected by each participant rather than *x* days. Consequently, this data will be analysed using the ARM and the information fed back to the participants via the web portal.

Acknowledgements. This research is supported by a research grant from the Engineering and Physical Sciences Research Council, UK (EP/K014420/1).

References

1. Centers for Disease Control and Prevention. Prevalence of autism spectrum disorders (2013). http://www.cdc.gov/ncbddd/autism/data.html. Accessed 01 Aug 2013
2. Dillenburger, K., Keenan, M., Doherty, A., Byrne, T., Gallagher, S.: Living with children diagnosed with autistic spectrum disorder: parental and professional views. Br. J. Spec. Educ. **37**(1), 13–23 (2010)
3. Mills, R., Marchant, S.: Intervention in autism: a brief review of the literature. Tizard Learn. Disabil. Rev. **16**(4), 20–35 (2011)
4. Smith, T., Buch, G.A., Gamby, T.E.: Parent-directed, intensive early intervention for children with pervasive developmental disorder. Res. Dev. Disabil. **21**(4), 297–309 (2000)
5. Foxx, R.M.: Applied behavior analysis treatment of autism: the state of the art. Child Adolesc. Psychiatr. Clin. North Am. **17**(4), 821–834 (2008). ix Oct 2008
6. Goldsmith, T., LeBlanc, L.: Use of technology in interventions for children with autism. J. Early Intensive Behav. **1**(2), 166–178 (2004)
7. Behavior Tracker Pro (2013). http://www.behaviortrackerpro.com/products/btp/BTP-for-iPhone.aspx. Accessed 02 Aug 2013
8. Catalyst' from DataFinch (2013). http://www.datafinch.com/products/catalyst. Accessed 02 Aug 2013
9. Autism Tracker (2013). http://www.trackandshareapps.com/Autism. Accessed 02 Aug 2013
10. ABC Logbook (2013). http://cbtaonline.com/drupal/products. Accessed 02 Aug 2013
11. Marcu, G., Tassini, K., Carlson, Q.: Why do they still use paper?: understanding data collection and use in Autism education. In: Proceedings of the SIGCHI Conference on Human Factors in Computing Systems, pp. 3177–3186 (2013)
12. SimpleSteps' ABC Chart (2013). http://www.peatni.org/directory/resources/article.asp?ArticleID=abc_chart_resource. Accessed 01 Aug 2013
13. Agrawal, R., Srikant, R.: Fast algorithms for mining association rules. In: Proceedings of 20th International Conference on Very Large Data Bases, VLDB (1994)
14. Scheffer, T.: Finding association rules that trade support optimally against confidence. In: Siebes, A., De Raedt, L. (eds.) PKDD 2001. LNCS (LNAI), vol. 2168, pp. 424–435. Springer, Heidelberg (2001)
15. Flach, P., Lachiche, N.: Confirmation-guided discovery of first-order rules with Tertius. Mach. Learn. **42**(1), 61–95 (2001)
16. Hall, M., Frank, E., Holmes, G.: The WEKA data mining software: an update. ACM SIGKDD **11**(1), 10–18 (2009)

Context and Situation Awareness

Ontology Based Context Fusion for Behavior Analysis and Prediction

Asad Masood Khattak, Amjad Usman, and Sungyoung Lee[⊠]

Department of Computer Engineering, Kyung Hee University,
Seoul, South Korea
{asad.masood,amjad.usman,sylee}@oslab.khu.ac.kr

Abstract. Current healthcare systems facilitate patients in provision of healthcare services by using their context information. However, the problem is that the context information received from various sources is of heterogeneous nature which is not useful for conventional systems. To overcome this issue, we propose an ontology-based context fusion framework in this research that fuses the related and relevant context information collected about the patient's daily life activities for better understanding of patient's situation and behavior. The fused context information is logged using ontological representation in Life Log deployed on cloud server. On top of the Life Log, behavior analysis and prediction services are developed to analyze the behavior of the patient and provide better healthcare, wellness, and behavior prediction services. System execution flow is demonstrated using a running case study that shows how the overall process is initialized and performed.

Keywords: u-Healthcare · Lifestyle · Activity recognition · Ontology · Context-awareness · Context fusion

1 Introduction

During the last couple of decades, the emergence of new technologies in the field of healthcare has shown tremendous improvement in healthcare and lifestyle of a person [5, 13]. In response to the needs, the use of smartphones and smartphone-based healthcare applications are increasing at a rapid pace [5, 12]. Activity recognition using such applications [12] is an example that is developed to analyze, recognize, and monitor the daily activities of a person [5, 12]. Other examples include healthcare systems to monitor health issues, nutrition intakes and social networks to keep track of social interactions of patient (user) [1, 5, 9, 12, 13]. The key to success in improving the lifestyle of a patient is to understand his/her behavior first. The services like personalized lifecare, recommendations, and behavior analysis can be provided by using the advanced technologies for capturing and fusing the context information like activity information, social interaction, diet and environment information.

Healthcare systems have been at the top due to its everlasting importance in our daily life. It is reported that 68 % of the healthcare cost in USA is due to the poor lifestyle of people. So there is a need of a system that can reduce the cost of healthcare services at both hospitals and home environment by integrating different context

© Springer International Publishing Switzerland 2015
C. Bodine et al. (Eds.): ICOST 2014, LNCS 8456, pp. 157–164, 2015.
DOI: 10.1007/978-3-319-14424-5_17

information emerging from diverse modalities in order to use them for behavior analysis, behavior recommendation and behavior prediction to facilitate patients and caregivers in provisioning of lifecare services.

The solution proposed to the above problems is to fuse the daily life context information of a patient coming from various sources and build patient's profile based on the emerging context information. The build profile is then used for behavior analysis, and prediction to attain better lifestyle. In order to fuse the context information received from various diverse sources (i.e., physical activities, social media interactions, diet information, and environment information), ontology based context fusion (horizontal and vertical) mechanisms are developed to fuse patient's context information at different time intervals of a day. As shown in Fig. 1, the context information is collected using smartphone and then forwarded to the main system deployed on cloud. The fused context information is then logged in a centralized ontology based Life Log. On top of Life Log, a behavior prediction algorithm is proposed in this research to predict patient's behavior based on their profile, current context and the existing behavior models stored in the Life Log repository.

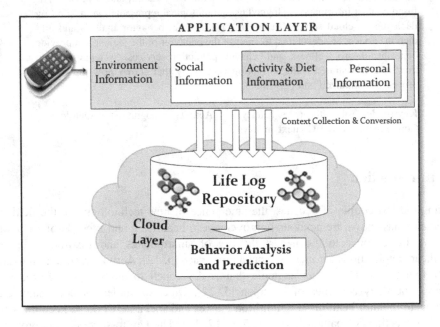

Fig. 1. Overview of the proposed solution

The research paper is arranged as follows: Sect. 2 describes the related research work in the area of healthcare and behavior analysis. Section 3 presents our proposed system with details on each component. Section 4 presents a case study as a working example of our proposed system. Section 5 concludes the research work and provides future research directions.

2   Related Work

Research in the area of healthcare using information technology is getting mature where various healthcare and wellness services are provided remotely [5, 12, 13]. In this area, ComMotion [1] and HYCARE [2] are activity reminding systems based on predefined schedule. Both these systems recognize human activities with the help of sensors and generate alerts for scheduled activities. Most recently an ontology-based reminder system [4] is developed that incorporates rules to manipulate the recognized activities of elderly persons. Some authors have focused on recognizing patient's real time activities using low-level sensory data coming from diverse sensors. In [7], the authors have used the information about activities recognized and the domain knowledge to analyze the situation with the help of experts designed rules. The research work in [6, 11] has focused on the social interaction of patients.

The context information collected is necessary for comprehensive and sophisticated recommendations generation; however, it is also a challenge to keep the context information in uniform representation and also relate (fuse) them to appropriate user [4]. The need of context representation and fusion is highlighted with the help of their uses in [4, 7]. Every context-aware system needs to formally represent the context after acquisition and fuse them with other relevant context if needed. In case of multiple and diverse sensors discussed in [4, 7, 13], the context from one sensor needs to be fused with other sensor's context to achieve a higher level context with more confidence on the monitored situation [5, 7, 13]. However, these systems are strict in representations and only consider multiple sensors of similar type.

The fused context is then logged in Life Log where all information about a patient life is logged. Patients and caregivers can refer back to any of the contents in the log easily and intelligently. The system in [14] has initially developed Life Log system and allowed users to build and exploit Life Log ontology. Microsoft research project MyLifeBits [9] stores the life activities of a person with the help of SenseCam that contains sensors like accelerometers, heat sensor and audio sensor. It provides a clear and understandable view of user's life and history which is a step towards user's behavior analysis. The logged context retrieved from diverse sources has potential to be used for behavior analysis and user's lifestyle monitoring. Morita [10] has developed a behavior monitoring system to capture user's interests from large amount of context information, whereas in [2], the authors have explained different limitations regarding recommendations generation using life log. To overcome these limitations, they made suggestions to provide support in the process by introducing multiple context resources. In [8], the authors presented behavior ontology to capture user behavior within a given context (i.e., time period and community) and used a semantic-rule based methodology to infer the role a user has within a community based on his/her exhibited behavior. The work has facilitated in analyzing the differences between communities and predicting community activities. In [12], the authors monitored daily activities of user for long term and then mine some irregular lifestyle patterns which can affect user health.

The main limitations of the existing systems are that majority of them uses one input modality for human activities and are not based on context information extracted from diverse input sources. Moreover, the existing developed systems are based on imperfect context information [3] which is the main cause of irregular service recommendation and decision making.

3 Proposed System

To provide better healthcare and lifestyle services, we need to understand the behavior of patient first. Current state of the art technologies are matured enough to help us in collecting patient's daily life routine information which can be later on processed to generate the required services. The proposed system architecture comprises of two main components as shown in Fig. 2 and discussed below.

3.1 Context Modeling

Context modeling component is responsible for collecting and modeling the context information in a unified format in order to be used by Behavior Modeling & Prediction component to analyze and predict patient's behavior. The proposed system collects patient's (1) profile information, (2) social media interactions, (3) diet information, (4) daily life activities information and (5) environment information from various sources using our lab developed systems [12, 13, 15]. To store the context information collected, an ontology-based Life Log repository is maintained in the system to provide basic descriptions for events, experiences, actions, activities and interactions. The goal of Life Log is to record and archive all information about a patient's life. The collected

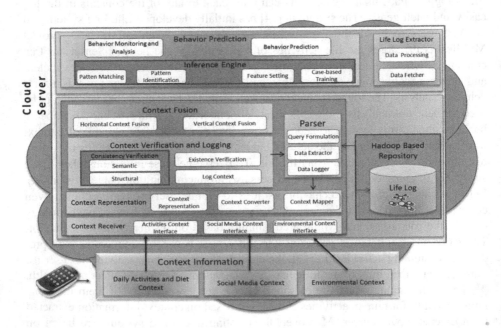

Fig. 2. Architecture of proposed system

context information is converted into a unified representational format acceptable by Life Log using the context conversion algorithms.

The logged context passes through the structural and semantic verification processes to check the information received for acceptable format and semantic conflicts if any. The relatedness and dependency of context information is achieved in proposed system by using the proposed context fusion (horizontal and vertical) mechanism. For example, context information like *walking, bending, sitting, standing* together is used for exercise if we apply horizontal fusion technique with specified time intervals. Similarly, a tweet *"exercise is good for health"* by a patient, and then after sometimes, performing exercise by the same patient means there exists some relationship between the tweet and the performed activity. So these contexts need to be fused in order to understand patient's interest and behavior in exercise.

3.2 Behavior Modeling and Prediction

This component analyzes and predicts the behavior of a patient using patient's profile from Life Log repository. Initially, patterns are identified in the profile and context information which are then matched against pre-classified patterns. In case of patient with abnormal life patterns, such situation is detected by system using pattern classification that patient behavior is not according to the prescribed behavior. This result can be viewed for both patient's recent past (short term) as well as patient's behavior pattern for a longer duration (long term) of time. This also facilitates patients and caregivers in analyzing patient's lifestyle. For the purpose of prediction, case-based reasoning scheme is used in the proposed system that first identifies prominent features in patient's context and then match against various trained behavior models. A match of patient activity, context and behavior results in prediction for the possibility of patient behavior in immediate future.

4 Case Study

In this section, we show the execution flow of proposed system with a running case study. Table 1 shows the context information received by proposed system regarding patient's daily life routine activities emerging from different sources [1, 5, 12, 13, 15]. Location sensor recognizes the patient in a restaurant at 14:00:00. Using smartphone,

Table 1. Context information received from various sources

`<activity type="Motion">`	`<activity type="Motion">`	`<activity type="Video">`
`<detectedBy>` Location Sensor	`<detectedBy>` Body Sensor	`<detectedBy>` Video Sensor
`</detectedBy>`	`</detectedBy>`	`</detectedBy>`
`<hasName>` Truc `</hasName>`	`<hasName>` Truc `</hasName>`	`<hasName>` Truc `</hasName>`
`<activityName>` In Restaurant	`<activityName>` Eating Lunch	`<activityName>` Increased Calories
`</activityName>`	`</activityName>`	`</activityName>`
`<id>` 666 `</id>`	`<id>` 987 `</id>`	`<id>` 1012 `</id>`
`<time>` 14:00:00 `</time>`	`<time>` 14:05:00 `</time>`	`<time>` 14:15:00 `</time>`
`</activity>`	`</activity>`	`</activity>`

Table 2. N3 representation of the fused context information

kb:ActivityInstance_145892	kb:ActivityInstance_145894	kb:ActivityInstance_145945
a: kb:Activity;	a: kb:Activity;	a: kb:Activity;
kb:hasId: kb:666;	kb:hasId: kb:987;	kb:hasId: kb:1012;
kb:hasName: kb:In Restaurant;	kb:hasName: kb:Eating Lunch;	kb:hasName: kb:Increased Calories;
kb:hasConnectedActivity: kb:null;	kb:hasConnectedActivity:	kb:hasConnectedActivity:
kb:resultedIn: kb:null;	kb:ActivityInstance_145892;	kb:ActivityInstance_145892,
kb:hasAction: kb:null;	kb:resultedIn: kb:null;	kb:ActivityInstance_145894;
kn:hasSensorType:	kb:hasAction: kb:null;	kb:resultedIn: kb:null;
kb:Location Sensor;	kn:hasSensorType: kb:Body Sensor;	kb:hasAction:
kb:lostFor:	kb:lostFor:	kb:RecommendationInstance_231;
kb:DurationInstance_3452612;	kb:DurationInstance_3452634;	kn:hasSensorType: kb:Video Sensor;
kb:performedBy:	kb:performedBy:	kb:lostFor:
kb:ActorInstance_345;	kb:ActorInstance_345;	kb:DurationInstance_3452762;
kb:atLocation:	kb:atLocation:	kb:performedBy:
kb:LocationInstance_245;	kb:LocationInstance_245;	kb:ActorInstance_345;
kb:dependsOn: kb:null;	kb:dependsOn: kb:null;	kb:atLocation:
		kb:LocationInstance_293;
		kb:dependsOn:
		kb:ActivityInstance_145892;

patient's eating activity is recognized which has resulted in increase of patient calories consumption at 14:05:00 and 14:15:00 respectively.

This information is converted into the designed ontological format, fused and later logged in Life Log repository. Table 2 shows the converted and fused N3 notations of the received context.

While fusing this context information with the profile information of the respective patient, the proposed system has proved its worth here by reporting that the current patient is a heart patient and the happenings of high calories and fats intake is not good for patient's health. The proposed system has encountered a negative situation about patient and the system is checking the history of the problem (associated to patient) to make appropriate analysis. Our proposed system has extracted Life Log information of the respective patient using the abstract sparql query given in Fig. 3 and has performed behavior analysis to see whether such situations occurred before or not.

```
SELECT ?activity ?performedBy ?time   ?topic ?hasConnectedActivities ?dependsOn ?Location ?Diet,
?interaction, ?Action
    WHERE { Lifelog:Activity :hasName ?activityName .
    …………
    Lifelog:Activity :hasPerformedBy ?performedBy .
    Lifelog:Activity :hasConnectedActivity ?hasConnectedActivities .
    Lifelog:Action :hasAction ?Action . }
```

Fig. 3. Sparql query for extraction of fused context from Life Log

The analysis report has stated that such situation has occurred before, and mostly it has happened after taking food at restaurants. The system generates alert for the patient about the adverse situation which may persist if patient maintains the same behavior in food selection. Finally, the system recommends him to go for a walk or any other

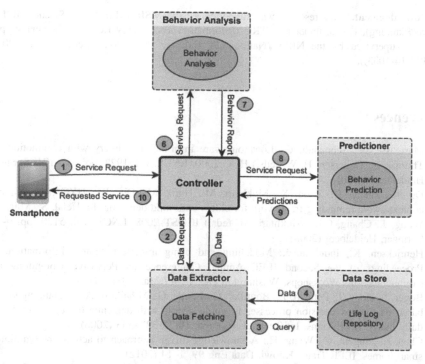

Fig. 4. The diagram showing execution flow for the behavior analysis and prediction services of proposed system

prescribed routine to burn some calories. Figure 4 shows component diagram of the execution flow for behavior analysis and prediction services.

It is visible from Fig. 4 that for the services of behavior analysis and prediction, the context information from Life Log is extracted which is then used in inference engines at behavior analysis and prediction module to generate appropriate services. The results of services are provided to patients on their smartphones as well as in audio reminders format.

5 Conclusion

Healthcare and behavioral services are important to analyze daily behavior and have better lifestyle. To facilitate the aspect of behavior analysis we have proposed a system that facilitates patients in provision of better lifestyle services, and behavior analysis and prediction. The system has used unified context representation related to the daily routine of a patient emerging from various sources of diverse nature. Context fusion techniques are developed to fuse related context which is then used for the analysis of the patient's behavior and for prediction of patient's behavior next state. The system is currently under development and will be deployed on cloud server to facilitate ease of access and low cost.

Acknowledgement. This research was supported by the MSIP (Ministry of Science, ICT & Future Planning), Korea, under the ITRC (Information Technology Research Center) support program supervised by the NIPA (National IT Industry Promotion Agency) (NIPA-2014-(H0301-14-1003)).

References

1. Marmasse, N., Schmandt, C.: Location-aware information delivery with commotion. In: Thomas, P., Gellersen, H.-W. (eds.) HUC 2000. LNCS, vol. 1927, pp. 157–171. Springer, Heidelberg (2000)
2. Du, K., Zhang, D., Zhou, X., Mokhtari, M., Hariz, M., Qin, W.: HYCARE: a hybrid context-aware reminding framework for elders with mild dementia. In: Helal, S., Mitra, S., Wong, J., Chang, C.K., Mokhtari, M. (eds.) ICOST 2008. LNCS, vol. 5120, pp. 9–17. Springer, Heidelberg (2008)
3. Henricksen, K., Indulska, J.: Modelling and using imperfect context information. In: Proceedings of the Second IEEE Annual Conference on Pervasive Computing and Communications Workshops, Washington DC, 14–17 Mar 2004
4. Boger, J., Hoey, J., Poupart, P., Boutilier, C., Fernie, G., Mihailidis, A.: A planning system based on markov decision processes to guide people with dementia through activities of daily living. IEEE Trans. Inf Technol. Biomed. **10**(2), 323–333 (2006)
5. Chen, L., Nugent, C., Wang, H.: A knowledge-driven approach to activity recognition in smart homes. IEEE Trans. Knowl. Data Eng **99**, 1–14 (2012)
6. Flouris, G., Manakanatas, D., Kondylakis, H., Plexousakis, D., Antoniou, G.: Ontology change: classification and survey. Knowl. Eng. Rev. **23**(2), 117–152 (2008)
7. IBM Press Room - Medens, IBM and ActiveHealth Management Collaborate to Transform Healthcare in Puerto Rico. http://www-03.ibm.com/press/us/en/pressrelease/33038.wss
8. IBM Smarter Planet – Smarter Healthcare. http://www.ibm.com/smarterplanet/uk/en/healthcare_solutions/examples/index.html
9. IBM Press Room - Medens, IBM and ActiveHealth Management Collaborate to Transform Healthcare in Puerto Rico. http://www-03.ibm.com/press/us/en/pressrelease/33038.wss
10. Piette, J.D., Mendoza-Avelares, M.O., Ganser, M., Mohamed, M., Marinec, N., Krishnan, S.: A preliminary study of a cloud-computing model for chronic illness self-care support in an underdeveloped country. Am. J. Prev. Med. **40**(6), 629–632 (2011)
11. Wen-Syan, L., Jianfeng, Y., Ying, Y., Jin, Z.: Xbase: cloud-enabled information appliance for healthcare. In: Proceedings of the 13th International Conference on Extending Database Technology (EDBT '10), pp. 675–680. NY, USA (2010)
12. Han, M.H., Vinh, L.T., Lee, Y.K., Lee, S.Y.: Comprehensive context recognizer based on multimodal sensors in a smartphone. Sensors **12**(9), 12588–12605 (2012)
13. Khattak, A.M., Truc, P.T.H., Hung, L.X., Vinh, L.T., Dang, V.H., Guan, D., Pervez, Z., Han, M.H., Lee, S.Y., Lee, Y.K.: Towards smart homes using low level sensory data. Sensors **11**(12), 11581–11604 (2011)
14. Lee, S., Gong, G., Hwang, I., Lee, S.G.: LifeLogOn: a practical lifelog system for building and exploiting lifelog ontology. In: 2010 IEEE International Conference on Sensor Networks, Ubiquitous, and Trustworthy Computing, pp. 367–373 (2010)
15. Batool, R., Khattak, A.M., Maqbool, J. Lee, S.Y.: Precise tweet classification and sentiment analysis. In: 12th IEEE/ACIS International Conference on Computer and Information Science (ICIS 2013), Toki Messe, Niigata, Japan, 16–20 June 2013

Quantifying Semantic Proximity
Between Contexts

Patrice Roy[1], Bessam Abdulrazak[1(✉)], and Yacine Belala[2]

[1] Université de Sherbrooke, 2500, boul. de l'Université,
Sherbrooke, QC, Canada
{Patrice.Roy,Bessam.Abdulrazak}@USherbrooke.ca
[2] INRS-EMT, 800, de la Gauchetière O., Montréal, QC, Canada
belala@emt.inrs.ca

Abstract. Autonomic Agents in Open intelligent space face a wide diversity of Context providers and formats. With a micro approach to Context-awareness, individual Agents perform their own assessment of individual Context relevance. This assessment relies in part on the semantic proximity between requested and candidate Contexts. We present a quantitative semantic distance function that supports subjective Context relevance assessment in Agents.

Keywords: Context · Context-awareness · Autonomic agents · Semantic distance · Semantic proximity

1 Introduction

Intelligent environments use context to represent complex information and relations between physical and software entities. In most pervasive systems, context describes information with respect to categories such as time, location, the user, the application and the way the latter two interact. With our approach, ContextAA, Context with a capitalized 'C' is formalized as a language that can express the aforementioned information, as well as the operations on Context and the Agents that act on Context.

Humans today tend to use or wear computing devices that fade into the background. Humans are mobile individuals and so are many of their devices. Humans in a traditional intelligent environment often experience a discontinuity of service when they leave an intelligent environment. The ability to remain connected even outside traditional intelligent environments is an opportunity for intelligent entities such as distributed agents to provide services in a more continuous manner.

Continuity of service and quality of service are not mutually exclusive but cannot always be maximized simultaneously. A typical traditional intelligent environment is feature-rich: services such as locating the user or detecting dangerous conditions (falling, experiencing a sudden change of course) can sometimes be maintained without discontinuity with minimal support from the environment. An agent on a mobile device that passes through a shopping mall faces a significant diversity of devices, services and data formats, the set of actuators and sensors that could concretely alter the environment to suit the needs of the user in that location is probably less tailor-made for its user's needs.

C. Bodine et al. (Eds.): ICOST 2014, LNCS 8456, pp. 165–174, 2015.
DOI: 10.1007/978-3-319-14424-5_18

In the intelligent environment without boundaries we name Open intelligent space [8], Agents that behave in an autonomic manner [5] are an asset. The micro approach to Context-awareness [1] taken by ContextAA helps such Agents adapt to the changing conditions of the environment. We define Context as Context *according-to* an Agent, allowing for as many formats and contents as there are Agents, and impose a common *syntax* for all Agents.

Due to the variety of formats and contents used to describe Context in complex settings such as urban pervasive space or with the Internet of things, and due to the potentially high number of Context providers at any given location, sorting available Context with respect to its relevance *according-to* an Agent and selecting from these candidate Contexts the most useful for this Agent is important. Quantifying the proximity between requested Context and candidate Contexts gathered from the environment helps achieve this goal.

In this article, we show how Agents in ContextAA evaluate Context proximity according to subjective, per-Agent criteria, and how this approach leads to an Agent-based, subjective Context quality assessment, otherwise expressed as Context relevance *according-to* an Agent. First, we present related work on research on Context proximity and Context quality assessment, after which our Context model is summarily described, including the way we model Agents as Context. Then, we explain how we approach Context proximity assessment, how we compute it, and show some empirical results. We conclude with a short description of the general utility of Context proximity, of our approach, and we briefly discuss extensions to our model that will make it even more useful for individual Agents.

Context relevance *according-to* an Agent is a key element in the way ContextAA's Agents achieve autonomicity and adapt to complex environments such as urban pervasive settings and Open intelligent space. Context proximity between what an Agent needs and what it finds yields a quantitative metric for Context relevance *according-to* that Agent.

2   Related Works

There has been some work on context distance and semantic distance, mostly (but not exclusively) in the realms of linguistics and automatic translation.

El Sayed et al. have presented context-based semantic distance in order to establish similarity between concepts in written texts [4]. The authors explain that similarity between concepts depends on the context in which they appear, and seek to provide a formal automated measurement for similarity with results close to those human specialists would obtain. They construct trees based on the taxonomy of words that describe these concepts and weigh the nodes in these trees based on what they call context-dependency to a corpus. Their approach is more specialized than ours, but their formal comparison of tree-like structures with weighed nodes is in many ways close to the way we define Context distance functions, semantic and other issues.

A similar problem is described by Andrade et al. [2], where they show a technique to find potential name translation pairs from domain-specific vocabulary in different languages. Their comparison function takes into account sub-domains and sub-topics, differences in word usage and the frequency with which pairs of words are found together in each language, and yields the probability of a match.

The approach used by Pilz et al. [7] seeks to disambiguate named entities found in unstructured contexts by comparing potential semantic matches to candidate Wikipedia entries. Associating meaning to words without the context in which these words are used is a difficult task at best. The authors extract disambiguated datasets from relevant Wikipedia entries and apply classification techniques to establish the best match from a set of candidates. Their thematic distance function, like our Context distance functions, establishes a probability based on a set of weighed criteria.

Keßler et al. [6] insist on the importance of context-modelling in similarity measurement, using the geospatial domain as an example. They propose a metric that compares trees with weighed nodes on an abstract level, using the algebraic properties of the nodes.

The aim of Cremene et al. [3] is to establish a service and context-independent adaptation mechanism to achieve dynamic service adaptation, particularly for services that cannot be stopped. The authors apply autonomic computing principles [5] to automate decisions related to service adaptation. Then, they define a service-context graph to model interaction with the service, annotate the graph with descriptive attributes and compose the resulting graphs. Their service-context distance function is a composite metric that uses information flow and resource utilization distance, an approach similar to our composite semantic distance function ρ described in Sect. 4. Function ρ in ContextAA is different, being defined in part by individual Agents' ontic frame.

3 Context Model

ContextAA uses a simple formal name-value representation for Context, where $c = n\{v\}$ means Context c has name n and value v, and where v is a set of Contexts. What follows is a short summary of our format; more information can be found in [1].[1] We express Context either in compact or in canonical form. The following Context is expressed in canonical form:

$$h\{a\{c\{q\{1\}val\{**\{Celsius\}\}\}\}\}$$

Expressed in compact form, the same Context is written as:

$$h : a : c\{q\{1\}val\{**\{Celsius\}\}\}$$

Context names can be expressed as character strings and are quoted when containing spaces. Symbol ':' is a delimiter when found outside of quote marks and expresses an aggregate of Contexts as a name in compact form. The parts of a name separated by ':' are called name elements.

---

[1] Briefly, if c is a Context of the form $a\{b\{c\}d\}$, then the name of c is a and its value is a set of two Contexts, $b\{c\}$ and d. In this case, c can be expressed as a tree with root a and depth 3, where child nodes of a are b and d and where leaves are c and d.

This simple format can describe such statements as "Context c is the temperature read by Agent a on Host h from sensor XYZ, and has value 19.03 degrees Celsius with a precision of 1×10^{-3}" in many ways, including:

$$h : a : c\{sensor\{name\{XYZ\}precision\{0.001\}\}value\{19.03\}unit\{Celsius\}\}$$

This expression of a Context associates precision with the sensor. Precision could also be associated with the actual sensor reading. Thus, a very similar idea could be expressed as Context c':

$$h : a : c'\{sensor\{name\{XYZ\}\}precision\{0.001\}value\{19.03\}unit\{Celsius\}\}$$

ContextAA's Context model does not require Context producers and Context consumers to structure Context the same way; we require Context to follow the basic syntactic rules given above. In these examples, Contexts c and c' might describe the same reality from different angles. Are they identical? Clearly not, as they have different structures and convey different biases. Are they similar? Can these similarities be quantified in practice? Most importantly: is their apparent similarity relevant to the observing Agent? These questions guide our definition of semantic Context proximity and influence our definition of subjective Context relevance.

3.1   Agents as Context

Our model uses Context-aware and Context-dependent Agents. Agents are executed on distributed processes we call Hosts. We support two distinct categories of Agents: standard Agents, that offer middleware-like services in each Host, and domain Agents, each of which performs a Context-related mission.

Standard Agents tend to be hard-coded. They can access the underlying hardware of their Host and perform a number of Context-related tasks for other Agents.

Domain Agents tend to be expressed as Context. We define domain Agent a as a 4-tuple of the form $a = \{M, O, S, R\}$ where M describes its mission, what a has to achieve; O describes its ontic frame, how a evaluates the quality and relative value of Context; S is its Context space, what a knows; and R describes its resource restrictions, what set of resources a requires to operate. Each of these four elements is expressed as Context.

3.2   Context Requests

In ContextAA, Agents express requests for Context as Context, more precisely as Context patterns. Every Context is a Context pattern, although we mostly use the word "pattern" when some names in a Context are subject to match more than one name. This architectural decision allows us to keep our software architecture small and simple by restricting it to process a single data format.

A self-evident example of exact Context matching would be:

$$c = a\{b\}, c' = a\{b\} \Rightarrow c = c'$$

Another example of exact Context matching would be:

$$c = a\{b\}, c' = a \Rightarrow c = c'$$

This unconventional equality results from the unicity of Context names: two Contexts with the same name are considered equal for most practical purposes when their names are considered equal. This decision has been made for efficiency purposes: shallow comparisons, limited to names, are performed much faster than deep comparisons, also supported but only used when explicitly required as they compare all nodes and are significantly more complex.

Context patterns can include wildcards, such as $*$ (match any one name), ? (match any one name element) or $**$ (match any number of names, recursively, typically until some specific name can be matched). Thus, below, Context c is matched by patterns p and p' but not by pattern p'':

$$c = h : a : id\{b\{c\}\}$$

$$p = ** \{c\}; p' = h : ? : id\{b\}; p'' = *\{c\}$$

4 Context Proximity

We define shallow name matching as equality between Contexts for efficiency, but equality is not the general case for autonomic Agents in Open intelligent space. In practice, we expect requested Context and published Context to match only partially in most cases. This partial match can be due to many factors, including:

- Differences in structure, such as a requester Context c associating the measurement precision of a sensor with the actual measurement while the published Context c' associates it with the sensor's description:

$$c = *\{temp\{value\{? = val\}unit\{Celsius\}prec\{0.01\}\}sensor\{name\{xyz\}\}\}$$

$$c' = a : h : id\{temp\{value\{20.5\}\}sensor\{name\{xyz\}unit\{Celsius\}prec\{0.01\}\}\}$$

- Differences in content, such as when, given Contexts c and c', there are elements c that are not part of c' or elements of c' that are not part of c:

$$c = a : h : id\{temp\{value\{20.5\}\}sensor\{name\{xyz\}unit\{Celsius\}location\{z3\}\}\}$$

$$c' = a : h : id\{temp\{value\{20.5\}\}sensor\{name\{xyz\}unit\{Celsius\}prec\{0.01\}\}\}$$

- Differences in measurement units, in such a way that Contexts c and c' are identical given the appropriate transformation:

$$c =* \{temp\{value\{? = val\}unit\{Celsius\}\}\}$$

$$c' = a : h : id\{temp\{value\{68.9\}unit\{Fahrenheit\}\}\}$$

Agents often do not encounter full match between requested Context and published Context; there can be a significant number of candidate Contexts for a given request, each of them partially matching the request. Agents seek proximity between Contexts, in order to sort candidates according to how close they seem to be with respect to what the Agent is requesting, after which the question becomes: which one matches the best candidates with the Agent's ontic frame.

This article focuses on Context proximity, but defines a number of distance functions, between names and between Contexts. In our model, if D represents distance, $P = 1 - D$ represents proximity.

4.1 Name Distance

Since Context is made out of names, all Context proximity functions are at least in part based on name distance.

Name distance $distance :: Name \rightarrow Name \rightarrow \mathbb{Q} \in [0..1]$ is defined as 0 when two names are identical and 1 when they are fully different. Partial name distances are possible: for example $n = h : a : c, n' = h : a' : c, a \neq a'$ implies $distance(n, n') = \frac{1}{3}$ as n, n' are two thirds identical. Wildcards are considered fully matching.

Names are read from left to right. When two names have a different number of elements, the rightmost elements from the name with the highest number of elements are considered non-matching: $distance(a : ? : c : d, b : x : c) = \frac{1}{2}$.

4.2 Structural Distance

We define structural distance σ to reflect the structural similarities between Contexts:

$$\sigma :: C \rightarrow C \rightarrow \mathbb{Q} \in [0..1]$$

$$\sigma(n\{\emptyset\}, n'\{v'\}) \triangleq 1$$

$$\sigma(n\{v\}, n'\{\emptyset\}) \triangleq 1$$

$$\sigma(n\{\emptyset\}, n'\{\emptyset\}) \triangleq distance(n, n')$$

$$\sigma(n\{v\}, n'\{v'\}) \triangleq \left\{ \begin{array}{l} Let\ small = smallest(v, v'), large = largest(v, v') \\ \dfrac{\left(distance(n,n') + \left(1 - \frac{size(small)}{size(large)}\right) + \frac{\sum_{e \in small}\left(\frac{min_{e' \in large}(\sigma(e,e'))}{size(small)}\right)}{}\right)}{3} \end{array} \right.$$

where *distance* is the distance between two Context names, *smallest* :: $Set \rightarrow Set \rightarrow Set$ accepts two sets and yields the one with the smallest cardinality, *largest* :: $Set \rightarrow Set \rightarrow Set$ accepts two sets and yields the one with the highest cardinality, and *size* :: $Set \rightarrow \mathbb{N}$ yields the cardinality of a set.

The definition of σ yields symmetric results: $\forall c, c' : \sigma(c, c') = \sigma(c', c)$.

For σ, root name similarity is the most important factor when comparing c with c'. The other two components of this function are a comparison of their respective values' sizes and an application of σ to elements of these values.

4.3   Content-Wise Distance

We define content-wise distance ϱ to reflect similarity in content between Contexts:

$$\varrho :: C \rightarrow C \rightarrow \mathbb{Q} \in [0..1]$$

$$\varrho(n\{v\}, n'\{\emptyset\}) \triangleq distance(n, n')$$

$$\varrho(n\{\emptyset\}, n'\{v'\}) \triangleq distance(n, n')$$

$$\varrho(n\{v\}, n'\{v'\}) \triangleq \left(\frac{distance(n, n') + \left(\frac{\sum_{e \in v} \frac{bestEquiv(e, v')}{size(v)}}{} \right)}{2} \right)$$

where: *bestEquiv* :: $C \rightarrow Set\langle C \rangle \rightarrow \mathbb{Q} \in [0..1]$, given Context c and set v of Contexts, yields Context c' from v that leads to the smallest value for $\varrho(c, c')$. Thus, ϱ gives equal weight to the similarity between names and the average ϱ for the best match found between Context values.

The definition of ϱ does not necessarily yield symmetric results, although symmetric ϱ results do occur. In practice, $\exists c, c' : \varrho(c, c') \neq \varrho(c', c)$.

4.4   Semantic Distance

Agents seek to establish a quantifiable measure of proximity between two Contexts: semantic distance ρ. Informally, a "good" ρ function implies that if c' is "more like" c than c'', then $\rho(c', c) < \rho(c'', c)$.

We define ρ as a weighed combination of Context distance functions f_i. Assuming $n : n > 1, n \in \mathbb{N}$, functions $f_i, 0 \leq i < n$ and weights $\omega_i, 0 \leq i < n$, we require that:

$$\rho :: C \rightarrow C \rightarrow \mathbb{Q} \in [0..1]$$

$$\left. \begin{array}{l} f_i :: C \rightarrow C \rightarrow \mathbb{Q} \in [0..1] \\ 0 \leq \omega_i \leq 1, \sum \omega_i = 1 \end{array} \right\} 0 \leq i < n$$

$$\rho(c, c') \triangleq \sum_{i=0}^{n-1} \omega_i f_i(c, c')$$

By default, $\omega_i = \frac{1}{n}$ but each Agent can weigh individual Context distance functions according to its ontic frame. The codomain of f_i being in $[0..1]$, we define proximity in terms of f_i as $1 - f_i$.

Given our Context *according-to* approach, what makes Contexts close to one another depends on the observing Agent, more specifically its ontic frame. Thus, the weights and Context distance functions depend on the Agent. By default, we use:

$$\rho :: C \to C \to \mathbb{Q} \in [0..1]$$

$$\rho(c, c') \triangleq \frac{\varrho(c, c') + \sigma(c, c')}{2}$$

Since ρ potentially depends on functions that can yield asymmetric results, there is no guarantee that ρ itself will yield symmetric results in practice.

5 Empirical Results

Running ρ, σ and ϱ on a wide array of Contexts provides insight in the behavior and utility of these metrics. For all three functions, as can be expected, the distance between a Context and itself is 0. Contexts used for these tests are shown in Table 1.

On average, ϱ tends to be more costly to compute than σ. Assuming *time* $:: F \to \Delta t$ a function that yields the execution time of some function F provided relevant arguments, we have $\frac{time(\sigma(c,c'))}{time(\varrho(c,c'))} \cong 0,88$ given current implementations of σ and ϱ. As could be expected, $time(\rho(c, c')) \cong (time(\sigma(c, c')) + time(\varrho(c, c')))$, but in practice, $time(\rho(c, c')) < (time(\sigma(c, c')) + time(\varrho(c, c')))$ can be expected.

An example of very close Contexts for σ in Table 1 involves c_0 and c_{11}, as $\sigma(c_0, c_{11}) = 0.117284$. The value of $\sigma(c_0, c_{11})$ would be closer to 0 if the root names were identical; the $\frac{1}{3}$ distance between these names impacts the results significantly. In practice, an Agent looking for c_0 might be satisfied with c_{11} (Fig. 1).

An example of Contexts that are $\approx 75\%$ structurally close to one another are c_3 and c_4, as $\sigma(c_3, c_4) = 0.22222$. In fact, they have the same (simple) structure but differ in content. The relevance of these differences depends on the ontic frame of the requesting Agent, where the relative importance of individual differences can be weighed.

There are of course Contexts that are totally different from one another using σ. For example c_6 and c_{13}: $\sigma(c_6, c_{13}) = 1$.

Applying ϱ to the same Contexts yields different results; for example, $\sigma(c_0, c_{11}) = 0.117284$ but $\varrho(c_0, c_{11}) = \varrho(c_{11}, c_0) = 0.19791$. Contexts c_0 and c_{11} remain similar to one another according to both σ and ϱ, but the relative weight of structure similarity has more impact in the case of σ. In the case of c_3 and c_4, $\sigma(c_3, c_4) = 0.22222$ but $\varrho(c_3, c_4) = \varrho(c_4, c_3) = 0.416667$: they are more similar in structure than in content.

Table 1. Contexts used for tests.

c_0	host0:agent0:1 {public {temperature {value {10 } unit {Celsius } precision {0.001 } } source {agent0 } } }
c_1	host0:agent1:1 {public {temperature {value {10 } } source {agent1 unit {Celsius } precision {0.01 } } } }
c_2	host0:agent2:1 {public {temperature {value {50 } unit {Fahrenheit } precision {0.001 } } source {agent2 } } }
c_3	h:a:0 {value {10 } }
c_4	h:a:1 {value {50 } }
c_5	h:a:2 {value {10 } unit {Celsius } }
c_6	h:a:3 {value {50 } unit {Fahrenheit } }
c_7	h:a:4 {value {10 } unit {Celsius } precision {0.001 } }
c_8	host0:agent2:2 {public {temperature {value {10 } src {unit {Celsius } precision {0.001 } agent2 } } } }
c_9	host0:agent3:1 {public {temperature {value {10 } unit {Celsius } precision {0.001 } } source {agent3 unit {Celsius } precision {0.001 } } } }
c_{10}	host0:agent4:1 {public {temperature {value {10 } } source {agent4 unit {Celsius } precision {0.001 } } } }
c_{11}	host0:agent0:2 {public {temperature {value {100 } unit {Fahrenheit } precision {0.1 } } source {agent0 } } }
c_{12}	host0:agent0:3 {public {humidity {value {100 } unit {kpa } precision {0.1 } } source {agent0 } } }
c_{13}	a
c_{14}	b {c}

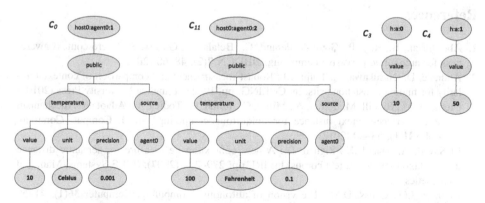

Fig. 1. Similarities between c_0 and c_{11} and between c_3 and c_4 (differences in boldface).

6 Conclusion

Agents use Context distance functions when a given Context request yields two or more candidate Contexts. When only one Context matches a given request, and when the match is perfect, there is no reason to discriminate between candidates; in Open intelligent space [1], this simple situation is not expected to be the common case.

In ContextAA, we formalize Context distance through functions such as semantic distance ρ, structural distance σ and content-wise distance ϱ in order to let Agents sort candidate Contexts according to their relevance, and make it easier to find those that might be truly useful to the Agent's mission.

For some Agent a, it is possible that the best match according to some distance function, including ρ, is not the most appropriate candidate Context according to the ontic frame of a. For example, if $\rho(c, c')$ is very small but if one of the differences between c and c' is irreconcilable according to the ontic frame of a, then c' can be excluded, leading a to prefer a more distant match.

Such an irreconcilable difference occurs when a finds a Context very close to its needs but that expresses a value using a measurement unit not understood by a and which a cannot translate into something it would understand. Another such difference occurs if a requires a measure performed with a precision of at least 10^{-3} but the best semantic match found Context produced by a less precise sensor. With our approach, the mission and ontic frame of a have precedence over more generic heuristics.

Functions σ and ϱ in ContextAA are not meant to cover the Context similarity evaluation needs of Agent a. Likewise, a is not required to give σ and ϱ equal weight as the default behavior of ρ suggests: the ontic frame of a overrides default behavior.

Through subjective Context proximity assessment, Agents in ContextAA can function in heterogenous environments such as Open intelligent space where the Context found in the environment does not always match precisely what the Agent requested. The resulting autonomicity enhancement contributes to a better continuity of service for ContextAA's Agents, and provides a general solution to the problem of continuity of service for Agents.

References

1. Abdulrazak, B., Roy, P., Gouin-Vallerand, C., Belala, Y., Giroux, S.: Micro context-aware-ness for autonomic pervasive computing. IJBDCN **7**(2), 48–68 (2011)
2. Andrade, D., Nasukawa, T., Tsujii, J.I.: Robust measurement and comparison of context simi-larity for finding translation pairs. In: COLING, pp. 19–27. Tsinghua University Press (2010)
3. Cremene, M., Riveill, M., Rarau, A., Miron, C., Iulian, B., Todica, V.: Adaptation mechanism based on service-context distance for ubiquitous computing. Int. J. Comput. Commun. Control **VII**(1), 53–60 (2012)
4. El Sayed, A., Hacid, H., Zighed, D.: A new context-aware measure for semantic distance using a taxonomy and a text corpus. In: IRI, pp. 279–284 (2007). (IEEE Systems, Man, and Cybernetics Society
5. Kephart, J.O., Chess, D.M.: The vision of autonomic computing. Computer **36**(1), 41–50 (2003)
6. Keßler, C.: Similarity measurement in context. In: Kokinov, B., Richardson, D.C., Roth-Berghofer, T.R., Vieu, L. (eds.) CONTEXT 2007. LNCS (LNAI), vol. 4635, pp. 277–290. Springer, Heidelberg (2007)
7. Pilz, A., Paaß, G.: From names to entities using thematic context distance. In: CIKM, pp. 857–866. ACM, (2011)
8. Roy, P., Abdulrazak, B., Belala, Y.: Approaching context-awareness for open intelligent space. In: Proceedings of the 6th International Conference on Advances in Mobile Computing and Multimedia, pp. 422–426 (2008)

Emotion Aware System for the Elderly

Hai Yu$^{(\boxtimes)}$, Celine Maria Amrita Anthony Sunderraj,
Carl K. Chang, and Johnny Wong

Iowa State University, 226 Atanasoff Hall, Ames, IA 50011, USA
{yuhair, celine, chang, wong}@iastate.edu

Abstract. The growth in elderly population challenges technologists to develop applications explicitly designed for the elderly which are innovative yet intuitive to use. According to recent studies in Gerontology, one of the challenges that an elderly person has to confront is solitude and boredom. With the detectability of emotions through Brain Computer Interfaces (BCI), one can provide reliable services to the elderly that address their emotional needs. In this paper the applications of the Emotiv EPOC, a BCI, is explained by developing a system called AWARE which helps mitigate loneliness in the life of an elderly and provides emergency services and other services based on their real-time emotional state. The AWARE system uses a model of computation that has taken pervasive computing to the next level by reducing the need for an explicit user input and facilitates the understanding of the user's emotions by the system to address theirs emotional needs.

Keywords: Emotiv EPOC headset · Brain Computer Interface (BCI) · Gerontechnology · AWARE · Emotional state

1 Introduction

Brain Computer Interfaces (BCI) includes the range of technologies which allow computers to communicate with the human brain. The non-invasive BCI Electroencephalogram (EEG) has numerous applications in clinical fields as well as research fields, such as Emotion Detection. Research in the field of Emotion Detection using brainwaves has shown immense progress, with the fundamental Valence Arousal Model introduced by James Russel [1] which maps various regions of the Valence-Arousal Graph to specific emotions, to the judicious detections of the Affectiv Suite of Emotiv EPOC which performs real-time emotion detection promptly and precisely. The EPOC headset is a wireless, 14-electrode, EEG detecting. The Emotiv EPOC SDK is composed of a set of three suites Expressiv, Affectiv and Cognitiv suites that process the raw EEG signals to reveal the facial expressions, emotions and identify thought processes respectively. The following emotional states are detected by the Affectiv Suite: Frustration, Meditation, Boredom, Instantaneous Excitement and Long-term Excitement.

BCI could be able to provide a combination of information and features that no other input modality can offer. Having such easily accessible yet capable devices in the market, one can apply them to address various issues related to the elderly and a good understanding of user's emotional state can help develop applications that cater to the

© Springer International Publishing Switzerland 2015
C. Bodine et al. (Eds.): ICOST 2014, LNCS 8456, pp. 175–183, 2015.
DOI: 10.1007/978-3-319-14424-5_19

deep needs of the elderly [2]. Gerontechnology, however, poses the challenge of developing applications that require a design intuitive to the elderly. Various modern technologies [3] aimed mainly at young users are often not very useful for elderly people and result in elderly people having difficulties with the user interface. Studies in Gerontological Design [4] has long helped understand designs that have revealed some of the effective designs such as the use of fewer buttons in applications and the use of visibly large buttons. The AWARE system described in the paper implements a Gerontological design to enable proper use by the elderly.

The AWARE system is a prototype developed in the Smart Home Lab which uses the Affectiv Suite to detect the emotional state of the person. It is developed for a smart phone running the Android OS and was designed and implemented for use by the elderly to help them tackle solitude and help in their successful ageing.

The remainder of this paper is organized according to the following roadmap. Section 2 talks about the exiting work in the field of Gerotechnology, Sect. 3 introduces the Aware System, Sect. 4 discusses some of the use cases of the AWARE System, Sect. 5 explains the Design of the Aware System, Sect. 6 concludes our study and provides ways of building upon this system to enhance additional features.

2   Existing Work

In modern society, the rapid development of Gerotechnology provides the potential to help elderly people to maintain physical fitness, cognitive function as well as social activity [5]. Communication applications under the context of the Internet as an important Information and Communication Technology (ICT) can remotely connect elderly people with family members and friends, which could help to mitigate elder loneliness [6]. Existing work focus on building assistive technologies for the elderly in order to provide for physical needs of the elderly such as location aware pervasive computing for the elderly, or communication systems for the elderly, which do not address most of the deep needs of the elderly [2]. The AWARE System described in the next section uses emotion awareness, to address the deep need for social touch. The AWARE System has introduced the novel idea of 'making elderly care systems emotion aware' and thereby increasing the appeal of the elderly care systems.

There are numerous emergency handling systems that detect emergencies such as medical emergencies using medical indicators [7]. Emergencies in an elderly person's life can be detected pervasively using various other sensors such as motion sensors which detect a fall or unusual absence of movement. AWARE also applies emotion awareness to Emergency handling which is an innovative concept.

3   AWARE System

The AWARE System is mainly designed to addresses the problem of boredom for the elderly and provide a technical solution for elderly care giving to the care givers and family or friends. It consists of three main components: (a) AWARE Android Application (b) Emotiv EPOC Headset (c) Interfacing Server.

The AWARE Android Application provides the necessary service to the elderly user. The range of services provided include Emergency Alert System, Entertainment and Emotion Logging. Emergency Alerts are triggered that notify the care taker or relatives when the elderly person experiences increased levels of frustration. The emergency alert functionality is based on the idea that such emotional states of frustration and anxiety are experienced during times of emergency such as a seizure or severe pain or trauma so in the AWARE system an increased level of frustration also serves as an emergency indicator [8]. The Entertainment module intends to help reduce boredom and frustration by playing the user's favorite music or connecting a Skype call to friends or family members. The Emotion Logging is done to maintain statistics of user's emotional state.

The Emotiv EPOC headset is to be worn by the user for the AWARE system to detect the user's real-time emotions using Emotiv's Affectiv Suite. The Interfacing Server runs the Java Application that uses the Emotiv EPOC SDK and Socket communication protocol in order to communicate the output of the Affectiv Suite to the AWARE Android Application.

4   Experiment

At the initial stages of the project, the idea was presented to a group of two elderly mentors from a local nursing home facility called Northcrest Retirement Community in Ames, Iowa. When asked 'Would a system that helps detect the mood of the person and responds to it, be welcomed among the elderly?' their answers were very positive. With this confirmation of our design, the prototype was implemented. Some modules of AWARE are presented below for which the threshold values are purely based on the authors' understanding of the Emotiv Detections.

For setting up the AWARE System, the Interfacing Server is first started and it listens to input from the Emotiv EPOC headset. The user needs to constantly wear the Emotiv EPOC headset in order to enable real time emotion detection. The AWARE app in the user's Android device can then connect to the Interfacing Server. Figure 1 is a screenshot of the Emotiv Control Panel that provides information about the signal strengths of brainwaves from each of the electrodes. Figure 2 shows the Affective suite giving a graphical output with the blue line showing the level of frustration and the red line showing the level of engagement/boredom. During the initialization phase emergency contacts and Skype Contacts are added to the system.

4.1   Emergency Alert

The output from the Emotion Detection module provides the levels of frustration or boredom experienced by the user. The Alert System monitors the level of frustration and when it exceeds a certain threshold (here 0.85), for example in a scenario where the user is experiencing a heart attack [8], it triggers an alert email and SMS to the emergency contacts. Figure 3 shows the Interfacing server that displays the detected

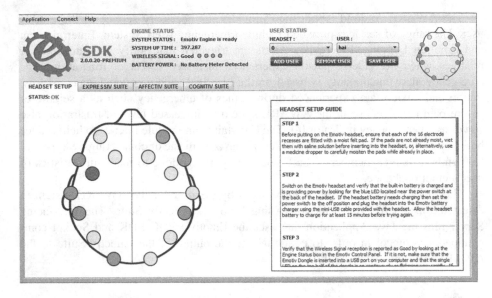

Fig. 1. Screenshot of the Emotiv EPOC Control Panel

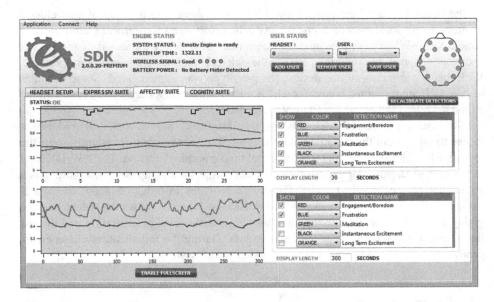

Fig. 2. Screenshot of the Affectiv Suite in the Emotiv Control Panel showing real-time emotions.

level of frustration and boredom. The Alert system is triggered in this case as the level of frustration is high (>0.85) and an email and a SMS are sent to the care-taker or family member or friend who is added to the list of emergency contacts.

4.2   Entertainment (Music)

Similar to the Alert module, the entertainment modules, namely Skype, Music Player and Video Player, continuously monitor the levels of frustration or boredom of the elderly user. When the levels of frustration or boredom cross certain thresholds (here >0.6 for frustration and <0.3 for boredom) then the music player is opened. The user's music preference list can be mined using machine learning techniques; however the current prototype allows the user to add music to this list in the initialization phase.

Fig. 3. Screenshot of the Interfacing server

4.3   Emotion Logging

The detected emotional states, as important analyzable data, will be logged by the emotion logging system into the database along with a timestamp for future statistical analysis. For instance, with this data one could analyze the most common time of the day that the elderly user has a feeling of loneliness. Table 1 shows the data collected during a regular day's use of the AWARE System. Similar kinds of analysis can be performed to obtain a better understanding of the user based on the Emotion logging system to provide customized services. The following formulae are used to calculate percentage of time the user showed Frustration (F) and Percentage of time the user showed Boredom (B) in Table 1.

$$F = \left(\frac{\text{Duration of frustration}}{\text{Total Duration}}\right) \times 100, \tag{1}$$

$$B = \left(\frac{\text{Duration of boredom}}{\text{Total Duration}}\right) \times 100. \tag{2}$$

The resulting Android AWARE Application was demonstrated to the same group of mentors from Northcrest Retirement Community towards the end of the project. The mentors were thrilled by the capability of the Emotiv EPOC headset and found the AWARE Application a handy tool to overcome boredom and identify emergency.

Table 1. Table showing the analysis of logged emotion

User	F		B	
	Morning	Evening	Morning	Evening
1	14.5 %	17.6 %	1.6 %	0 %
2	2.1 %	5.6 %	0 %	2 %

5   Application Design/Architecture

In the process of AWARE System implementation, the Model-View-Controller (MVC) [9] software pattern is adopted. Central component model mainly deals with the operations about data collected from Emotiv EPOC and AWARE's database. The output is the representation of information (view) based on Android user interface. The controller analyzes input data and triggers command to the model or view to finish a service. Figure 4 gives the Architecture Diagram of the Aware System which is explained in two aspects: AWARE Android application and interactions between the Interfacing server and the application.

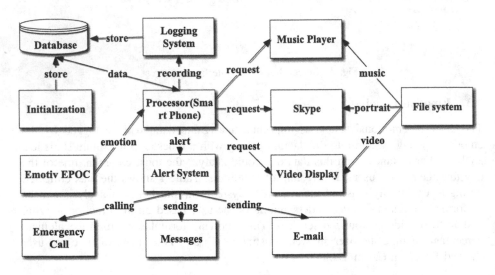

Fig. 4. Architecture Diagram of AWARE System

5.1   AWARE Android Application

For the design of frontend, we emphasize on simplicity and usability of the features. In the Skype calling feature, the contacts information is shown as a gallery of head portraits of people that is loaded from the Skype component. The user can associate the Skype account for each portrait by touching on the picture and then input the corresponding Skype account. And then a long press will initiate the Skype call to the person whose Skype account is associated with the image that is pressed. This interface with minimal options makes it easier for use by the elderly. The Emotion logging and Alert systems are transparent to the elderly user and only the emergency contacts need to be updated for the Alert system.

Music player interface is also made as simple as possible. It only contains a playlist of user's favorite music and buttons for basic operations which are labeled with word rather than with the icon, which usually confuse the elderly people who have little experience with common icons. Features like downloading music from the Internet, sharing music with friends, commenting music, etc. are not supported by AWARE because they will make the music player more complicated to use for the elderly people.

5.2 Interaction Between Emotiv EPOC and AWARE Android Application

We adopt the client-server model to connect the AWARE system and Emotiv EPOC. In the interfacing server, the Emotive EPOC SDK is installed and is used for EEG data collections and emotion detection and analysis. AWARE Android client part will receive emotion information from the server and then provide appropriate service to the user according to the detected emotion data. Socket API (Application Programming Interface) is used to connect the server and the client. We use the structured analysis and design technique (SADT) [10], a software engineering methodology to describe their interaction as shown in Fig. 5. The SADT diagram is composed of boxes representing functions and four types of arrows input, output, control and mechanism. On the horizontal segment, input entering from the left side of the box represents things that will be transformed by the box and the output leaving from right side is the transformed data. On the vertical segment, control entering the top of the box affects how the box transforms input and mechanism pointing up into the bottoms of the box represents who/how/what physical resources performs the function. Consider the function 'Detecting Emotion', Brain waves as input enter the box and a tuple with the detected emotion and the detected level of the same emotion is the output of the box, and the two types of emotions detected are frustration and boredom and their levels scale from 0 to 1. Emotion model describing emotions in valence and arousal dimensions and fast Fourier transform (FFT) analyzing and transforming electroencephalogram (EEG) signals to emotion, play a role of control for the 'Detecting Emotion' box and the mechanism, the Emotiv EPOC as a Bain Computer Interface (BCI) is used to detect brainwave; affective suite deciphers user's emotions; Emotiv Software development kit (SDK) provides a software tool to retrieve emotion data for use in the AWARE application. Considering the function 'Detecting Emotion', Brain waves are input and a tuple with the detected emotion and the detected level of that

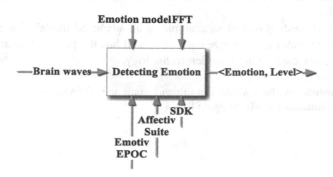

Fig. 5. Structure Diagram of the Emotion Detection function

emotion is the output; the two types of emotions detected are frustration and boredom and their levels scaling from 0 to 1. Models describing emotions in valence and arousal dimensions and fast Fourier transform (FFT), play a role of control; and for the mechanism, the Emotiv EPOC is used to detect brainwaves; Affective suite deciphers user's emotions; Emotiv Software development kit (SDK) provides a software tool to retrieve this data for use in the AWARE application.

6 Conclusion and Future Work

The AWARE System is a model that successfully uses the potentials of current day BCI and realizes the idea of a computer system comprehending human emotions. It is a stepping stone for systems that can facilitate a two-way understanding between the system and the user of the system. This prototype is a part of a bigger idea which is a 'Personal Pal'. The Personal pal can be a mobile application taking the form of any animated character which the user of the application tends to virtually pet and nurture, and this is often a one-way relationship where the virtual pet does not respond to the emotions of the user. This idea can be extended to establish a two-way relationship between the Application and the user, where the application responds to user's real-time emotions. In case the user, is bored the application could initiate a game interface. If the user is happy the application should try to log voice or video reports of the user in order to create a memory such as in Digital Life. One can enhance this prototype to achieve this goal.

Following are some additional enhancements; Along with logging the emotional state, one can also track other information like the music or videos or contacts the user prefers. With some statistical analysis and machine learning, one may provide smarter services to the user that are completely pervasive and offline, not requiring the wearing of the headset. One could apply other techniques of emotion detection such as utilizing facial expression in order to improve the reliability of the detection result. In order to detect emotions that are not recognized by the Affectiv suite, one may process the raw EEG through filtering and feature recognition, to provide more customization. One would desire a more compact headset with less number of electrodes, or find ways to achieve high accuracy with increased compactness of the device, and remove the need for an interfacing server, if the Emotiv EPOC headset could directly communicate with a mobile device.

The AWARE system is thus an example of an advanced model of user-computer interaction in the realm of pervasive computing and has the potential to transform the scenario in elderly care giving and Gerotechnology.

Acknowledgements. Authors would like to thank some the AWARE project team members Mr. Abhinav Vinnakota and Mr. Swagoto Roy.

References

1. Colibazzi, T., Posner, J., Wang, Z., Russell, J.A., et al.: Neural systems subserving valence and arousal during the experience of induced emotions. Emotion **10**(3), 377–389 (2010)
2. Zejda, D.: Deep design for ambient intelligence: toward acceptable appliances for higher quality of life of the elderly. In: Sixth International Conference on Intelligent Environments, pp. 277–282 (2010)
3. Fukuda, R.: Gerontechnology for a super-aged society. In: Kohlbacher, F., Herstatt, C. (eds.) The Silver Market Phenomenon. Marketing and Innovation in the Aging Society, pp. 79–89. Springer, Heidelberg (2011)
4. Tacken, M., Marcellini, F., Mollenkopf, H., Ruoppila, I., Széman, Z.: Use and acceptance of new technology by older people. Findings of the international MOBILATE survey: enhancing mobility in later life. Gerontechnology **3**(3), 126–137 (2005). Web: 6 Apr 2014
5. Chen, K., Chan, A.H.S.: The ageing population of China and a review of gerontechnology. Gerontechnology **10**(2), 63–71 (2011). doi:http://dx.doi.org/10.4017/gt.2011.10.2.001.00
6. Cotten, S.R., Anderson, W., McCullough, B.: The impact of ICT use on loneliness and contact with others among older adults. Gerontechnology **11**(2), 161 (2012)
7. Hua, H.M., Liu, B.J., Wang, T.E.: A decision support system for medical emergencies of older adults in Taiwan. Gerontechnology **6**(3), 169–174 (2007)
8. Lane, A.M., Godfrey, R.: Emotional and cognitive changes during and post a near fatal heart attack and one-year after: a case study. J. Sports Sci. Med. **9**(3), 517–522 (2010)
9. Grove, R.F., Ozhan, E.: The MVC-WEB DESIGN PATTERN. In: 7th International Conference on Web Information Systems and Technologies, 6–9 May 2011
10. Marca, D.A.: SADT/IDEF0 for Augmenting UML, Agile and usability engineering methods. In: Escalona, M.J., Cordeiro, J., Shishkov, B. (eds.) ICSOFT 2011. CCIS, vol. 303, pp. 38–55. Springer, Heidelberg (2013)

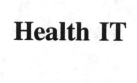

Health IT

Dual Locks: Partial Sharing of Health Documents in Cloud

Mahmood Ahmad[1]($\boxtimes$), Zeeshan Pervez[2], and Sungyoung Lee[1]

[1] Department of Computer Engineering, Kyung Hee University, Seoul, South Korea
{rayemahmood,sylee}@oslab.khu.ac.kr
[2] School of Computing, University of the West of Scotland, Paisley PA1 2BE, UK
zeeshan.pervez@uws.ac.uk

Abstract. While working with the sensitive data e.g., related to health, there is a barrier of mistrust while selecting cloud services. To overcome this barrier various standards of cryptosystem are used like encrypted outsourcing, attribute based encryption and oblivious access policies. The default access model of authorization on encrypted data gives full access permission to its user. To narrow down the access scope as a subset on given authorization is a non-trivial task. To design such systems multiple encryption and decryption keys, data partitioning or attribute based encryption are few available options. These techniques involve extra computation cost and complex issue of key management. In this paper we have proposed a framework to restrict authorization on encrypted data with selective access. The underlying model is independent from complex issue of key management. The proposed model also avoids one dimension of side channel attacks on secure data and that is to learn from the patterns of encrypted traffic. Our experimental results show that selective authorization based on proposed model is compute efficient and create random pattern for user access even for similar queries.

Keywords: Health data · Data sharing · Cloud computing · Security and privacy

1 Introduction

The enormous volume of data in todays era of digitization is ready to be explored and shared by scientists, research institutes and enterprise organizations for enhanced knowledge exploration. Ease of accessing the internet, widespread of e-applications, user awareness, obvious benefits of digitized world on humanity are main reasons for this data proliferation. With same trend in health care domain, services like Personal Health Record (PHR) allow its users to create, manage and share its medical records with entities like physicians, friends and family members [8]. Due to the management and maintenance cost of systems like PHR, they are outsourced to third parties or cloud infrastructure [9,12]. Besides these potential advantage of cloud infrastructure, health data requires optimal level of security too. From the consumers' and data sharing perspective,

© Springer International Publishing Switzerland 2015
C. Bodine et al. (Eds.): ICOST 2014, LNCS 8456, pp. 187–194, 2015.
DOI: 10.1007/978-3-319-14424-5_20

these concerns remain the primary inhibitor for adoption of cloud computing services [2]. Besides PHR, hospital information management systems (HIMS)and electronic medical records (EMR) require even greater level of security due to the larger volume and variety of data. At a fine grained level the personal health information (PHI) or the electronic health records (EHR) are required to be protected in terms of their storage and utilization. Other than threat of mistrust from third party or cloud service provider, the inside rouge user pose an equal threat for the privacy breach of same information. A similar example is give in [8] where a user took the PHI data home of 26.5 million users without prior permission of his employer. With all these concerns encrypted storage of sensitive data is highly recommended while availing service of cloud infrastructure [3,7]. Encrypted storage maximizes the privacy aspect of data however; at the cost of lower scope of its utility. Encrypted data requires decryption keys by authorized user to avoid its unsolicited disclosure. To minimize the usage of network bandwidth and to avail optimal computation powers of cloud infrastructure various searchable encryption SE schemes have been proposed [1,4]. With SE, if Alice is an authorized user, she does not need to download the entire data from cloud to her machine for decryption and then searching, rather, her encrypted query can be evaluated efficiently with the help of available SE schemes. The SE schemes allow users to access entire data for which authorization has been granted by the owner.

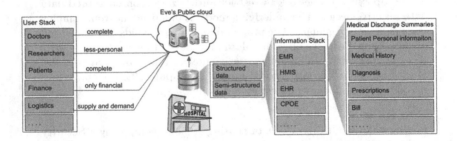

Fig. 1. Overall architecture

Another challenge beyond authorized access on sensitive data is to restrict authorization for selective segments of information which comes under the category of fine grained access control over encrypted data [5]. Consider an example where a National Hospital (NH) is using HIMS and its IT infrastructure is utilizing services of public cloud owned by Eve. To narrow down our example, we will consider the scenario for medical discharge summaries. In medical discharge summaries various sections like medical history, prescription, allergies, diagnosis and accounts information is entered and kept as record. These documents hold value for various analytical processing e.g., frequently prescribed medicines, prevalent diseases or the financial statements. The overall architecture is shown in Fig. 1. To perform any sort of analysis, it is required that personal information of patient should not be disclosed to anyone else other than the clinicians.

Information on drug usage is required to be shared with the supply department and account section need to look into the billing section of this summary. A single document now has multiple users with definite restrictions as imposed by the data access policy of hospital. This issue can be handled by disintegrating the clinical discharge summary document into various sections(bins) and then assign each bin to its intended recipient. This approach might work for trivial access structure ignoring the additional leakage of information which is explained through an example.

Alice and Bob are two researchers in the hospital having access on the disease and drug sections. Recently it is reported that diabetic patients aged 40 and above have serious reaction with certain drug usage. Alice and Bob investigate the information with repetitive queries. Although the information is encrypted in the cloud, yet similar queries encrypted with same keys can reveal a common pattern on Eves' cloud. These common pattern in shape of similar queries or replies might help the curiosity of Eves by learning beyond required. To overcome, both Alice and Bob may require different keys, however, it will make the overall key management a complex process and process of segregating the segments(bins) useless. Considering all these concerns as motivation to our proposed solution we have formalized a *Dual-Lock* mechanism to overcome the aforesaid limitations. The proposed methodology is analogous to real world scenario of banking lockers. The bank locker can be opened by two keys, where one key is held with the bank and other is kept with the consumer. The unlocking process is possible only when bank administration and owner has right pair of keys. The rest of the paper is structured as below. Section 2 is about related work. Main idea and proposed methodology is given in Sect. 3. Section 4 covers the evaluation and results. Conclusion is given in Sect. 5.

2   Related Work

The trend in sharing health data between its stakeholder is not as much progressive as in other disciplines due to the sensitivity and security issues related with that [11]. This issue persist despite knowing the fact that its sharing can greatly helps researchers to minimize the rate of illness and can save human lives. The direct concern of security with health data is usually dealt with encrypted storage [3, 7] where it can be shared with authorized parties conveniently. Health data sharing take place between person to person e.g., PHR systems, between hospitals through HIMS and standards like HL7. Personal health record (PHR) is an emerging patient-centric model of health information exchange, which is often outsourced on computer clouds. However, there have been wide privacy concerns as personal health information could be exposed to those third party servers and to unauthorized parties. For PHR system security Attribute based encryption (ABE) is proposed [8]. In this system the concept of multi authority ABE has been introduced. The proposed idea mainly relies on keys which is a costly operation. A system that works with multiple keys becomes cumbersome for consumer in terms of remembering and managing these keys. In another technique [6] that uses the ABE. After highlighting the importance of data and security concerns while storing it in the untrusted domain of cloud computing, they emphasis is to protect data and authorize access is permitted only if the patient attributes meet the ABE construction.

Besides protecting data from unauthorized access, inferred knowledge is another challenge while dealing with the sensitive data. To protect inferred knowledge also known as additional slip away of information techniques like k-anonymization [13] and l-diversity [10] with their various variations are used. The purpose of all these techniques is to protect data either from unauthorized access or avoiding the additional leakage of information. In between these two concerns we have proposed a new methodology with least instrumentation to provide further selective access on authorized data.

3   Main Idea

The motivation behind proposed idea is to exploit optimal resources in cloud environment with flexible, controlled and trace-free recourse sharing. With optimal resources utilization we mean that for every request call, a constant operation will output the required result. The controlled resource sharing will ensure that a user does not learn anything for which it is not authorized. The proposed algorithm also gives no clue to infer any additional knowledge by an honest but curious cloud service provider from user request logs. The proposed methodology also protects the pattern discovery of network traffic if intercepted by an eavesdropper or malicious user. The same strength is also effective for inside intruders.

3.1   Notations and Assumptions

The notations used in proposed system is given in Table 1.

Table 1. Notations used in the descriptive detail of *Dual Locks*

Notation	Description
$D = \{f_1, f_2, .., f_n\}$	D is a data containing set of files
$f_i = s_1, s_2, s_3, ..., s_m$	Each file consist of m set of sections/attributes
$P(x, y)$	A polynomial P defined over roots x and y
$\Delta_{y_1...n}$	Each Δ uniquely identified a section $s_i \in f_i$
$\ell\{\gamma, \delta\}$	To unlock each section of $f \in D$, ℓ holds one and only one combination of γ and δ for a particular section s. Formal proof of this concept is given in next section
$ER_P(x)$	Evaluation result of a polynomial P with root x

3.2   Methodology

Sara is a security expert and looks after the automation process for the National Hospital. The encrypted Data D of hospital is outsourced to a public cloud owned by Eve. As a public cloud owner, Eve is considered as trusted but curious. With trust we mean that data storage and policy of sharing this data with authorized users is rightfully executed by Eve however for its curiosity Eve tries to learn beyond obvious and permitted information disclosure. Authorized users on this data holds a valid key to access the information. Recently medical discharge summaries have also been uploaded on the cloud. There is a range of user groups within the hospital that will be accessing the information on these documents. To avoid unnecessary disclosure of information it is required that an employee working in logistic department should only be able to view relevant information related to logistics. Similarly people working in research department has nothing to do with supply and demand issues. To achieve fine grained level of access either multiple keys per group are required to be generated or data has to be categorized in sub categories. To achieve it a dual lock mechanism is followed that fits into the infrastructure already running. The fist locking component is constructed using the unique identifier δ for each section s of a file with in D. This unique identifier is used to construct a polynomial $P(x, y)$ where x and y are two large random numbers such that $|x - y| = \delta$. The second locking component is constructed using the same mechanism and is handed over to authorized user which we call as γ. The value of γ is send with user request to Eve Cloud. Eve then calculates the composite polynomial using δ and γ. This composite polynomial is then evaluated on x and y pair that were used in constructing δ and γ. This operation will end up in $ER_p(r1)$, $ER_p(r2)$, $ER_p(r3)$ and $ER_p(r4)$. The Fig. 2 shows how these values are dealt with XOR and NOR logical gates. The output result of gate operation is then multiplied with the user public key and reply is encrypted with that key. In case of valid request the output will remain decipherable by the user secret key and in case of invalid request the output will not be recoverable.

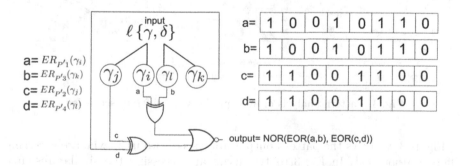

Fig. 2. Internal working of Dual Locks operations

3.3   Proof of Valid Roots for Composite Polynomial

In this section we will prove that a composite polynomial constructed with a finite set of roots satisfies the basic principle of proposed methodology. We well show that only complete and exact participation of roots can result in required output as manipulated with logical gates.

Let $\gamma_{1...n}$ be the set of valid roots. γ_i, γ_j, γ_k, γ_l have been used to construct two polynomials $P_1(\gamma_i, \gamma_j)$ and $P_2(\gamma_k, \gamma_l)$ such that $\gamma_i < \gamma_j < \gamma_k < \gamma_l$. Also $\gamma_j - \gamma_j = \gamma_l - \gamma_k = \Gamma$, where Γ is an integer value. These polynomials are then added together resulting in P'. This newly constructed polynomial P' is then evaluated as $ER_{P'1}(\gamma_i)$ $ER_{P'2}(\gamma_j)$, $ER_{P'3}(\gamma_k)$ and $ER_{P'4}(\gamma_l)$. The proposed methodology works only when Eq. 1 is satisfied.

$$ER_{P'1} = ER_{P'3}, ER_{P'2} = ER_{P'4} \tag{1}$$

Let us consider that there exist another root value $\gamma_x | \gamma_x \notin \{\gamma_i, \gamma_j, \gamma_k, \gamma_l\}$ for which equality of Eq. 1 still holds. But while constructing the P_1 and P_2, γ_x has not been used therefore if equality holds for Eq. 1, that means γ_x is used while constructing the polynomial and it is equal to at least one of $\{\gamma_i, \gamma_j, \gamma_k, \gamma_l\}$.

4   Evaluation and Results

The signature for Encrypted data varies either with different key or variant input plain text. In our experimental evaluation we have used it without using any encryption technique. The output pattern revealed by our proposed methodology is random and trace free even without encryption to find out the pre encryption resistance for pattern trace. After applying encryption on these inputs will generate different output with similar keys.

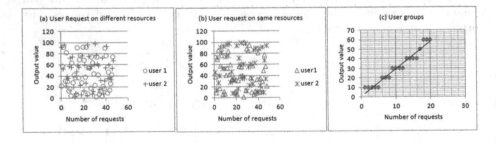

Fig. 3. Pattern analysis of user queries with different scenarios

Figure 3(a) shows the pattern output analysis of two users who are accessing different resources[1]. In Fig. 3(b) two users are accessing the similar resource again and again but both Fig. 3(a) and (b) are hard to distinguish. In Fig. 3(c)

---

[1] The results in Fig. 3 are normalized to lower scale as shown on y-axis whereas x-axis represents the number of user requests.

we showed the output patterns without using the mechanism of dual locks. In this figure, Fig. 3(c), if users are requesting the same resource they will end up in forming a cluster of similar queries.

5   Conclusion

In this paper we have proposed a framework that is used to narrow down user authorization for selective attributes only. The goal of proposed framework is two fold. First, It avoids using complex management of encryption keys and is usable in existing systems where encrypted access is required for selective authorization. Second, For every user request, irrespective from similar query or users from same groups, the output pattern always end up in random pattern. This random pattern helps to avoid additional leakage of information especially while availing services of public cloud.

Acknowledgment. This research was supported by the MSIP(Ministry of Science, ICT&Future Planning), Korea, under the ITRC(Information Technology Research Center) support program supervised by the NIPA(National IT Industry Promotion Agency) (NIPA-2014-(H0301-14-1003)).

References

1. Abdalla, M., Bellare, M., Catalano, D., Kiltz, E., Kohno, T., Lange, T., Malone-Lee, J., Neven, G., Paillier, P., Shi, H.: Searchable encryption revisited: consistency properties, relation to anonymous IBE, and extensions. In: Shoup, V. (ed.) CRYPTO 2005. LNCS, vol. 3621, pp. 205–222. Springer, Heidelberg (2005)
2. Chen, D., Zhao, H.: Data security and privacy protection issues in cloud computing. In: 2012 International Conference on Computer Science and Electronics Engineering (ICCSEE), vol. 1, pp. 647–651. IEEE (2012)
3. Chow, R., Golle, P., Jakobsson, M., Shi, E., Staddon, J., Masuoka, R., Molina, J.: Controlling data in the cloud: outsourcing computation without outsourcing control. In: Proceedings of the 2009 ACM Workshop on Cloud Computing Security, pp. 85–90. ACM (2009)
4. Curtmola, R., Garay, J., Kamara, S., Ostrovsky, R.: Searchable symmetric encryption: improved definitions and efficient constructions. In: Proceedings of the 13th ACM Conference on Computer and Communications Security, pp. 79–88. ACM (2006)
5. Goyal, V., Pandey, O., Sahai, A., Waters, B.: Attribute-based encryption for fine-grained access control of encrypted data. In: Proceedings of the 13th ACM Conference on Computer and Communications Security, pp. 89–98. ACM (2006)
6. Ibraimi, L., Asim, M., Petkovic, M.: Secure management of personal health records by applying attribute-based encryption. In: 2009 6th International Workshop on Wearable Micro and Nano Technologies for Personalized Health (pHealth), pp. 71–74. IEEE (2009)
7. Kamara, S., Lauter, K.: Cryptographic cloud storage. In: Sion, R., Curtmola, R., Dietrich, S., Kiayias, A., Miret, J.M., Sako, K., Sebé, F. (eds.) RLCPS, WECSR, and WLC 2010. LNCS, vol. 6054, pp. 136–149. Springer, Heidelberg (2010)

8. Li, M., Shucheng, Y.: Scalable and secure sharing of personal health records in cloud computing using attribute-based encryption. IEEE Trans. Parallel Distrib. Syst. **24**(1), 131–143 (2013)
9. Löhr, H., Sadeghi, A.-R., Winandy, M.: Securing the e-health cloud. In: Proceedings of the 1st ACM International Health Informatics Symposium, pp. 220–229. ACM (2010)
10. Machanavajjhala, A., Kifer, D., Gehrke, J., Venkitasubramaniam, M.: l-diversity: Privacy beyond k-anonymity. ACM Trans. Knowl. Discov. Data **1**(1), 3 (2007)
11. Pisani, E., AbouZahr, C.: Sharing health data: good intentions are not enough. Bull. World Health Organ. **88**(6), 462–466 (2010)
12. Steinbrook, R.: Personally controlled online health data-the next big thing in medical care? N. Engl. J. Med. **358**(16), 1653 (2008)
13. Sweeney, L.: k-anonymity: A model for protecting privacy. Int. J. Uncertainty Fuzziness Knowl. Based Syst. **10**(05), 557–570 (2002)

Biomedical Ontology Matching as a Service

Muhammad Bilal Amin[✉], Mahmood Ahmad, Wajahat Ali Khan,
and Sungyoung Lee

Department of Computer Engineering, Kyung Hee University, Seoul, South Korea
{mbilalamin,rayemahmood,wajahat.alikhan,sylee}@oslab.khu.ac.kr

Abstract. Ontology matching is among the core techniques used for integration and interoperability resolution between biomedical systems. However, due to the excess usage and ever-evolving nature of biomedical data, ontologies are becoming large-scale, and complex; consequently, requiring scalable computational environments with performance and availability in mind. In this paper, we present a cloud-based ontology matching system for biomedical ontologies that provides ontology matching as a service. Our proposed system implements parallelism at various levels to improve the overall ontology matching performance especially for large-scale biomedical ontologies and incorporates third-party resources UMLS and Wordnet for comprehensive matched results. Matched results are delivered to the service consumer as bridge ontology and preserved in ubiquitous ontology repository for future request. We evaluate our system by consuming the matching service in an interoperability engine of a clinical decision support system (CDSS), which generates mapping requests for FMA and NCI biomedical ontologies.

Keywords: Biomedical ontologies · Ontology matching · Cloud computing · Software as a service

1 Introduction

Over the recent years, semantic web technologies especially ontologies are contributing in biomedical systems for greater benefit. These ontologies are getting used for annotation of medical records [1], standardization of medical data formats [2], medical knowledge representation and sharing, clinical guidelines (CG) management [3], clinical data integration and medical decision making [4]. As a consequence of this vast usage, biomedical researchers are investing more time in generating more and comprehensive biomedical ontologies. Therefore, biomedical community has in depth ontology repository like Open Biomedical Ontologies (OBO) [9]; furthermore, biomedical ontologies like the Gene Ontology (GO) [5], the National Cancer Institute Thesaurus (NCI) [6], the Foundation Model of Anatomy (FMA) [7], and the Systemized Nomenclature of Medicine (SNOMED-CT) [8] have emerged.

Biomedical ontologies are complex in nature and contain overlapping information. Utilization of this information is necessary for the integration, aggregation, and interoperability; for example, the plethora of web-based medical

© Springer International Publishing Switzerland 2015
C. Bodine et al. (Eds.): ICOST 2014, LNCS 8456, pp. 195–203, 2015.
DOI: 10.1007/978-3-319-14424-5_21

information resources provides related information over the Internet. If these resources are annotated by ontologies, software agents can automatically aggregate information for biomedical professionals and biomedical querying systems. For example, NCI ontology defines the concept of "Myocardium" related to the concept "Cardiac Muscle Tissue", which describes the muscles surrounding the human heart. Concept "Cardiac Muscle Tissue" is defined in FMA ontology; therefore, a biomedical professional or a system integrating knowledge regarding human heart requires mappings between candidate ontologies FMA and NCI [10]. Likewise, GO is a highly organized structure of medical knowledge facilitating medical genetics. It is widely used by biomedical researchers in numerous genetical research fields including gene group-based analysis for discovering the hidden links overlooked by the single-gene analysis [11]. Finding mappings between GO ontology and FMA ontology can be used by molecular biologist in understanding the outcome of proteomics and genomics in a large-scale anatomic view [12]. Moreover, mappings by ontology matching have also been used for heterogeneity resolution among various health standards [13].

Ontology matching systems developed over the years have taken biomedical ontologies into consideration and have implemented possible resolutions. However, these resolutions are more focused on optimization of the matching algorithms and partitioning of larger ontologies into smaller chunks for performance benefits [14]. Incase of biomedical ontologies, matching algorithms utilizes third-party resources like Unified Medical Language System (UMLS) [15] and WordNet [16]. Slow and comprehensive nature of these resources adds onto the performance bottlenecks during matching. Ontology matching being a quadratic complexity problem with an addition of slow third-party resources can go to a certain extent in gaining performance by optimizing only the algorithms over localized computational resources. Furthermore, these ontology matching systems are tools with confined deployments, which can be utilized locally with very limited computational ability and scalability over time. Therefore, an opportunity emerges of building a biomedical ontology matching system that can improve or sustain the ontology matching performance. Such system should not only be confined as a localized deployment; it should be a shareable resource of ontology matching that is available for biomedical researchers and biomedical systems to benefit from. So far in ontology matching, the performance improvement based-on exploitation of newer hardware technologies has largely been missed. Among these technologies are affordable parallel systems which are easily available as distributed platforms [17]. One such platform is Cloud Computing.

This paper presents a biomedical ontology matching system that benefits from the cloud resources and provides biomedical ontology matching as a service to the consumer. Our proposed system avails the opportunity of multicore nature of cloud instances and performs parallel ontology loading and matching to improve overall ontology matching performance. Even with utilization of slow third-party resources, the performance fall is far less due to its parallel nature. Matched results are returned to the consumer as a bridge ontology and preserved in a centralized ontology repository for the same matching requests in future.

Due to the ubiquitous nature of the cloud, matching services are available for researchers and biomedical systems without downtime.

The rest of the paper is organized as follows. In Sect. 2 we describe the related work in the field of biomedical ontology matching. Section 3 provides the details of our proposed system. Section 4 describes a primilinary evaluation of our system performed by consuming the matching service in an interoperability engine of a Clinical Decision Support System (CDSS). Section 5 concludes this paper.

2   Related Work

Among the systems for biomedical ontology matching, SAMBO [18] is a pioneering system which provides a framework for aligning and merging ontologies. SAMBO's implementation is focused towards its matcher algorithms which integrates WordNet, UMLS, and PubMed [19] as third-party resources. Despite the fact that this integration is highly beneficial for accuracy, slow nature of these resources creates performance bottlenecks while matching. To overcome this bottleneck, SAMBO fails to provide any resolution.

Similar to SAMBO, ASMOV [20] with its computational performance directly associated with its matching algorithms, authors of [20] acknowledged that effort is required to improve the computational complexity of the system. With high coupling between ASMOV's performance and computational complexity of matching algorithms, and its sequential execution, it is unlikely for ASMOV to avail any performance benefits from parallel platforms.

ServOMap [21] is another biomedical ontology matching system, but built with the motivation of matching large-scale biomedical ontologies. Instead of using lexical resources like WordNet and UMLS, ServOMap relies on information retrieval and ontology repository technique. ServOMap does not implement any performance gain techniques that can exploit parallelism over available multicore platforms for the benefit of biomedical ontology matching.

In current state-of-the-art generic ontology matching systems, i.e., AgrMaker [22], LogMap [23], and GOMMA [24], performance has been given a considerable focus to complement accuracy of these systems. AgrMaker with its tightly integrated implementation between matching algorithms and the system's user interface, relies on user interactions and feedback. Performance of AgrMaker depends upon the iterative execution of matching algorithms as sample set for the following matching algorithms gets reduced. LogMap, is claimed as highly scalable from the perspective of ontology matching; however, this scalability is not of any parallel or distributed nature. After further research, it was found that one of the LogMap's associated research group has proposed a concurrent classification approach for reasoning over ontologies; nonetheless, its utilization for improving performance during ontology matching in LogMap is unclear. GOMMA on the other hand, implements parallelism with its techniques mentioned in [14,25]. In [25], authors acknowledge the fact that very little research has been performed in devising parallelism for matching problems; furthermore, it describes size-based partitioning scheme to perform parallel matching. Research presented in [25] discusses entity matching in general with no concentration or evaluation over ontologies. In [14] however, authors specifically discuss parallelism techniques pertaining to life science ontologies. They propose inter- and intra-matcher parallelism techniques, which uses parallel and distributed infrastructure for ontology matching to achieve better performance.

In contrast with above-mentioned techniques and systems, the focus of our proposed system is on facilitating the consumers with ontology matching as a service. Instead of localized implementation, it is deployed over cloud platform and scales according to the usage needs. To provide a performance efficient solution it implements parallelism at various levels. As the performance gain in our system is achieved by exploiting the parallelism from the multicore cloud instances, our system contributes largely to overcome performance bottlenecks encountered by using slow third-party biomedical resources and thesauri (e.g., UMLS, PubMed, and WordNet).

3 Methodology

Overall stack-like architecture of our proposed system is illustrated in Fig. 1. The primary objective of our system is to exploit the available resources of cloud platform and provide a service-based interaction to our system, taking the benefit of the ubiquitous nature of the cloud computing.

Request of matching biomedical ontologies can be generated from several resources including, biomedical professionals and researchers, biomedical and bioinformatics system, or even third-party healthcare information services running over cloud platforms. Match request encapsulates the ontologies to be matched as source and target ontologies. Matched results are returned to the consumer as "bridge ontology".

Starting from the top of the stack illustrated in Fig. 1, Consumer Interaction component provides an ontology matching RESTful web service for clients to consume. The matching service provides four trivial arguments as service bindings for consumption.

1. *match (sourceOntologyURI/File, targetOntologyURI/File)*
2. *match (sourceOntologyURI/File, targetOntologyURI/File, returnEmail)*
3. *match (sourceOntologyURI/File, targetOntologyURI/File, matchingAlgorithms [ ])*
4. *match (sourceOntologyURI/File, targetOntologyURI/File, matchingAlgorithms [ ], returnEmail)*

Among the arguments, collection of matching algorithms and return email are extended parameters used for matching request customization. In case of first request, all the algorithms present in the matching library will execute. This matching will take more time; however, will have higher accuracy. Incase of trivial and far less complicated ontologies, consumer can select the matching

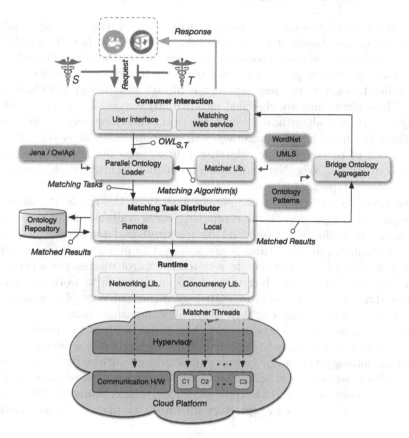

Fig. 1. Proposed architecture

algorithms to be executed as collection of matching algorithms (Request 3 and 4). For large-scale ontologies, where the evaluation time can exceed from 20 min or later, URL of the bridge ontology to-be is provided and can be returned over a particular email address (Request 2 and 4). After matching, the active URL will reference the bridge ontology.

Adjacent to the Web service, Consumer Interaction component encapsulates the matching web service in a user interface (UI). This UI provides a web-based direct interaction between a biomedical professional or a researcher who wants to benefit from matching service and our system.

Parallel Ontology Loading component benefits from the multicore nature of cloud instances and loads the source and target ontologies by thread-level parallelism. These ontologies are parsed in parallel and populated in multiple thread-safe ontology model objects. Each object encapsulates the information required by a single matching algorithm during runtime. Furthermore, redundancy like URI based names of concepts etc., is removed during this process. This keeps the system to load un-necessary and redundant information in main memory during execution, preventing memory strains at runtime. For ontology parsing, available OWL frameworks, Apache Jena and OWLApi are used. Although these frameworks provide comprehensive ontology models; due to these models not being thread-safe, our system provides its own ontology model implementation.

Matcher Library component provides a library of ontology matching algorithm. These algorithms are classified into primary, secondary, and complementary type. Primary algorithms execute for every matching request, secondary algorithms execute for higher accuracy, and complimentary algorithms execute with respect of ontology scope. Matcher Library also utilizes external third-party resources, i.e., WordNet and UMLS for higher accuracy in secondary and complementary type algorithms.

Matching Task Distributor component partitions the candidate ontologies as subsets and assigns over to the computing cores available. Several partitioning schemes including size-based and complexity-based partitioning are used. For local resources, matcher threads are assigned to perform parallel matching invoking available cores. For remote resources, control messages are generated for participating nodes regarding their chunk of partition to work and matching algorithm to execute. Each node after receiving the control message loads performs parallel matching over their available computing cores.

Every participating node(s) generates their respective matched results. Bridge ontology aggregator, accumulates these results and generate a bridge ontology file. Bridge ontology aggregator provides an interface to bridge ontology patterns to be used for pattern-based bridge ontology generation. Bridge ontology file is returned as a response or a URL to physical file to the consumer. This ontology is also be persisted in ontology repository for future use in case of same matching requests.

4   Evaluation

We have evaluated our system over a tri-node private cloud platform. Each Virtual Machine is equipped with 4 cores, 4 GB RAM, and Windows 7 based guest OS. These VMs are hosted over a Xen Hypervisor using Intel(R) Core(TM) i7 CPU, and 16 GB of memory as infrastructure.

For execution scenario, matching web service is consumed by an interoperability engine of a clinical decision support system (CDSS). Matching requests encapsulates small and whole versions of FMA and NCI biomedical ontologies for small and large matching requests respectively. All primary matching algorithms with quadratic or higher computational complexity were executed for this evaluation and the results are described in Table 1.

As it can be seen from results, a substantial amount of time is taken by ontology loading in contrast with matching which is a more complicated task. Although source and target ontologies are loaded and parsed in parallel, the time taken is due to the slow single-threaded nature of Jena. If Jena is replaced with a performance-based ontology parser, a substantial improvement in performance can be seen, especially in case of large matching requests.

Table 1. FMA with NCI evaluation

	Parameter	Small request	Large request
	Loading time	11.2 s	52.2 m
	Matching time	19.3 s	228 m
Total time		30.47 s	4.65 h
F-measure	Refined UMLS	0.857	0.710
	Original UMLS	0.863	0.715

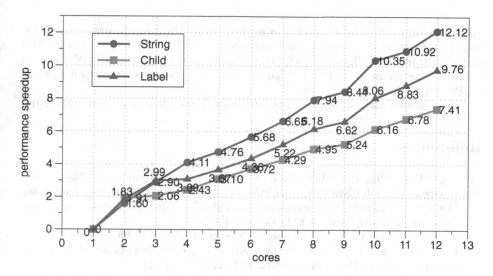

Fig. 2. Matching request scaling over cloud

To evaluate the scaling of the larger volume of matching tasks over cloud platform, the matching web service receives whole versions of FMA and NCI ontologies. The matching task distributor scales this large matching request from single-node sequential to tri-node parallel. Results are illustrated in Fig. 2. String-based, child-based and label-based matching algorithms are used from the matching library and after scaling it over all the available computing resource we observe a performance speedup of 12.12, 7.42, and 9.76 times respectively.

5   Conclusion

In this paper, we presented biomedical ontology matching system as a service that utilizes clouds computational resources and its ubiquitous nature for service availability. Our system provides a RESTful matching service for biomedical ontologies and provides comprehensive results by using UMLS and WordNet in the form of a bridge ontology. Matched results are preserved in a centralized repository for future use. Our system implements parallelism during ontology loading and matching over multicore cloud instances; consequently, improving the ontology matching performance. The ontology matching service is currently being used in our lab by various biomedical systems with ontology matching needs and have shown promising results. Our current system scales single matching request at a time over cloud platform; however, in future we plan on evaluating our platform with multiple matching requests constituting various sizes and requiring various matching algorithms. We plan on extending our work by implementing a performance based ontology parser and exploring several other methods of parallization to further improve the overall performance.

Acknowledgment. This research was supported by Microsoft Research Asia, Beijing, China, under the research grant provided as MSRA Project Award 2013–2014 and MSIP(Ministry of Science, ICT&Future Planning), Korea, under IT/SW Creative research program supervised by the NIPA(National IT Industry Promotion Agency) (NIPA-2013-(H0503-13-1010).

This research was also supported by Microsoft Azure4Research Award 2013–2014.

References

1. López-Fernández, H., Reboiro-Jato, M., Glez-Pea, D., Aparicio, F., Gachet, D., Buenaga, M., Fdez-Riverola, F.: BioAnnote: a software platform for annotating biomedical documents with application in medical learning environments. Comput. Methods Programs Biomed. **111**, 139–147 (2013)
2. Cimino, J., Zhu, X.: IMIA Yearbook of Medical 1, 124–135 (2006)
3. Isern, D., Snchez, D., Moreno, A.: Ontology-driven execution of clinical guidelines. Comput. Methods Programs Biomed. **107**, 122–139 (2012)
4. De Potter, P., Cools, H., Depraetere, K., Mels, G., Debevere, P., De Roo, J., Huszka, C., Colaert, D., Mannens, E., Van de Walle, R.: Semantic patient information aggregation and medicinal decision support. Comput. Methods Programs Biomed. **2**, 724–735 (2012)
5. Gene Ontology Consortium: The Gene Ontology (GO) database and informatics resource. Nucleic Acid Res. (Database issue) **32**, D258–D261 (2004)
6. Golbeck, J., Fragoso, G., Hartel, F., Hendler, J., Oberthaler, J., Parsia, B.: The National Cancer Institute's Thesaurus and ontology. Web Semant. Sci. Serv. Agents World Wide Web **1**, 75–80 (2003)
7. Rosse, C., Mejino, J.L.: A reference ontology for biomedical informatics. J. Biomed. Inform. **36**, 478–500 (2003)
8. Schulz, S., Cornet, R., Spackman, K.: Consolidating SNOMED CT's ontological commitment. Appl. Ontol. **1**, 1–11 (2011)
9. Smith, B., Ashburner, M., Rosse, C., Bard, J., Bug, W., Ceusters, W., Goldberg, L.J., Eilbeck, K., Ireland, A., Mungall, C.J., OBI Consortium, Leontis, N., Rocca-Serra, P., Ruttenberg, A., Sansone, S.A., Scheuermann, R.H., Shah, N., Whetzel P.L., Lewis, S.: The OBO Foundry: coordinated evolution of ontologies to support biomedical data integration. Nat. Biotech **25**, 1251–1255 (2007)
10. Jimnez-Ruiz, E., Meilicke, C., Cuenca Grau, B., Horrocks, I.: Evaluating mapping repair systems with large biomedical ontologies. In: 26th International Workshop on Description Logics. LNCS. Springer (2013)

11. Sun, X., Li, J.: pairheatmap: comparing expression profiles of gene groups in heatmaps. Comput. Methods Programs Biomed. **112**, 599–606 (2013)
12. Gennari, J.H., Silberfein, A.: Leveraging an alignment between two large ontologies: FMA and GO. In: Seventh International Protege Conference (2004)
13. Khan, W.A., Hussain, M., Afzal, M., Amin, M.B., Saleem, M.A., Lee, S.: Personalized-detailed clinical model for data interoperability among clinical standards. Telemed. e-Health **19**, 632–642 (2013)
14. Gross, A., Hartung, M., Kirsten, T., Rahm, E.: On matching large life science ontologies in parallel. In: Lambrix, P., Kemp, G. (eds.) DILS 2010. LNCS, vol. 6254, pp. 35–49. Springer, Heidelberg (2010)
15. Schuyler, P.L., Hole, W.T., Tuttle, M.S., Sherertz, D.D.: The UMLS Metathesaurus: representing different views of biomedical concepts. Bull. Med. Libr. Assoc. **81**, 217–222 (1993)
16. Princeton University, What is WordNet? (2013)
17. Shvaiko, P., Euzenat, J.: Ontology matching: state of the art and future challenges. IEEE Trans. Knowl. Data Eng. **25**, 158–176 (2013)
18. Lambrix, P., Tan, H.: SAMBO-A system for aligning and merging biomedical ontologies. Web Semant. **4**, 196–206 (2006)
19. National Center for Biotechnology Information, U.S. National Library of Medicine, PubMed (2013)
20. Jean-Mary, Y.R., Shironoshita, E.P., Kabuka, M.R.: Ontology matching with semantic verification. Web Semant. **7**, 235–251 (2009)
21. Ba, M., Diallo, G.: Large-scale biomedical ontology matching with ServOMap. IRBM **34**, 56–59 (2011)
22. Cruz, I.F., Antonelli, F.P., Stroe, C.: AgreementMaker: efficient matching for large real-world schemas and ontologies. Proc. VLDB Endow. **2**, 1586–1589 (2009)
23. Jiménez-Ruiz, E., Cuenca Grau, B.: LogMap: logic-based and scalable ontology matching. In: Aroyo, L., Welty, C., Alani, H., Taylor, J., Bernstein, A., Kagal, L., Noy, N., Blomqvist, E. (eds.) ISWC 2011, Part I. LNCS, vol. 7031, pp. 273–288. Springer, Heidelberg (2011)
24. Kirsten, T., Gross, A., Hartung, M., Rahm, E.: GOMMA: a component-based infrastructure for managing and analyzing life science ontologies and their evolution. J. Biomed. Semant. **2**, 6 (2011)
25. Kirsten, T., Kolb, L., Hartung, M., Gross, A., Köpcke, H., Rahm, E.: Data partitioning for parallel entity matching. In: 8th International Workshop on Quality in Databases (2010)

Short Contributions

Action Prediction in Smart Home Based on Reinforcement Learning

Marwa Hassan$^{(\boxtimes)}$ and Mirna Atieh$^{(\boxtimes)}$

Faculty of Economic Sciences and Business Administration,
Lebanese University, Hadat, Lebanon
{marwahassan, matieh}@ul.edu.lb

Abstract. This paper presents an "intelligent" environment that can be occupied by an elderly or handicapped person. It is characterized by its online learning and continuous adaptation based on a new algorithm called "Planning Q-learning Algorithm (PQLA)". The user can make feedback promptly which simulates an algorithm that reconfigures the existing plans. The software adaptation is run under middleware "WCOMP" based on the aspect of assembly concept to adapt to the environmental changes.

Keywords: Ambient computing · Intelligent environment · Online learning · Reinforcement learning · Software adaptation

1 Introduction

Ambient computing environments are enriched with devices that are present everywhere and minimized with a lot of computational capabilities. One of its main applications is ambient assisted living and smart homes [1] where the user expects many services that assist him in his daily living concerning health status, activities, and control home appliances [2].

In this work we present architecture of a smart home that adapts dynamically based on continuous learning process to the changes in the environment. It may be occupied by an elderly or handicapped person that can use an assistive platform. The system automates actions by predicting them according to continuous monitoring of the inhabitant behavior. To satisfy calmly the user intents we combine high level learning and reasoning with Low level adaptation to context changes. We monitor user's actions and context using planning system and machine learning to generate online plans. The plans are modeled based on Markov Decision Process (MDP). The main application is run over a context aware middleware (WCOMP) to adapt to environmental changes. In this contribution we focus on the interaction between the resident and the system. Unlike existing systems where plans are predefined and static, our planning system generates dynamic plans of user's activities and prompt feedbacks online. In the first section challenges of ambient computing with the categories of user interactions with the smart environment are described. In second section the approach is detailed. Section three presents the whole architecture with its modules. In section four the model of the plan and its parameters is shown. The PQLA is deliberated in section five and section six provides a conclusion.

© Springer International Publishing Switzerland 2015
C. Bodine et al. (Eds.): ICOST 2014, LNCS 8456, pp. 207–212, 2015.
DOI: 10.1007/978-3-319-14424-5_22

2 Problem Statement and Related Work

In ambient environments, for the services to be provided abstractly, two main challenges should be taken into consideration. First ambient assisted living system should provide user with abstract service that is adapted to the context and device changes. It should be heterogeneous, dynamic, and open [3]. Second the user should interact with the smart space to adapt to his needs. The ways of interaction can be categorized into three types: user configuration, predefined rules and system learning. In user configuration category inhabitants configure their own space by programming languages or through natural languages [4, 5]. In predefined rules category the designers may monitor users for a specific period of time [6], ask them about their preferences [7], or even depend on expert's knowledge. In this case user may be unable to express his needs exactly, or he may forget different details. Also humans change their behaviors by time in addition they may feel that they are obliged with system's decision. The above limitations motivate us to use the learning tools. For the environment to be more intelligent, the interaction with the system should be reduced [8]. Machine learning techniques could be offline where created patterns are fixed like in [9, 10] or online learning where patterns are dynamic and may change over time due to environment dynamicity and inhabitant's behavior changes. Few works targeted the online learning like in [11]; they detect the changes in the behavior of the inhabitants from the user himself or by a smart detection method. Our work differs by its online and continuous learning. The system learns the change of user's behavior by allowing him to make feedback actions directly on the devices manually.

3 Our Approach

Many works addressed the low level self-adaptation to context changes like [12] or the high level learning and reasoning to satisfy calmly the user intents. In this work we merge between those two levels by using:

A planning, reasoning and machine learning system to learn and predict user actions: planning and decision-making have been well studied in the AI community [13]. We present planning system based on MDP model coupled with q-learning. This system observes the user's actions in various situations, context and the environmental changes then constructs online plans of those actions. The learning system will learn when to execute automatically user needs in the future. The system accepts user rejection (feedback) of a taken decision that leads to a reconfiguration of an existing plan. The new configuration is taken into consideration in the next prediction.

Context adaptive middleware to reconfigure the running application: the application is run on a context adaptive middleware (WCOMP) [3] that satisfies the challenges mentioned above. The output of the plan execution is the input that simulates the adaptation of the running the software application.

4   Architecture of the System

Based on our previous architecture [14] we present the detailed architecture of an intelligent system (Fig. 1). The environment is equipped with set of devices, sensors actuators where the user acts. Three types of interactions with the environment can change the overall state: interaction from user, interaction from environment or inter-action from system. The ontology describes different devices in the smart space. The system retrieves information about devices from this ontology. The monitoring and classification module senses the incoming events and retrieves information about it and its device. It also infers the time zone of the incoming event. The inference module searches in the plan library for a plan corresponding to the incoming context.

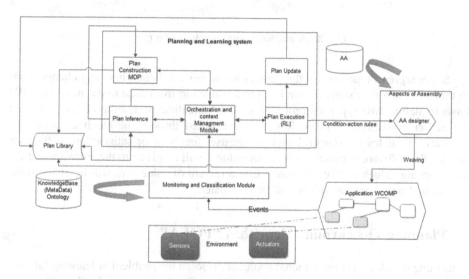

Fig. 1. The detailed architecture of the intelligent system

We consider the time and location of the event as the contextual information since they are the main labels that characterize user actions. Orchestration and context management module sends the incoming event and the received context information to the appropriate module. In the plan construction module the system creates the new plans. All the new incoming events are recorded in new plans and saved in plan library. In [15, 16] they define plan library as a set of plans or predefined steps. In this proposition plan library is constructed online through monitoring the user. The execute plan module executes inferred plan following the policy of a new algorithm based on Q-learning algorithm [17] called PQLA. It calculates the Q values based on the returned reward. The update plan module receives the needed information about feedback. It updates the existing plan, adds the new changes due to feedback, recon-figures the probabilities and saves the changes in the plan library.

5 Plan Model: Markov Decision Process

Plans are constructed based on Markov Decision Process (MDP's) model. Below we define each of the MDP parameters in our plans (Fig. 2):

Fig. 2. A graphical representation of a plan

States represent the state of the devices in the environment where any change leads to transition to a new state. Action leads to a transition from state to the next state. We have to define two types of probabilities the transition probability $P(S1/S, a)$ and the action probability $P(a/S)$. Reward is specified through online interaction; the software calculates the reward based on the user feedback or satisfaction. If the user accepts the software decision, a reward of value 1 will be given to the software and the new learning values will be calculated. Else a reward of value zero will be given to the system and new learning values will be calculated.

6 Planning Q-Learning Algorithm "PQLA"

Q learning develops a computational approach to solve the problem of learning through interaction [18]. It allows the machine to learn its behavior based on feedback from the environment. We define a new Q-learning algorithm based on the knowledge extracted from the generated plans "PQLA" used to make decisions to predict the future actions. In PQLA the agent doesn't learn only from the immediate rewards but it depends on the learnt knowledge from the generated plans. This knowledge is used to initialize two matrices in the algorithm the probability table and the policy table. The probability table contains the probabilities for each pair of state and action. The policy table contains the sum of the Q-values table and the probability table for each pair of state and action. This algorithm will choose the actions not randomly but according to the values in the policy table.

PQLA algorithm

1. Set the alpha and gamma parameters;
2. Rewards are not set before. Rewards are based on the users satisfaction;
3. Initialize Q matrix (based on previous experience);
4. Initialize Probability matrix (based on probabilities from the plans);

5. Calculate the Policy matrix (Add the Q matrix and the Probability matrices).
6. For each inferred plan

  Go from the environment state
    Do while the final node in the selected path hasn't reached yet.
    a. Select an action based on the Policy matrix;
    b. Wait to get the user reaction;
    • If satisfied the r=1; Calculate Q; State = next state and go to a;
    • Else r=0, Calculate Q; Check the reached state:
    • If has another next state in the plan; Go to a;
    • Else
      o If context condition satisfied; Record user's actions;
      o Else if; Break;
    End Do
  Go to update Plan
  End For

7 Software Adaptation Middleware

The main software application will be run on WCOMP middleware [3] where the adaptation to the environment changes is based on the aspect of assembly concept. Each executed action in the plan will produce an output of the condition-action form that will lead to a selection of a set of aspects of assembly "AAs". Those AAs (Fig. 3) are deployed in WCOMP and adaptation to changes will occur.

```
===Aspect: AA1=== (Abstraction)
Pointcut:
Device1 is a (Type: PIR, Location: Kitchen)
Device2 is a (Type: Light, Location: Kitchen)
----------------------------------------------
Advice:
Boolean a;
Device1.changestate(a)^->Device2.turn(a)
```

Fig. 3. AA example

8 Conclusion and Perspectives

We presented architecture for a smart environment that can be occupied by an elderly. We conciliate between a machine learning approach and context aware adaptation approach. At the high level a planning, reasoning and learning system is used to monitor user and predict the future actions. The user is always in the loop since he can do feedbacks to the system that reflects his satisfaction. At the low level layer the application is run under a context aware middleware WCOMP. This application is reconfigured based on the changes in the environment.

References

1. Augusto, J.C., Nugent, C.D. (eds.): Designing Smart Homes. LNCS (LNAI), vol. 4008. Springer, Heidelberg (2006)
2. Abowd, G., Mynatt, E.D.: Designing for human experience in smart environments. In: Cook, D.J., Das, S.K. (eds.) Smart Environments: Technology, Protocols and Applications, pp. 153–174. Willey, New York (2005)
3. Tigli, J.Y., Riveill, M., Rey, G., Lavirotte, S., Hourdin, V., Cheung-Foo-Woo, D., Callegari, E.: A middleware for ubiquitous computing: Wcomp. Research Report, Sophia Antipolis University – I3S Laboratory, Nice (2008)
4. Jara, A.J., Zamora, M.A., Skarmeta, A.F.: An architecture for ambient assisted living and health environments. In: Omatu, S., Rocha, M.P., Bravo, J., Fernández, F., Corchado, E., Bustillo, A., Corchado, J.M. (eds.) IWANN 2009, Part II. LNCS, vol. 5518, pp. 882–889. Springer, Heidelberg (2009)
5. Fontaine, E.: Programmation d'espace intelligent par l'utilisateur final. Ph.D. thesis, Brenoble University - Informatic Laboratory, France (2012)
6. Baldoni, R., Di Ciccio, C., Mecella, M., Patrizi, F., Querzoni, L., Santucci, G.: An embedded middleware platform for pervasive and immersive environments for-All. IEEE, Rome (2009)
7. Davis, G., Wiratunga, N., Taylor, B., Craw, S.: Matching SMARTHOUSE technology to needs of the elderly and disabled. In: ICCBR 03, Norway, pp. 29–36 (2004)
8. Dix, A., Finlay, J., Abowd, G., Beale, R.: Human–Computer Interaction, 3rd edn. Pearson/Prentice Hall, Harlow (2004)
9. Jakkula, V.R., Youngblood, G.M., Cook, D.J.: Identification of lifestyle behavior patterns with prediction of the happiness of an inhabitant in a smart home. AAAI, Boston (2006)
10. Sajal, K., Diane, J., Bhattacharya, A., Heierman, E., Tze-Yun, L.: The role of prediction algorithms in the MavHome smart home architecture. IEEE Wireless Commun. **9**(6), 77–84 (2002)
11. Rashidi, P., Cook, D.: An adaptive sensor mining model for pervasive computing applications. ACM, Cyprus (2004)
12. Wang, Q., Cheng, L.: AwareWare: an adaptation middleware for heterogeneous environments. In: IEEE International Conference on Communications, Paris (2004)
13. Russell, S., Norvig, J.: Artificial Intelligence: A Modern Approach. Prentice Hall, Upper Saddle River (2003)
14. Hassan, M., Mougharbel, I., Meskawi, N., Tigli, J.-Y., Riveill, M.: Design considerations for assistive platforms in ambient computing for disabled people - wheelchair in an ambient environment. In: Abdulrazak, B., Giroux, S., Bouchard, B., Pigot, H., Mokhtari, M. (eds.) ICOST 2011. LNCS, vol. 6719, pp. 246–250. Springer, Heidelberg (2011)
15. Snoeck, N., Kranenburg, H., Eertink, H.: Plan recognition in smart environments. In: IEEE ICDIM 07, Lyon, France (2007)
16. Boger, J., Hoey, J., Poupart, P., Boutilier, C., Fernie, G., Mihailidis, A.: A planning system based on Markov decision processes to guide people with dementia through activities of daily living. IEEE Inf. Technol. Biomed. **10**(2), 323–333 (2006)
17. Szepesvari, C.: Reinforcement Learning Algorithms for MDPs. Synthesis Lectures on Artificial Intelligence and Machine Learning. Morgan & Claypool, San Rafael (2009)
18. Sutton, R.S., Barto, A.G.: Reinforcement Learning: An Introduction Adaptive Computation and Machine Learning. MIT Press, Cambridge (1998)

A Mobile Survey Tool for Smoking Dependency Among Native Americans

Golam Mushih Tanimul Ahsan[1(✉)], Drew Williams[1], Ivor D. Addo[1],
S. Iqbal Ahamed[1], Daniel Petereit[2], Linda Burhansstipanov[3],
Linda U. Krebs[3], and Mark Dignan[4]

[1] Marquette University, Milwaukee, WI, USA
{golammushihtanimul.ahsan,drew.williams,ivor.addo,
sheikh.ahamed}@marquette.edu
[2] Rapid City Regional Hospital, Rapid City, SD, USA
dpetereit@regionalhealth.com
[3] Native American Cancer Initiatives, Pine, USA
lindab@natamcancer.net, linda.krebs@ucdenver.edu
[4] University of Kentucky, Lexington, USA
mbdign2@uky.edu

Abstract. Smoking and tobacco related cancers are very common among Native Americans. Gathering information during different phases of smoking cessation can help us understand different factors that may work during smoking cessation. In this paper, we will present a survey system designed to collect data for several phases of smoking cessation. We designed and developed a survey system that helps researchers to collect data from people who are going through different phases of smoking cessation. We evaluate this system from the experiences of end users and by generating reports.

Keywords: Smoking cessation · Phase based model · Behavioral studies · mHealth

1 Introduction

Smoking is one of the leading causes of cancer. According to the US Center for Disease Control and Prevention (CDC) [1], smoking is responsible for more deaths than the aggregate of drug abuse, suicide, motor accidents, murder, and AIDS. A lot of people die each year from first hand and second hand smoking. The toll of death from smoking related illness is very high.

A person goes through several phases during stopping to smoke. To understand the different factors for motivation, we need to create extensive surveys to question those who are in the act of stopping smoking. From a well-organized survey, we are able to collect enough data that will show us patterns in behavior, which will eventually lead us to the main objective, to understand the behavior of someone who hopes to stop smoking, and how to make smoking cessation programs more effective. Smoking is a leading cause of death in US that is preventable [2]. It has a higher percentage of occurrences among Native Americans than any other ethnicities in US. The system we

© Springer International Publishing Switzerland 2015
C. Bodine et al. (Eds.): ICOST 2014, LNCS 8456, pp. 213–218, 2015.
DOI: 10.1007/978-3-319-14424-5_23

developed is used to study smoking dependence in the Native American population in the Northern Plains of South Dakota.

2 Motivation

There are several scenarios currently plaguing researchers that we are hoping to address in the creation of this survey software. They are as follows:

Scenario 1: A researcher wants to create a survey questionnaire for a controlled group. She/he wants the questionnaire to be available only to a particular group of participants.

Scenario 2: A researcher wants to have some trained personnel to help participants to take the survey. The participants may live in remote places. The trained personnel should be able to carry around the device that is used for the survey. The personnel want to submit survey responses remotely.

Scenario 3: A researcher wants to check progress of a participant under the study via reports, graphs etc. She/he needs an interface for generating these reports.

To address these problems, we are presenting our survey application system. Using this system, a researcher can create a questionnaire for the control group via website. The trained personnel can collect user data in their iPad using the survey application.

3 Required Features

We've identified several characteristics and functionalities that may better a survey application system like our own. They are as follows:

3.1 Modularity

The survey system should be such that it can be divided into several independent components that can communicate between themselves. The necessity of independent components is to ensure the rest of the system is running, even if a part of it is not working. For example, even if the question generation component is not working at this moment, the system should not stop users to get the existing surveys and submit a response.

3.2 Questionnaire Generation

A survey has a set of questions. The set of questions can be divided into several sections. An interface is required for this questionnaire generation. This interface should only be accessed by the administrator/researcher and should be simple enough for a person to generate surveys with many sections and many questions.

3.3   Parsing

If we want to design a dynamic survey application system, we must ensure that the questionnaire can change over time. So, it is not feasible to store survey questionnaire in local devices. There are transfers of questionnaire that may vary from user to user over time. That is why; the application should be able to parse complicated data types such as our survey with several sections, each section containing several questions of different types and possibly having single or multiple responses. To accommodate all these, it's easy to see that an elaborate parser is needed at the client application end.

3.4   Dynamic Application

As we understand from the previous discussion, the user end application should be very dynamic. It should be able to render different questionnaires. The application should show different types of questions with their responses correctly. The application should be able to change itself depending on the participants and their status.

3.5   Control of Data

The most important part of a survey system is the survey response data. The control over data is twofold. Firstly, the data should be stored in such a way that the anonymity of the participants are ensured. On the other hand, the response data should be available to the researchers for further analysis. This data will be used to generate different reports. It should also be available to the researchers in supportive format.

4   Related Work

Raw et al. [3] proposed some healthcare recommendations and guidelines for restricting smoking dependence. Baker et al. [4] presented a phase-based framework for smoking cessation that described these phases: motivation, pre-cessation, cessation and maintenance. Ajzen [5] proposed the Theory of Planned Behavior (TPB) with a mathematical model. This theory tries to find the relationship between a person's behavior and attitudes and the factors that are related to these. Norman et al. [6] used TPB to predict the intention and attempts to quit with behavioral intentions correctly.

This survey solution is a part of a study of smoking cessation among Native Americans. The survey tool ensures detailed data capture from the different phases of the smoking cessation. The questionnaires include questions regarding Theory of Planned Behavior. So, our solution will help understanding the behavior of a participant who is going through the process of smoking cessation.

5   Our Approach

To solve the problem of creating a dynamic, modular survey system, we've developed the survey system explored here. The system consists several components, and ensures correct flow of survey questionnaire generation, performing survey and report generation. Here we will discuss the functionalities and the architecture of our system, and how we developed and deployed the system (Fig. 1).

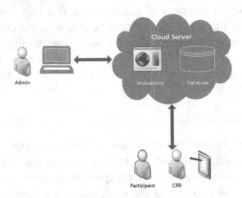

Fig. 1. Data flow diagram

5.1   Functionalities

In our system, the admin can create survey questions from the website, where there is an interface for creating these surveys. A survey, as mentioned, can have several sections each having several questions. The question types can be single answer, multiple choice or simple text. Only the admin has the privilege to add questions in surveys.

In our system, the survey is performed by an iPad application. End users (data collectors) use this application to collect data from the participants in the survey. The application communicates with the server and collects the questionnaire depending on the phase the participant is in. The application stores the information collected from participant and saves it in the server.

5.2   Architecture

In the server component, the database lies in the bottom. It can be accessed only by the web services on top of it. The server has one layer that has several web services. This web services are used to communicate with the database. The web client is hosted in the cloud server and from it an admin can add survey questionnaires, generate survey reports and monitor improvements among participants. The iPad application communicates with the web services to collect questionnaire and submit survey responses. All the clients use SOAP to communicate with the web services.

5.3   Development and Deployment

The web interface was developed using C#, ASP.NET, HTML5 and CSS technologies. The web service interface was designed in C#. For the database structure, a relational database management system (RDBMS) was used (MS SQL Server 2012) was used. A Windows Azure cloud server hosted the database, the web services and the website. The survey application was developed for iOS platform, and iPad devices were used to run the application in testing and production.

6 Evaluation

6.1 Modularity

The system we designed has some basic components. There is a website for generating different survey questionnaires and reports. The iPad application is in the client end and helps in allowing a medical professional administer the survey and submit the responses. Other components are the web service interface and the database. These independent components communicate among themselves.

6.2 Questionnaire Generation

By using the website, the researcher (working as an admin) can create survey questionnaires. Any number of surveys can be created each having several sections and many questions. The question creation page is very intuitive and easy to use. The survey questionnaires can be modified, updated and deleted from this interface.

6.3 Parsing

The survey application in the iPad can communicate with the database by using web services. It can ask for a specific survey according to the participant and their status. After getting the set of questions, the application parses this into a data type for its understanding so that it can be shown later to the user correctly. We have an elaborate parser that helps us to parse complex XML files consisting of the questionnaire (Fig. 2).

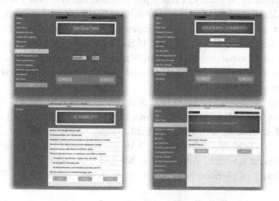

Fig. 2. Dynamic pages of the application

6.4   Dynamic Application

The application we developed was very dynamic. In the Smoking Cessation project, there are 16 groups and each person has to go through 11 visits of surveys. Our application can fetch the questionnaire for that survey and change itself accordingly. Dynamic pages help the applications to work for a variety of types of questions.

6.5   Control of Data

In our system we used a HIPAA compliant server. We ensured in our system that the participants' identity and anonymity are protected. As we set up our own database, it is much easier for us to generate the reports and show them in the website. Even if there is a new change in the database, the change can be implemented in the client sides as well. The updates of the application are usually very swift.

7   Conclusion

Smoking related health hazards are life threatening and it is important that a proper study is conducted to understand the status of people who are going through smoking cessation and also what are the motivating factors. For all these, we need a survey tool that helps us in generating questions, conducting surveys, and generating reports. In this paper we described our solution and showed how it is making the survey more effective, which will lead to an efficient study of the smoking cessation problem.

Acknowledgments. The application was developed for a project funded by NIH that studies the smoking dependence in Native Americans in the Northern Plains.

References

1. CDC, Tobacco-Related Mortality, Center for Disease Control and Prevention. http://www.cdc.gov/tobacco/data_statistics/fact_sheets/health_effects/tobacco_related_mortality/
2. U.S. Department of Health and Human Services: The Health Consequences of Smoking: A Report of the Surgeon General, Atlanta: U.S. Department of Health and Human Services, Centers for Disease Control and Prevention, National Center for Chronic Disease Prevention and Health Promotion, Office on Smoking and Health (2004). http://www.cdc.gov/tobacco/data_statistics/sgr/sgr_2004/index.htm
3. Raw, M., McNeill, A., West, R.: Smoking cessation: evidence based recommendations for the healthcare system. BMJ (British Medical Journal) 318, 182–185 (1999)
4. Baker, T.B., Mermelstein, R., Collins, L.M., Piper, M.E., Jorenby, D.E., Smith, S.S., Christiansen, B.A., Schlam, T.R., Cook, J.W., Fiore, M.C.: New methods for tobacco dependence treatment research. Ann. Behav. Med. 41, 192–207 (2011)
5. Ajzen, I.: The theory of planned behavior. Organ. Behav. Hum. Decis. Process. 50(2), 179–211 (1991)
6. Norman, P., Conner, M., Bell, R.: The theory of planned behavior and smoking cessation. Health Psychol. 18(1), 89–94 (1999)

Smart Built Environments and Independent Living: A Public Health Perspective

Blaine Reeder[1](✉), George Demiris[2], and Hilaire J. Thompson[2]

[1] University of Colorado Anschutz Medical Campus, Aurora, CO, USA
blaine.reeder@ucdenver.edu
[2] University of Washington, Seattle, WA, USA
{gdemiris,hilairet}@uw.edu

Abstract. To address the projected global shortfall of gerontological health care workers, we outline a research approach that is informed by the past successes of public health toward the goal of developing and implementing smart homes at the community-level to support independent living. Specifically, we discuss the epidemiologic triad consisting of host, environment, and agent factors in relation to other person-environment fit models. We propose this model as the underlying framework for a smart homes development approach that focuses on creating task advantages to support independence at home. We provide recommendations to implement the approach by including community-level stakeholders and policy makers in research that uses a model well-recognized by public health professionals.

Keywords: Smart homes · Public health · Independent aging · Older adults

1 Introduction

The number of adults over 65 in the United States will almost double between 2005 and 2030 [1]. This growth in the population of older adults will result in a projected shortage of workers in the gerontological health care workforce [2]. The projected shortage of gerontological health care workers and the continuous rise in health care costs make finding ways to improve efficiency and reduce the cost of care a priority for informal caregivers, health care providers and policy makers. Rice and Fineman note the challenge of supporting functional independence at home through a variety of in-home services due to the growing numbers of chronically ill and disabled elderly [3]. Identified ways to meet the future demand for gerontological care services include focusing on the development of new technologies [4], integrating successful models of chronic care delivery for older adults [5] and making changes to public policy for care of aging populations [6]. Given the challenges of many health care systems, including uncertain economics and workforce issues, innovative solutions are needed to help maintain independence and improve quality of life for community-dwelling older adults.

E-health and smart home technologies integrated into the built environment have the potential to support independent living. E-health is the use of information systems, telecommunications and mobile technologies to support healthcare delivery and

© Springer International Publishing Switzerland 2015
C. Bodine et al. (Eds.): ICOST 2014, LNCS 8456, pp. 219–224, 2015.
DOI: 10.1007/978-3-319-14424-5_24

education [7]. Smart home technologies refer to residential settings equipped with infrastructure to enable passive monitoring of residents' well-being and support proactive responses to residents' needs and safety, promoting independence [8]. These technologies include sensors in smart homes [9], mobile phone applications [10], and wearable and non-wearable fall detection devices [11]. Smart home studies have demonstrated evidence that home automation [12] and lifestyle monitoring technologies [13] can support independence in older adults. With regard to cognitive function, research using in-line arrays of motion sensors suggests that monitoring gait speed and its variability in the home may allow for detection of changes in cognitive status [14]. Research using body-worn global positioning system (GPS) technology has shown differences in performance of cognitively-demanding tasks between cognitively health participants and those with dementia [15]. Other recent research has shown that a room-to-room location sensing technology can track occupancy of participants aging with disability with accuracy ranging from 62 % to 87 % [16].

Smart home systems may support independent living at population levels if systematically deployed across communities. However, small feasibility studies have been the primary focus of smart home technology research to date [17] and have not addressed scalability of smart home technologies at the macro level in the context of population-based planning for independent living. Expanding the focus of current smart home research activities to address their public health implications is essential since most advances in population health in the past century have been due largely to public health efforts [18]. In this paper, we propose consideration of smart home technologies in relation to the epidemiologic triad model from public health to aid development and implementation of community-level technology-enhanced programs to support independent living.

2 Conceptualizing Independence

One way to conceptualize independence is as a function of interactions between personal capacity and environmental resources in relation to a threshold of independence. When the results of interactions between capacity and resources fall below this threshold, the ability of a person to live independently is compromised. Those persons who function at a level just above the threshold of independence are considered vulnerable to disability and loss of independence. Efforts to help vulnerable persons maintain independence should target person-environment *interactions* in cognitive, physical and social areas that improve opportunities to live independently. In addition, those below the threshold are targets for support to move them up to independence.

3 Epidemiologic Triad and Smart Home Technologies

The epidemiologic triad is an ecological model that comprises relationships between host, agent and environment that result in a state of relative health and wellness [19]. Traditionally, this model has been used to determine causes of communicable diseases and inform interventions to interrupt disease transmission. In modern times, the epidemiologic triad has been applied to improve population health outcomes for other conditions such as injuries [20] and obesity [21]. In particular, improvement in public health through reduction in motor-vehicle-related injuries and deaths is considered to be one of the ten great public health achievements of the 20th century [18]. Specifically, the death rate from motor vehicle injuries in the United States decreased by 90 % from the year 1925 to the year 1997 and this decline is attributed to systematic prevention efforts using a strategy based on the epidemiologic triad [22]. We believe that a similar strategy that relies on smart home and e-health technologies can be used to improve population health outcomes by maximizing independence and minimizing disability in an aging population.

In our smart homes version of the epidemiologic triad, the host is a person and his or her capacity to perform tasks where *task* is defined as specific work done to achieve a goal [23]. The environment is characterized by *affordances* that are defined as environmental properties that allow performance of actions [24]. The agent is defined as person-environment interactions that determine whether tasks are successfully performed. Smart home technologies aim to enhance personal capacities and improve environmental affordances to ultimately create *task advantages* that reduce barriers to performance of tasks required for independent living. Specifically, a task advantage is the relative ease with which a technology-supported task is performed as compared to performance of the same task without support. This concept is consistent with the fundamental theorem of biomedical informatics that states that a person supported by an informatics resource is "better" than that same person unassisted [25]. Figure 1 illustrates the relationship between person, affordances, interactions and smart home technologies in the smart homes version of the epidemiologic triad.

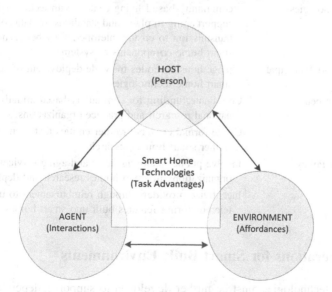

Fig. 1. The epidemiologic triad illustrating *host* as a *person* with capacity to perform tasks, *environment* as characterized by *affordances*, *agent* as person-environment *interactions*, and *smart home technologies* that create *task advantages* for independent living.

Other ecological models of health are congruent with this version of the epidemiologic triad and define elements that match its definitions. Corresponding to task, the
person-environment-occupation model from occupational therapy research defines
"occupation" as "self-directed, functional tasks and activities in which a person
engages over the lifespan" [26]. Corresponding to capacity, the competence/press
model from gerontology research defines "competence" as individual levels of
"physical or mental health, intellectual capacity or ego strength" [27]. Corresponding to
interactions, Iwarsson and Stahl define "accessibility" as "the encounter between the
person's or group's functional capacity and the design and demands of the physical
environment" [28]. However, personal capacity in the smart homes epidemiologic triad
goes beyond simple physical function given diverse notions of independence that are
informed by psychosocial factors [29].

Table 1. Critical factors and recommendations for smart built environments.

Factor	Recommendation
Community-Based Participatory Research and Participatory Design	Support shared decision-making pertaining to design and implementation among stakeholders that include older adults, family members, community planners and local, state and national policy makers
Model Development and Testing	Define and refine interactions between people, the aging process and smart home environments to enhance innovation, development, implementation and adoption of new smart home technologies
Standardization of Smart Home Technologies	Develop standards for the successful retrofit of homes and community-based living centers with technologies to support aging in place, and standards for data collection and transmission to ensure interoperability between different smart home components or systems
Community and Municipal Planning	Change housing codes for wide deployment of standardized smart home technologies
Fiscal Commitment	Coordinate funding for community-based initiatives by national research and practice organizations
	Create formal centers or other entities that focus on and further smart homes research
Public Health Policy Change	Involve public health agencies and aging services organizations in smart homes research and deployment
	Incentivize providers through reimbursement to use telemonitoring features built into smart homes

4   Considerations for Smart Built Environments

Smart home technologies must be further developed to support independent living in
built environments. Table 1 shows a list of critical factors and recommendations at
fundamental and community levels to achieve successful development and diffusion of
smart home systems. The technologies that are appropriate for specific groups to

improve health outcomes are still unknown. In addition, new technology applications are often not adopted due to a variety of barriers or concerns pertaining to usability, reliability and cost and these issues must be resolved. Future research activities should involve older adults, family members and health care providers to promote translation of technologies that support integrated approaches to independent living.

5   Conclusion

Smart home and e-health research conducted in conjunction with community planning has the potential to support independent living, reduce costs of care, improve health outcomes and equalize health inequities between demographic groups for aging populations at local and national levels. We believe these goals can be reached through widespread adoption of smart home technologies to create a built environment that allows a greater number of people to live independently. Toward this end, we outlined recommendations for smart home designers to engage public health policy makers and community planners in the research process by considering long-term community planning and modification of building codes to accept standardized smart home technologies in the built environment. In order to support a public health perspective, smart home design engagement should include the scientific approaches of epidemiology, environmental health, health behavior research and other public health research.

References

1. Institute of Medicine: Retooling for an aging America: building the health care workforce. Institute of Medicine (2008)
2. Cohen, S.A.: A review of demographic and infrastructural factors and potential solutions to the physician and nursing shortage predicted to impact the growing US elderly population. J. Publ. Health Manage. Pract. **15**, 352–362 (2009)
3. Rice, D.P., Fineman, N.: Economic implications of increased longevity in the United States. Annu. Rev. Publ. Health **25**, 457–473 (2004)
4. Koch, S., Hägglund, M.: Health informatics and the delivery of care to older people. Maturitas **63**, 195–199 (2009)
5. Boult, C., Green, A.F., Boult, L.B., Pacala, J.T., Snyder, C., Leff, B.: Successful models of comprehensive care for older adults with chronic conditions: evidence for the institute of medicine's "Retooling for an Aging America" report. J. Am. Geriatr. Soc. **57**, 2328–2337 (2009)
6. Houde, S.C., Melillo, K.D.: Public policy – caring for an aging population: review of policy initiatives. J. Gerontological Nurs. **138**, 8 (2009)
7. Eysenbach, G.: What is e-health? J. Med. Internet Res. **3**, e20 (2001)
8. Demiris, G., Hensel, B.K.: Technologies for an aging society: a systematic review of "smart home" applications. Yearb. Med. Inf. **47**(Suppl 1), 33–40 (2008)
9. Reeder, B., Meyer, E., Lazar, A., Chaudhuri, S., Thompson, H.J., Demiris, G.: Framing the evidence for health smart homes and home-based consumer health technologies as a public health intervention for independent aging: a systematic review. Int. J. Med. Inf. **82**, 565–579 (2013)

10. Joe, J., Demiris, G.: Older adults and mobile phones for health: a review. J. Biomed. Inf. **46**, 947–954 (2013)
11. Chaudhuri, S., Thompson, H., Demiris, G.: Fall detection devices and their use with older adults: a systematic review. J. Geriatr. Phys. Ther. **37**(4), 178–196 (2013)
12. Tomita, M.R., Mann, W.C., Stanton, K., Tomita, A.D., Sundar, V.: Use of currently available smart home technology by frail elders: process and outcomes. Top. Geriatr. Rehabil. **23**, 24 (2007)
13. Brownsell, S., Blackburn, S., Hawley, M.S.: An evaluation of second and third generation telecare services in older people's housing. J. Telemed. Telecare **14**, 8–12 (2008)
14. Dodge, H.H., Mattek, N.C., Austin, D., Hayes, T.L., Kaye, J.A.: In-home walking speeds and variability trajectories associated with mild cognitive impairment. Neurology **78**, 1946–1952 (2012)
15. Wettstein, M., Wahl, H.-W., Shoval, N., Oswald, F., Voss, E., Seidl, U., Frölich, L., Auslander, G., Heinik, J., Landau, R.: Out-of-home behavior and cognitive impairment in older adults: findings of the SenTra project. J. Appl. Gerontol. **68**(5), 691–702 (2012)
16. Chen, K.-Y., Harniss, M., Patel, S., Johnson, K.: Implementing technology-based embedded assessment in the home and community life of individuals aging with disabilities: a participatory research and development study. Disabil. Rehabil. Assistive Technol. **9**, 112–120 (2014)
17. Reeder, B., Chung, J., Lazar, A., Joe, J., Demiris, G., Thompson, H.J.: Testing a theory-based mobility monitoring protocol using in-home sensors: a feasibility study. Res. Gerontol. Nurs. **6**, 253–263 (2013)
18. Ten great public health achievements–United States, 1900–1999. MMWR Morb Mortal Wkly Rep. 48, 241–243 (1999)
19. Clark, M.J.: Community Health Nursing: Advocacy For Population Health. Prentice Hall, Pennsylvania (2007)
20. Haddon, W., Jr.: Advances in the epidemiology of injuries as a basis for public policy. Publ. Health Rep. (Washington, D.C. 1974), **95**, 411–421 (1980)
21. Egger, G., Swinburn, B., Rossner, S.: Dusting off the epidemiological triad: could it work with obesity? Obes. Rev. **4**, 115–119 (2003)
22. Motor-vehicle safety: a 20th century public health achievement. MMWR Morb Mortal Wkly Rep. 48, 369–374 (1999)
23. Whittaker, S., Terveen, L., Nardi, B.A.: Let's stop pushing the envelope and start addressing it: a reference task agenda for HCI. Hum. Comput. Interact. **15**, 75–106 (2000)
24. McGrenere, J., Ho, W.: Affordances: clarifying and evolving a concept. In: Graphics Interface, vol. 2000, pp. 179–186. Graphics Interface, Montreal (2000)
25. Friedman, C.P.: A "Fundamental Theorem" of biomedical informatics. J. Am. Med. Inform. Assoc. **16**, 169 (2009)
26. Law, M.: The person-environment-occupation model: a transactive approach to occupational performance. Can. J. Occup. Ther. **63**, 9–23 (1996)
27. Lawton, M.P.: An ecological theory of aging applied to elderly housing. J. Aging Environ. **31**, 8–10 (1977)
28. Iwarsson, S., Stahl, A.: Accessibility, usability and universal design–positioning and definition of concepts describing person-environment relationships. Disabil. Rehabil. **25**, 57 (2003)
29. Demiris, G.: Independence and shared decision making: the role of smart home technology in empowering older adults. In: 2009 Annual International Conference of the IEEE, Engineering in Medicine and Biology Society, EMBC 2009, pp. 6432–6436 (2009)

iCanLearn: A Mobile Application for Creating Flashcards and Social Stories™ for Children with Autism

Aaron Zaffke[1], Niharika Jain[1(✉)], Norah Johnson[2],
Mohammad Arif Ul Alam[1], Marta Magiera[1],
and Sheikh Iqbal Ahamed[1]

[1] Department of MSCS, Marquette University, Milwaukee, WI, USA
{Aaron.Zaffke,Niharika.Jain,Mohammadariful.Alam,
Marta.Magiera,Sheikh.Ahamed}@marquette.edu
[2] College of Nursing, Marquette University, Milwaukee, WI, USA
Norah.Johnson@marquette.edu

Abstract. This paper describes the design, implementation, and evaluation of iCanLearn, a mobile flashcard application (app) that can also be used for creating social stories for children with Autism Spectrum Disorders (ASDs). The app allows users to create personalized content using text, pictures and audio on their mobile devices (smartphones and tablets). Users of this application software can also share the content by connecting their devices over Wi-Fi. An evaluation of the app from both the perspective of children with ASD and their caregivers suggests that the app is easy to use.

Keywords: Computer-mediated communication · User-centered design · Design methods · Mobile application · Assistive technology

1 Introduction

The prevalence of autism spectrum disorders (ASDs) has increased to an estimated 1.47 % of the US population [1], presenting new teaching and learning challenges for parents, teachers and the children with ASD. An additional challenge is the great variability in the level of functioning of children with ASD, who present with a range of mild to severe communication, social interaction and behavioral problems [2]. However, mobile computing is a flexible and popular medium for teaching children with ASD [3] and therefore holds promise for the development of innovative interventions that are adaptable for variable treatments and interventions.

It is believed that with effective treatment and intervention, many children with ASD will improve their level of functioning and subsequently their quality of life. One technique that is effective for teaching children with ASD is breaking down an activity into steps, and replacing words with pictures [3]. Another technique, called Social Stories™ [4], uses a series of pictures with words representing the steps of a routine (e.g. getting a hair cut) along with scripting of expectations for the child (e.g. "I might

© Springer International Publishing Switzerland 2015
C. Bodine et al. (Eds.): ICOST 2014, LNCS 8456, pp. 225–230, 2015.
DOI: 10.1007/978-3-319-14424-5_25

have to wait"). Literature shows that the stories help to improve the child with ASD's understanding of social expectations [5].

iCanLearn, a mobile flashcard application allows the creation and review of individualized learning content adaptable to the child's level of functioning. The content helps children learn skills related to activities of daily living. The iCanLearn app allows the user to connect multiple devices together in a teacher-learner relationship. We evaluated the app for ease of use, which is recommended for assistive technology [6] and report on the findings of the evaluation in this paper.

2 Related Work

With the advancement in mobile technologies, mobile devices provide a flexible way of learning where the content, timing, and location of a learning schedule can be arranged according to user's preference [7]. A mobile device is usually equipped with camera, microphone, and speaker, which can aid in the content design of educational software and is very helpful while working with children with ASD [8].

Flashcards are widely used as an instruction medium for teaching specific skills for example, reading, spelling, and phonetics. Moreover, flashcards have been shown to be an effective method for teaching children with learning disabilities, such as ASD [9]. The flashcard-based system and mobile technology can be combined, in order to get the maximum benefits of these two learning means.

Many ABA flashcard apps [10] are available, however, the software usually lacks one or more useful feature and none of them allows real-time data sharing through remote control. Table 1 compares features of mobile software we reviewed.

Table 1. Comparison of Features in Mobile Software.

Mobile Software	Custom Content	Control Remotely	Audio	Pictures
Where's my Water?	✗	✗	✓	✓
Shape Builder	✗	✗	✓	✓
iWriteWords	✗	✗	✓	✓
Little Speller Site Words	✗	✗	✓	✓
Rocket Speller	✗	✗	✓	✓
Emotions	✓	✗	✓	✓
Actions	✗	✗	✓	✓
Social Stories	✓	✗	✗	✓
iCanLearn	✓	✓	✓	✓

3   iCanLearn – A Mobile Application

iCanLearn is a flashcard educational app that allows users to create their own flash cards with text, pictures, and audio. The uniqueness of iCanLearn lies in the ability to connect multiple devices in a teacher-learner relationship over a Wi-Fi network.

3.1   Features and Design

The features and challenges in the process of development of the app are described below.

Appearance and Text. The design theme for iCanLearn is simple and uncluttered. A sentence case with sans serif font was selected for ease of reading.

Navigation. Navigating the transition from screen to screen is accomplished by a visual flip with 3-D animation. The storyboard feature of Xcode was helpful in laying out the screens and managing transitions between them (see Fig. 1).

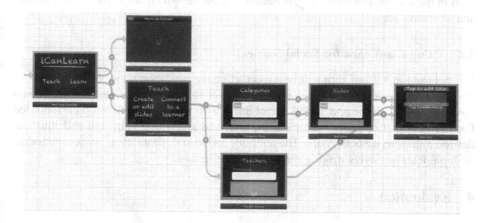

Fig. 1. Storyboard of iCanLearn in XCode.

Images. Implementing pictures was difficult due to trouble with the storage and retrieval of the images. For example, storing the images in a Core Data, SQLite database would have a negative effect on the performance of the app, so the images are written to a disk and a file path is stored as a string in Core Data. Another challenge to overcome was that the image view components displaying the images in the flashcards are sized differently depending on the device (iPad, iPhone or iPod touch). Furthermore, cameras and retina displays varies in quality across devices. Therefore, it was decided to store the image in their original state, and each device will resize it appropriately for its screen.

Audio. As with the images, we elected to store the audio on the device's hard drive and store the file path as a string in Core Data. Most of the audio being recorded was going to be spoken by users and played back by the tiny speakers of the mobile devices, so quality was not as important as file size and app performance. Therefore, a single channel, low quality recording with a sample rate of 44.1 kHz was chosen. The audio capability of the flashcards allows for the recording of the voices of the child's parents or teacher. The familiar voices may help children feel comfortable and possibly aid in their learning the material.

Playback Control. Standard playback symbols were chosen for the playback controls: triangle for play, square for stop, and circle for record. Buttons with words on them were not selected as they can cause problems when translating an app into another language.

Sharing Capabilities. The main feature that differentiates iCanLearn from other flashcard apps [11] is its slide sharing capabilities by connecting two or more devices over Wi-Fi. Children can have devices running iCanLearn in learner mode and still receive slides from another device that is running in teacher mode, which can then be displayed on their screen. iCanLearn is quite versatile and very useful in a classroom setting. For example, a teacher can make custom flashcards for teaching a variety of topics to their class, tailored to the specific needs of their children. Some flashcard apps apply tracking; however, tracking was not integrated into iCanLearn. When this app is used in the teacher-learner setting, a teacher can decide which slides the student should and shouldn't see.

3.2   Using iCanLearn for Social Stories

It is believed that iCanLearn will be a more effective educational tool for children with ASD if people use it to tell and illustrate social stories. Parents and teachers could create a category in the app, called Social Story where they could develop personalized flashcards in that category with pictures, text, and audio that helps tell and illustrate desired routine as a Social Story. The auditory and visual stimulation can accommodate multiple learning styles making the tool more effective.

4   Evaluation

4.1   Measures

Since, parenting a child with ASD can be demanding and comes with its unique anxiety producing stresses [12], using a new technology can be overwhelming for parents. We wanted to see if using the 'iCanLearn' app has any adverse effects on the anxiety being experienced by parents or not. For this, we used the six-item self-rated short form of the Spielberg State-Trait Anxiety Inventory (STAI) [13]. To assess the feasibility and usability of 'iCanLearn' app in terms of its features and design considerations, we created a web-based survey tool.

4.2   Participants and Procedure

Parents of children with ASD for the study were contacted by posting flyers in newsletters for the local affiliates of the Autism Society. This study was approved by University's Institutional Review Board (IRB) and was conducted in two parts. For the web-based pre-survey, participants were told to think about a situation where they were trying to teach a certain activity to their child. They were asked to self-rate themselves for anxiety levels and were given instructions on how to install 'iCanLearn' on their Apple devices. They were advised to use the app for next two weeks. At the end of two weeks, they were provided a post-survey link. Post-survey had 3 parts: (1) self evaluation for measuring the anxiety level, (2) mobile application evaluation (16 items) and (3) demographic questionnaire (8 items). Each participant was given an Amazon.com gift card worth $15 after the completion of post-survey.

4.3 Results and Discussion

The evaluation of the app has its limitation in small sample size. For the initial survey, there were 20 participants and 5 of these also completed the post-survey questionnaire. The average anxiety score of participants during pre-study was 13.4 and during post-study was 10.8 (high score indicates more anxiety). All the participants agreed that how the app is easy to use for parents as well as their children (average score on 'ease of use' being 3.6/4). The users' range of topics for the social stories and flashcards, as well as the comment about not needing an in person demonstration of how to use the app validates the acceptability and feasibility of the app. Below is a parent's feedback in his/her own words:

> "...I made a set for washing dishes, 6 steps. It took about 5 minutes to build it, SO easy, and fun! You just snap a picture, record your instruction, and give it a title. It could not be any easier. I love it!"

One participant commented that there was no instruction that the participant should have numerically labeled each slide in order to keep slides in correct sequence.

5 Conclusion

This paper describes the design, implementation, and evaluation of iCanLearn, a mobile flashcard application that can also be used for creating social stories for children with ASDs. Mobile computing is useful in the education of children with ASDs. An evaluation of the iCanLearn flashcard application suggested that the app has good acceptability and feasibility for a small sample of intended users. The app did not adversely affect the anxiety level of caregivers in this study. Thus there is real potential that iCanLearn could have a broad impact on our society by simplifying the process of custom creation of social stories that will improve the way we conduct autism interventions and education. Future developments that will improve the app include allowing devices to connect without Wi-Fi and allowing people to draw pictures instead of taking them.

References

1. Baio, J.: Prevalence of Autism Spectrum Disorders Among Children Aged 8 Years: Autism and Developmental Disabilities Monitoring Network, 11 Sites, United States, 2010. Morbidity and Mortality Weekly Report. Surveillance Summaries, Centers for Disease Control and Prevention, 63 (2014)

2. American Psychiatric Association: Diagnostic and Statistical Manual of Mental Disorders (DSM-5™), 5th edn. American Psychiatric Publishing, Arlington (2013)
3. Kagohara, D.M., van der Meer, L., Ramdoss, S., et al.: Using iPods® and iPads® in teaching programs for individuals with developmental disabilities: a systematic review. Res. Dev. Disabil. **34**, 147–156 (2013)
4. Gray, C.A.: Social stories and comic strip conversations with students with Asperger syndrome and high-functioning autism. In: Schopler, E., Mesibov, G.B., Kunce, L.J. (eds.) Anonymous Asperger Syndrome or High-Functioning Autism?, pp. 167–198. Springer, New York (1998)
5. Ozdemir, S.: The effectiveness of social stories on decreasing disruptive behaviors of children with autism: three case studies. J. Autism Dev. Disord. **38**, 1689–1696 (2008)
6. Dawe, M.: Desperately seeking simplicity: how young adults with cognitive disabilities and their families adopt assistive technologies. In: Proceedings of the SIGCHI Conference on Human Factors in Computing Systems, pp. 1143–1152 (2006)
7. Peters, K.: M-learning: positioning educators for a mobile, connected future. In: Ally, M. (ed.) Mobile Learning, p. 113. AU Press, Edmonton (2009)
8. Yee, H.S.S.: Mobile technology for children with autism spectrum disorder: major trends and issues. In: IEEE Symposium on E-learning, E-Management and E-Services, pp. 1–5 (2012)
9. Erbey, R., McLaughlin, T., Derby, K.M., et al.: The effects of using flashcards with reading racetrack to teach letter sounds, sight words, and math facts to elementary students with learning disabilities. Int. Electron. J. Elementary Educ. **3**, 213–226 (2011)
10. App Store Downloads on iTunes. https://itunes.apple.com/us/genre/ios/id36
11. Flashcard Apps. http://www.flashcardapps.info/
12. Sharpley, C.F., Bitsika, V., Efremidis, B.: Influence of gender, parental health, and perceived expertise of assistance upon stress, anxiety and depression among parents of children with autism. J. Intellect. Dev. Disabil. **22**, 19–28 (1997)
13. Marteau, T.M., Bekker, H.: The development of a six-item short-form of the state scale of the Spielberger State—Trait Anxiety Inventory (STAI). British J. Clin. Psychol. **31**, 301–306 (1992)

A Comparison Between Ambient Assisted Living Systems

Molham Darwish[1(✉)], Eric Senn[2], Christophe Lohr[1],
and Yvon Kermarrec[1]

[1] Ecole Nationale Supérieure des Télécommunications de Bretagne,
Technopôle Brest-Iroise, CS 83818, 29238 Brest Cedex 3, France
{molham.darwish, christophe.lohr,
yvon.kermarrec}@telecom-bretagne.eu
[2] Lab-STICC (CNRS), Centre de Recherche, European University of Brittany,
Université de Bretagne-Sud, BP 92116, 56231 Lorient Cedex, France
eric.senn@univ-ubs.fr

Abstract. The growing number of older people emerges the need to consider autonomy concerns for those people and their need for intensive care. Plenty of researches, such as those in the domain of Ambient Assisted Living Systems, have been carried out to create enhanced conditions for older people and people with disabilities, based on providing ICT solutions that enhance the well-being of elderly people and provide them with well independent daily living. This paper discusses how the efficiency for AAL solutions is achieved, through the identification and introduction of different essential requirements that should be realized to meet the objectives of ALL systems towards their various users, including family members and caregivers. Set of systems has been introduced with their solutions and architectures, to reach the main goal of this work, by evaluating these systems based on the proposed requirements, whether they meet the requirements, by studying system functionalities.

Keywords: Ambient assisted living · Interoperability · Adaptability · Reconfiguration · Distributed access points

1 Introduction

The growing number of older people [1] will cause considerable issues for most European countries, since these aging people are living alone and need intensive care. Various researches such as Ambient Assisted living (AAL) systems have been carried out to create improved medication adherence for older people as well as people with disabilities [2] through the use of information and communication technology. Therefore, in order to accomplish their objectives, the solutions which are provided by these systems should have specific features that increase systems efficiency towards user expectations. These features could, for instance, provide cost effective solutions with the consideration of user needs involvement, and privacy, as well as considering the participating of all related users, such as caregivers, family members and medical staffs, in the utilization of the system [3].

C. Bodine et al. (Eds.): ICOST 2014, LNCS 8456, pp. 231–237, 2015.
DOI: 10.1007/978-3-319-14424-5_26

The contribution in this work is to identify a set of crucial features for Ambient Assisted Living systems to increase the idealism of these systems towards user needs and expectations, and surveying various projects to investigate what features they maintain in their functionalities.

This paper is organized as follows. Section 2 defines the specific features of AAL systems and introduces the main requirements of an AAL system. Section 3 presents number of systems that are developed under various programs and approaches, to provide ambient assisted living services for elderly people and people at home. Section 4 makes evaluation of the proposed systems in Sect. 4, according to the stated requirements defined in Sect. 3. The paper make conclusion in Sect. 5.

2 Ambient Assisted Living Systems

Recent years, we are seeing the raise of technologies dedicated to make houses "intelligent", by providing different devices and services to people with disabilities (due to age or disease), which allow a more comfortable life and better safety [4].

Diverse researches, such as the Ambient Assisted Living (AAL) approach, have been conducted to use the latest technologies and facilities to enhance the well-being and support the independent living of older people at home, by the use of ICTs to enable the older persons to live autonomously in their own homes [5] and provide more efficient and more productive solutions [6]. Services provided by AAL systems can be categorized into emergency treatment services, autonomy enhancement services as well as comfort services which significantly improve the quality of life [7]. To develop such a system, users and deployment environments have number of specificities that should be considered when a system is developed, to fulfill user requirements [8], as well deployment environment (living space).

As the AAL systems considered as pervasive software systems [5], different non-functional requirements need to be considered in any system, Such as [9] adaptability, interoperability, availability, distributed access points, maintainability, price, acceptability, etc. Some of these requirements are specific to home automation support systems [10], which can summarized as follows:

- Adaptability: The ease with which a system or component can be modified for use in applications or environments other than those for which it was specifically designed [11]. Different needs for various users, according to their capabilities and disabilities, in addition to the evolution of these requirements must be addressed, as well as the evolution of the living space [12].
- Interoperability: The ability of two or more systems or components to exchange information and to use the information that has been exchanged [11]. Smart home environment includes various types of heterogeneous systems and services [13]. The heterogeneity of systems is considered as an essential challenge for the integration of all devices according to a standard mechanism that makes the heterogeneous systems interoperable and "speak the same language" apart from the used technology [14].

- Reconfiguration: "A process to perform changes to the system to ensure correct suitability to the current context. Changes can be made to the software, the hardware, or to both, and are triggered due to either objective changes (adaptively), or to service failures (fault-tolerance)" [15]. In other words, it is the ability to overcome the failure of service implementation through the definition of different scenarios during the design time. Reconfiguration is performed using statically defined reconfiguration rules in resource descriptions [16], or in a dynamic manner based on reconfiguration rules generated in execution time.
- Distributed access points: The degree to which a component, including devices, systems, resources or services, can be used by as many people as possible [19] from different locations.

3 Overview of AAL Systems

In recent years, the EU has funded different projects promoting independent living for elderly. As examples of these projects, the project funded by ICT Policy Support Programme under the Competitiveness and Innovation framework Programme (CIP) [20] and the Seventh (FP7 -2007-2013) Framework Programmes for Research and Technological Development [21], and the solutions funded by Ambient Assisted Living Joint Program (AALJP) [22].

In this paper, four systems have been chosen to be evaluated according to specified requirements. Choosing of those systems are based on the well documentation provided with each of them, in addition to the scientific papers related to each system, in which the provided services are illustrated in details. The four projects are briefly described in the following sub sections.

3.1 GiraffPlus

GiraffPlus (Jan. 2012–Dec. 2014) is an EU-running project funded by CIP and FP7 [23] in the area of ICT for ageing well. This project deals with enhancing the well-being of elderly people and extends their independency of living, by the early detection of possible health problems to decline them and providing services to assist them [24]. The system consists of a network of physiological and environmental sensing devices. Collected data from these sensors are interpreted by an intelligent system which in turn prompts alarms or reminders for two kinds of users, the elderly users at home and related caregivers and health professional. It consists also of telepresence robot, the Giraff robot, which is controlled over internet by a remote user to move inside the home, in order to assist elderly users to sustain their social contacts with other users. Further information about GiraffPlus can be obtained from [25].

3.2 InCASA

"Integrated Network for Completely Assisted Senior citizen's Autonomy (InCASA)" (April 2010–September 2012) deals with citizen- centric technologies and public/ private services network, to help and protect independent elderly people, prolonging the time they can live well in their own home by increasing their autonomy and self-confidence [11, 26], by providing services to monitor health conditions of users when they are at their homes and providing General Practitioners (GPs) and health professionals with technological facilities to remotely analyze and control elderlies' health conditions [27]. Therefore, InCASA architecture is organized into three main tiers (Front-End, Back-End and healthcare applications) and is illustrated in [28].

3.3   eCAALYX

The project eCAALYX (2009–2012) (Enhanced Complete Assisted Living Experiment) aims to provide a solution in order to improve the well-being of elderly people at home and extend their independency for longer periods, by developing home and outdoors 24/7 health telemonitoring / telehealthcare services for older people, including those with multiple chronic conditions. The system architecture consists of three main interconnected subsystems which are Home Subsystem, Mobile Subsystem and Caretaker Subsystem. This architecture is figured out with more details in [29, 30].

3.4   Danah

This project is one of seven projects that are emerged by the team MOCS in Lab-STICC laboratory in France. The research area of these projects is particularly "pervasive systems to help the handicaps" [10]. The main objective of Danah project (2006) is to set out the different scientific issues from previous projects to improve the propositions that have been made [17]. The project proposed a middleware that integrates a process of multilevel reconfiguration of home automation services, in addition to the topological reconfiguration of paths for the movement of an intelligent wheelchair [18]. Danah middleware is based on client-server architecture [10, 15].

4   Evaluation of the Systems

Following the identification of AAL requirements in addition to the introduction of different AAL projects, this section evaluates the previous projects according to AAL system requirements which have been introduced in Sect. 2, and Table 1 summarize this evaluation.

- GiraffPlus is configured to have an important feature that makes the system adaptive in a way allowing for adding and removing services easily and related sensors that provide these services [24]. In addition, the system includes not only the users at home, but also their family members and caregivers who are able to connect and control Giraff robot, as well as have access through PCs to the information and activities of the elderly people. This also applied for the medical stuff that are also can access the system to obtain health measurements [23], so that the system allow for distributed access points to the services. GiraffPlus system architecture is designed by integrating a middleware infrastructure that hiding the heterogeneity of the computational resources used in the living space, since that the services provided by the system components are developed using different technologies and connecting with each other using different protocols.

- InCASA system is developed using an architecture that undertake the heterogeneity of protocols, which are used in the Body Sensor Network and in the Home Sensor Network [11, 26]. InCASA architecture are realized using four levels of communication at home and with external users, which give different users the ability to use the system and interact with it from different locations.
- eCAALYX is performing the provided services depending on a system architecture that permits customization of the services, which makes these services adaptive to each user needs including the changing condition of the users at home [30]. The interoperability between different system components is also underlined, since eCAALYX builds on "Continua Version One standard and the Broadband Forum TR-069 CWMP specification" [30]. "Continua" is a defined standard that aim to develop ICT based healthcare systems following interoperability guidelines [31].
- Danah is considered the reconfiguration of services in case of failure by defining a set of reconfiguration scenarios in the resource description. The developed middleware in the system allows deploying Danah in heterogeneous living space, regardless of the communication technology and used technologies [18].

Table 1. Evaluation of AAL systems

	Adaptability	Interoperability	Reconfiguration	Distributed Access Points
GiraffPlus	X	X	-	X
InCASA	-	X	-	X
eCAALXY	X	X	-	-
Danah	-	X	X	-

5 Conclusion

An Ambient Assisted Living system is characterized by its functional and nonfunctional properties that need to be addressed to meet users' expectations and needs. The efficiency and effectiveness of a system is achieved when it has as many features as possible to reach its objectives. The main contribution of this paper is to evaluate number of Ambient Assisted Living Systems in order to characterize the main features that these systems have included. By studying different AAL systems according to the stated requirements, it is outlined that these systems meet the requirements partially. Thus, the attempt is to propose a system that meets all requirements so that it can be govern that the system meets all users' expectations. From this study, it is also stated that reconfiguration as an essential requirements is not considered systemically in most AAL systems, even though reconfiguration and failure tolerance in case of error occurrence, is considered a crucial requirement for systems that deals with health conditions and assistance such as AAL systems.

References

1. http://epp.eurostat.ec.europa.eu/portal/page/portal/eurostat/home/
2. Tang, L., et al.: MHS: a multimedia system for improving medication adherence in elderly care. IEEE Syst. J. 5(4), 506–517 (2011)
3. Sun, H., et al.: The missing ones: key ingredients towards effective ambient assisted living systems. J Ambient Intell. Smart Environ. 2(2), 109–210 (2010)
4. Helal, A., Mokhtari, M., Abdulrazak, B.: The Engineering Handbook of Smart Technology for Aging, Disability and Independence (2008). ISBN 978-0-471-71155-1
5. Virone, G., Sixsmith, A.: Toward information systems for ambient assisted living. In: The 6th International Conference of the International Society for Gerontechnology, Pisa, Italy, 4–7 June 2008
6. Liang, Y., et al.: Energy-efficient motion related activity recognition on mobile devices for pervasive healthcare. Mobile Netw. Appl. 19(3), 303–317 (2013)
7. Jean-Baptiste, L., et al.: A design process enabling adaptation and customization of services for the elderly. In: International Workshop on Ambient Assisted Living, Valancia, Spain (2010)
8. Jean-Baptiste, L., et al.: Design process enabling adaptation in pervasive heterogeneous contexts. Pers. Ubiquitous Comput. 15, 353–363 (2011)
9. Schneider, D., Becker, M.: Runtime models for self-adaptation in the ambient assisted living domain. In: 3rd Workshop on Models@run.time at MODELS 2008. Toulouse, France (2008)
10. Allegre, W.: Flot de conception dirigé par les modèles pour la commande et la supervision de systèmes domotiques d'assistance. Ph.D. thesis, UBS, Lorient (2012)
11. 610.12-1990 - IEEE Standard Glossary of Software Engineering Terminology. 31 Dec 1990
12. Lamprinakos, G.:. An integrated architecture for remote healthcare monitoring. In: 14th Panhellenic Conference on Informatics (2010)
13. Perumal, T., et al.: Interoperability among heterogeneous systems in smart home environment. In: IEEE International Conference on Signal Image Technology and Internet Based Systems (2008)
14. Miori, V., Tarrini, L., Manca, M.: An open standard solution for domotic interoperability. IEEE Trans. Consum. Electron. 52(1), 97–103 (2006)
15. Lankari, S., Philippe, J.L.: Multi-level reconfiguration in the DANAH assistive system. In: IEEE International Conference on Systems, Man and Cybernetics, San Antonio, USA (2009)
16. Lankari, S., et al.: Service reconfiguration in the DANAH assistive system. In: Proceedings of the 7th International Conference on Smart Homes and Health Telematics, France (2009)
17. Lankri, S., et al.: Architecture and models of the DANAH assistive system. In: SIPE 2008: Proceedings of the 3rd International Workshop on Services Integration in Pervasive Environments, New York (2008)
18. Lankri, S.: Services et navigation pour personnes dépendantes en environnements domotiques. Ph.D. thesis, UBS, Lorient (2009)
19. Queirós, A., et al.: Usability, accessibility and ambient-assisted living: a systematic literature review. Universal Access in the Information Society, Oct 2013

20. http://ec.europa.eu/information_society/activities/ict_psp/index_en.htm
21. http://cordis.europa.eu/fp7/ict/
22. http://www.aal-europe.eu/
23. Coradeschi, S., et al.: GiraffPlus: combining social interaction and long term monitoring for promoting independent living. In: Proceedings of the HSI (2013)
24. Cesta, A., et al.: Steps Toward end-to-end personalized AAL services. In: Workshop Proceedings of the 9th International Conference on Intelligent Environments (2013)
25. http://www.giraffplus.eu/
26. Prestileo, A., di Fiore, R.: inCASA project –Smart telemonitoring. TeleMediCare (2012)
27. M2M Journal, ISSN 1868 – 9558, March 2013. Page 11
28. Lioudakis, G.V.: Introducing privacy-awareness in remote healthcare monitoring. In: 3rd International Symposium on Applied Sciences in Biomedical and Communication Technologies (ISABEL) (2010)
29. Boulos, M.N.K., et al.: Connectivity for healthcare and well-being management: examples from six European projects. Int. J. Environ. Res. Public Health 6, 1947–1971 (2009)
30. Boulos, M.N.K.: ECAALYX: Towards a real-world ambient assisted living solution that delivers in non-technical environments and is sustainable. In: Proceedings of the Third Middle East Conference of Health Informatics, Beirut, Lebanon (2010)
31. Carroll, R., et al.: Continua: an interoperable personal healthcare ecosystem. IEEE Pervasive Comput. 6, 113–127 (2007). 4 October–December

Access My Campus

Kevin Michael Amaral[1(✉)], Ping Chen[1], William S. Carter[2],
and John Sanchez[2]

[1] University of Massachusetts Boston, Boston, Massachusetts, USA
Kevin.M.Amaral@gmail.com
[2] IBM Cambridge Research Center, Cambridge, Massachusetts, USA

Abstract. Access My Campus is a mobile phone application in development to make college campuses more accessible to students and visitors. Navigating a new college environment is a difficult task for anyone who has not fully explored it. This task is even harder for students and visitors with disabilities, such as visual impairments. Access My Campus seeks to help these students by tracking their position through Wi-Fi triangulation and providing information about classrooms, offices, and other notable landmarks within proximity. Students will also be able to plan routes and be actively guided to their destination.

Keywords: Accessibility · Mobile development · In-building navigation · Wi-Fi triangulation

1 Introduction

Providing smart physical and information access is an essential service to provide to higher-educational setting. The University of Massachusetts, Boston (UMB) and IBM have formed a Collaborative Innovation Center to create inclusive societal access through smarter policy, education and technology. IBM has a storied tradition of providing an inclusive work environment for our employees so that everyone has access to the tools and information required to be successful in their work [4]. UMB has a long standing commitment to supporting students with disabilities, and has recently introduced new advanced degree programs through their School of Global Inclusion and Social Development.

Many higher-ed institutions are located in densely populated urban environments or spread out on sprawling rural or suburban campuses. A typical campus usually involves a large and diverse population of students, faculty/staff, and visitors, which can serve as a controlled yet practical research environment for proving out smart access approaches. UMass Boston, for example, is a vibrant rapidly expanding campus with 7 buildings—and more on the way—10 parking lots and thousands of people accessing the campus every day. Traffic congestion and multiple active construction projects make streamlined navigation to/from/around campus more important than ever. However, with hundreds of vehicles, bicycles, public transport vehicles connected by a network of roads and pathways–navigating UMass Boston campus can be challenging for entire campus community. If the individual is aged or has a physical/cognitive disability the challenge is even tougher.

© Springer International Publishing Switzerland 2015
C. Bodine et al. (Eds.): ICOST 2014, LNCS 8456, pp. 238–241, 2015.
DOI: 10.1007/978-3-319-14424-5_27

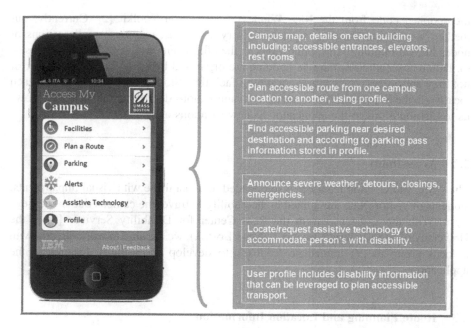

Fig. 1.

A Smarter Campus transportation strategy can help administrators improve the campus experience for all–students, faculty, staff, and visitors, and also comply with accessibility requirements such as Section 508 of the Americans with Disabilities Act and the UN Convention on the Rights of Persons with Disabilities. Both IBM and UMB are committed to finding innovative solutions to make our campuses accessible to everyone. Figure 1 shows a concept for a mobile application to enable faculty, staff, students, and visitors to locate accessible facilities, efficiently navigate the campus, find available parking, access real-time shuttle information, and know exactly where to go in an emergency.

2   Access My Campus Project

The Access My Campus application is being developed using the IBM Worklight Framework [1] to be deployable on any mobile device platform, allowing for the application to be available anyone and everyone with a smartphone. Since a smart phone is a very common accessory in this day and age, utilizing a smartphone prevents us from needing to burden our target audience with additional equipment.

2.1   Wi-Fi Triangulation

One of the pilot features of the application is the navigation feature, which uses Wi-Fi triangulation to pinpoint the location of the smartphone in the building. To do this, we incorporated code from the Rice Wireless Localization Toolkit [2]. Currently, our method is to collect location signatures every 1.5 yards, mapping small sections or nodes in each building. The application can then determine which node you are closest to. Different locations within the building are organized by category, as to whether or not they are offices, class rooms, or dining facilities. Storing Wi-Fi signature of each location in the Worklight server, along with annotations describing the location, allows us to distribute this to the application as new locations are scanned.

2.2 Accessibility

The AMC's navigation feature is also intended to assist those with visual impairments; students or visitors who are limited in their ability to travel the campus due to their eye sight. With the assistance from the Ross Center for Disability Services [3] at the University of Massachusetts Boston (UMass Boston), we are able to work directly with a focus group to get immediate feedback to develop accessibility features in the application.

2.3 Route Planning and Location Information

Combined with the navigation feature, the AMC application will include crowd-sourced route planning. Users will pick destinations they wish to travel to, such as a professor's office, a class room, or the rest room, and the application will provide them with a route. This route will either be calculated or sampled from routes others have taken to the same destination. Users will be organized into two groups: trusted users and general users. Trusted users would be able to submit these paths to the Worklight server to be used by all users for route planning purposes. Along with path information, trusted users would be able to annotate locations, providing pictures and textual information about them.

3 Work in Progress

The AMC application is far from a complete deliverable in its current state. In this paper we discussed many features which are currently in development. We are modeling the application after a previous work by IBM called Access My City [4], an application designed for New York City. In the future we hope to further develop these features to provide the applications to universities and other such educational institutions.

Our navigation feature is currently too low resolution to accurately navigate narrow hallway environments. Increase our location scanning resolution from one point per 1.5 yards (5 feet) to roughly one point per foot. There is also a matter of signal noise when scanning Wi-Fi signals. We will be pursuing noise reduction solutions.

We hope to automate the signature scanning process to allow for quickly profiling buildings for use with AMC. The current procedure is a manual scanning using a prototype of the application, which could take upwards of 8 hours of continuous scanning to profile a single floor.

Earlier in the paper, we mentioned working with the Ross Center to adapt the application to users with disabilities. Our cooperation with them in the future will be active and on-going through the development of this application. We will also be working with accessible User Interface researchers from IBM Watson to ensure the application interface meets accessibility standards.

4 Conclusion

Access My Campus is a mobile application designed to help users of all degrees of ability to navigate college campuses. For this purpose, it uses Wi-Fi triangulation to be easily deployable in existing college environments. Future development will perfect this navigation feature and may expand the scope of the application to larger campuses.

References

1. IBM Worklight. http://www-03.ibm.com/software/products/en/worklight/
2. Haeberlen, A., Flannery, E., Ladd, A.M., Rudys, A., Wallach, D.S., Kavraki, L.E.: Practical robust localization over large-scale 802.11 wireless networks. In: Proceedings of the 10th Annual International Conference on Mobile Computing and Networking (MobiCom '04), pp. 70–84. ACM, New York (2004). doi:10.1145/1023720.1023728. http://doi.acm.org/10.1145/1023720.1023728
3. UMB Ross Center. http://www.umb.edu/academics/vpass/disability
4. IBM Access My City. http://www.ibm.com/able/accessibility_research_projects/AccessMyCity.html

Immersive Physiotherapy: Challenges for Smart Living Environments and Inclusive Communities

Nirmalya Roy[1]([✉]) and Christine Julien[2]

[1] Department of Information Systems,
University of Maryland Baltimore County, Baltimore, USA
nroy@umbc.edu
[2] Department of Electrical and Computer Engineering,
University of Texas at Austin, Austin, USA
c.julien@mail.utexas.edu

Abstract. The ability to deliver therapeutic healthcare remotely relying on pervasive computing technologies requires addressing real research
challenges ranging from sensing people and their interactions with the
environment to software abstractions to move data from low-level signals into representations that are understandable and manipulatable by
domain experts who are not computer scientists. In this position paper,
we inspect the potential for *immersive physiotherapy*, just one of many
potential application of real smart health. The time is right for delivering real services for immersive physiotherapy, as many technological
solutions for remote monitoring of patients and their interactions are
ready for prime time. In this paper, we take a critical look at remaining
tasks, to propose novel concepts for data processing and service delivery of remote physiotherapy applications. We go beyond the obvious
integration tasks to uncover real and tangible research challenges that
are solvable in the near term and, when solved, will make the vision of
immersive physiotherapy possible.

Keywords: Smart health · Middleware · Immersive physiotherapy

1 Introduction

Recent visions of pervasive computing have considered the potential for using
emerging technologies in support of *smart health* in a variety of ways. Black
et al. [1] envisioned that as pervasive computing develops, there will be an evolution from isolated "smart spaces" to more integrated enterprise environments
where the dream of unconstrained, ubiquitous, pervasive computing will face
the realities of enterprise requirements, market forces, standardization, government regulation, security, and privacy. The authors defined pervasive healthcare,
based on pervasive computing, as the conceptual system of providing healthcare
to anyone, at anytime, and anywhere by removing the restraints of time and location while increasing both the coverage and quality of healthcare. Physiotherapy,
or physical therapy, refers to the act of treating disease, pain, or malformations

© Springer International Publishing Switzerland 2015
C. Bodine et al. (Eds.): ICOST 2014, LNCS 8456, pp. 242–248, 2015.
DOI: 10.1007/978-3-319-14424-5_28

of the body through exercise and stimulation rather than through surgery or medication.

Physiotherapy treatment includes physical examination of joints' ranges of motion, muscle length, and muscle power. Given assessments of needs, physiotherapists advise caregivers and family members on appropriate exercise regimens, however there is no way to ensure that these regimens are correctly followed or even carried out on a regular basis. Current practice requires frequent manual examinations, coupled with expensive equipment for assessment and therapy. This approach requires the physical proximity and dedicated attention of a highly trained physiotherapist, potentially making insufficient use of his skills and expertise. Furthermore it necessitates transportation of the patient (who is often elderly) from his home or nursing home to the hospital for each visit or for the therapist to perform services in the home.

Given the increasing availability of pervasive computing technologies, patients implicitly find themselves immersed in environments capable of supporting complicated physiotherapy routines in a transparent and natural way that encourages the patient's interaction with both the physical and digital environments. Briefly, our vision of pervasive computing assisted physiotherapy is one in which a patient can follow a prescribed exercise and physiotherapy regimen at anytime and in any place while being monitored and guided by digitally augmented physical objects embedded in their natural spaces. Therapists can be provided detailed dynamic and adaptive regimens and can monitor their patients' progresses and capabilities at a very fine grain. In this paper, we describe this vision, novel concepts on architectural and middleware design and identify key research challenges that exist in making it a reality. At a high level, our identified research challenges fall in the following categories:

- **Augmenting the environment.** Realizing the vision of immersive physiotherapy includes ensuring that the physical and digital environments are connected through sensing and actuation. Objects must be embedded with the ability to capture physiotherapeutic measures, and the algorithms and protocols that calibrate, sense, aggregate, and communication environmental data must support relevant physiotherapy data.
- **Defining regimens.** Therapists must be able to define physiotherapy polices, which requires a detailed representation of the physical objects in the immersive environment, their therapeutic capabilities, and their ability to measure their own interactive physical aspects. This representation must be abstracted to a level of understanding that matches the therapist's ability to define a therapy regimen, and the policies must feed back into the immersive environment's smart objects and the patient's interactions with them.
- **Middleware for delegation and integration.** The heterogeneity of patients' immersive environments, the distribution of therapists, patients, and their smart objects, and the vast quantities of information generated require a set of abstractions embodied in a middleware that coordinates the right amount of information to the right components or users at the right time.
- **User interfaces.** Building on the wealth of research that exists in interactive interfaces with digitally augmented objects, immersive physiotherapy requires

interactive constructs tailored to the therapy domain, which include the ability to give instructions on physical movements and to provide a wealth of feedback, including tactile feedback, using metrics of those physical movements.

The advancement of sensing, computing and communication technology and the omnipresence of smart devices in our everyday space can bring this vision of immersive physiotherapy to millions of users in their home environments. In particular, an immersive physiotherapy system can act as a virtual doctor who follows and monitors patients through their routine everyday tasks in their natural spaces. In this position paper, we explore how pervasive computing research can help to make this vision a reality and expand on these fundamental research challenges. A framework that supports this vision of immersive physiotherapy has other obvious potential use cases and benefits, for example as a fitness monitor [2] and assistant [5] or as an assistant in working with special needs children [4].

2   Research Challenges

The challenges in realizing the vision of immersive physiotherapy as we have described it are many. Several of the challenges, especially those related to resource discovery and network infrastructure (e.g., related to *cloudlets*) have been addressed or are the focus of significant other efforts. In this section, we highlight challenges that are inherent to the pervasive physiotherapy and their integration with other existing advancements. Specifically, we focus on challenges in four categories: (*i*) augmenting the environment; (*ii*) defining regimens; (*iii*) middleware for delegation and integration; and (*iv*) user interfaces. This vision also demands real interdisciplinary collaboration between engineers and clinicians to understand the various requirements and their impacts from a medical perspective.

2.1   Augmenting the Environment

Immersive physiotherapy is a true pervasive computing application in which the physical and digital worlds are inherently intertwined. People, the environment, and objects in that environment are all actors in the application and must all be augmented with devices that can sense and actuate.

One of the crucial related challenges relates to sensor placement and calibration. This has to include managing sensor signal variations due to the ambient conditions, including the nature of surrounding materials (e.g., clothing, skin, walls). However, extracting meaningful semantics from sensor data requires a mapping from signals to semantics, which may itself be dependent on a wide variety of context components. Manual calibration of these myriad sensors in the wide potential environments is, in the best case tedious and likely impossible. Therefore immersive physiotherapy demands *in situ* and on-going autonomous sensor calibration wherein individual sensor-specific calibration functions and parameters are learned while the application is live. Redundancy in sensing and actuation devices can aid in this process.

Further, these sensor networks integrated with the body, the environment, and objects in the environment present challenges in how to stream data from multiple sensor devices and synchronize those multiple sensor data streams simultaneously. For capturing fine grained human body movement, it may be necessary to transmit raw sensor data at high update rates [8]. This may deplete the battery power of the devices quickly and increases the challenges of supporting multiple sensing devices simultaneously. Alternatively, we must explore processing the sensor data locally on each device or on small clusters of devices and transmitting estimated features at a lower frequency. To perform in-network data processing and feature extraction, it is necessary to design a low complexity filtering algorithms suitable for these low powered devices and potentially tailored to the physiotherapy/fitness domain.

Traditional human motion capture technologies implicitly assume that movement of different segments of the body are independent and estimate their movement separately; therefore, the estimated motions often contain serious distortion [9]. To solve such distortion problems, algorithms must explicitly consider the skeleto-muscular structure of the human body. The degrees of freedom for any segment and the parameters to represent movement should be selected according to this structure. As a single example, the human body movement can be captured using angular velocities from gyroscopes and accelerations from accelerometers sensor. The collected acceleration and angular rate information can be fused by a Kalman filter [10] to reconstruct orientations of body segments in real time.

2.2   Defining Regimens

Therapists are not computer scientists. A high-level understanding of sensing and actuation must be enough for them to define complex regimens that can incorporate high degrees of expressiveness from the available sensors and actuators without requiring low-level sensor/actuator programming skills or even understandings. This has ramifications in two directions: (*i*) the level of abstraction with which users think about information in the immersive physiotherapy environment and (*ii*) the language and interfaces therapists, doctors, and caregivers use to get information out of the system and to define complex regimens.

In the first case, users of the immersive physiotherapy system think about high level pieces of information that are, at times, greatly distant from the low-level data that sensors acquire about the environment. What is required in these instances are mappings from these high-level specifications to the low-level sensors and actuators in the environment [6]. Such mappings should be automatic and transparent to the users.

In the latter case, what is necessary for the end user is an intuitive way to interact with a policy specification engine. Our previous work has looked at intuitive interfaces that build on web-programming techniques to provide natural ways for users to connect sensors and actuators in their environments [3]. For the immersive physiotherapy environment, what is needed is an additional layer of abstraction that frames these connections in terms of exercises and activities a patient can do given the available capabilities of the objects and the environment and the target state of therapy, whose progress is measured by the sensors.

2.3 Middleware for Delegation and Integration

The immersive physiotherapy environment will consist of a variety of wireless sensor devices which constitute the BSN, ESN and OSN. These devices will be highly heterogeneous, and the variability in a given deployment will be unpredictable. Given the availability of sensors to collect information about the environment and actuators to provide interaction, particular attention must be focused on selecting the *right* set of devices, given the defined regimen(s), the user and network requirements (e.g., on energy and communication costs), and the available capabilities. We have applied model-based regression techniques to select the most appropriate set of sensors to meet specified fidelity requirements for a high-level sensing task [6]; such approaches must be extended to also consider actuation and the joint optimization of competing regimens.

Different algorithms need to be evaluated and integrated into a middleware system that spans the immersive physiotherapy architecture, ranging from sensor information processing, data fusion, classification and clustering, human skeleton structure modeling, forward kinematic analysis, motion recognition, exercises assessment, etc.

Perhaps most importantly, delegation mechanisms must be designed that monitor the context and choose the best set of infrastructure components to meet the required tasks given the available resources. For example, if the patient is away from his home, the middleware must decide how to allocate processing capabilities to available cloudlets given the user's requirements for processing, dynamics, and data privacy. These aspects must be traded off against the need to seamlessly monitor the patient's interactions with his environments. Similar problems have been tackled in choosing the right sets of network interfaces for a task [7]; we will focus on extending these ideas to consider the context of processing in addition to network interfaces.

2.4 User Interfaces

An immersive physiotherapy or fitness system must be intuitive to use. It is inevitable that, to capture users' spontaneous interactions with different devices and sensors present in the surrounding environment, it is necessary to employ advanced gesture and natural interaction recognition. We do not want users to have to learn to interact with the environment and the therapy objects; we want the environment and the objects to learn how the user interacts with them. For example, time series algorithms such as dynamic time warping may be useful in measuring and learning the similarities between two time series of sensor readings for comparing them and drawing conclusions.

In addition, the points at which the patient and caregiver interact with the system must be user friendly and attractive. The system should be designed to inherently motivate normal users to follow their regimens without being insulting or annoying and without requiring constant guidance from the therapist.

The displays may need to incorporate three-dimensional graphics for rendering aspects of the therapy regimen. In addition, relying on elements of the environment, including objects in the environment to serve as part of the user interface is important for ensuring continuous and correct interactions between the patient and his therapeutic environment.

3   Conclusion

Our vision of immersive monitoring of individuals' health and wellness, specifically, in this paper, as it pertains to physiotherapy is an essential component of the vision of future home-based healthcare. While we have maintained a focus on the use of remote monitoring for supporting physiotherapy, many other application domains share a very similar structure and purpose. Clearly, monitoring the fitness of generally healthy individuals and the manner in which their daily activities support a specified fitness plan is quite similar, although potentially without some of the detailed monitoring and timing constraints necessary for physiotherapy. The same notions of instrumenting the environment, measuring the user's interactions with that environment, and using elements of the environment to motivate behavior are the same. Recent work has also looked at how to use pervasive computing to assess, motivate, and reach special needs children [4]; this infrastructure, when targeted to the characteristics and activities particular to a specific need can be used to support *in situ* monitoring of these children, which will lead to more natural interactions and information.

References

1. Black, J.P., Segmuller, W., Cohen, N., Leiba, B., Misra, A., Ebling, M.R., Stern, E.: Pervasive computing in health care: Smart spaces and enterprise information systems. In: MobiSys 2004 Workshop on Context Awareness (2004)
2. Fitbit. http://www.fitbit.com
3. Holloway, S.: Simplifying the Programming of Intelligent Environments. Ph.D. thesis, The University of Texas at Austin, May 2011
4. Kientz, J.A., Hayes, G.R., Westeyn, T.L., Starner, T., Abowd, G.D.: Pervasive computing and autism: Assisting caregivers of children with special needs. IEEE Pervasive Comput. 6(1), 28–35 (2007)
5. Myomo. http://www.myomo.com
6. Roy, N., Misra, A., Julien, C., Das, S.K., Biswas, J.: An energy efficient quality adaptive multi-modal sensor framework for context recognition. In: Proceedings of IEEE International Conference on Pervasive Computing and Communication, pp. 63–73, March 2011
7. Su, J., Scott, J., Hui, P., Crowcroft, J., de Lara, E., Diot, C., Goel, A., Lim, M.H., Upton, E.: Haggle: Seamless networking for mobile applications. In: Proceedings of the 9th International Conference on Ubiquitous Computing, pp. 391–408 (2007)
8. Young, A.D.: Comparison of orientation filter algorithms for realtime wireless inertial posture tracking. In: Proceedings of the 6th International Workshop on Wearable and Implantable Body Sensor Networks, pp. 59–64, June 2009

9. Zhang, Z., Wu, J.K., Wong, L.: Wearable sensors for 3d upper limb motion modeling and ubiquitous estimation. J. Control Theory Appl. **9**(1), 10–17 (2011)
10. Zhang, Z., Wu, Z., Chen, J., Wu, J.-K.: Ubiquitous human body motion capture using micro-sensors. In: PerCom Workshops, pp. 1–5, March 2009

Evaluation of the Barthel Index Presented on Paper and Developed Digitally

Elizabeth Sarah Martin[1(✉)], Chris Nugent[1], Raymond Bond[1],
and Suzanne Martin[2]

[1] School of Computing and Mathematics, University of Ulster,
Jordanstown, Northern Ireland, UK
martin-e17@email.ulster.ac.uk,
{cd.nugent,rb.bond}@ulster.ac.uk
[2] School of Health Sciences, University of Ulster,
Jordanstown, Northern Ireland, UK
s.martin@ulster.ac.uk

Abstract. Within medical applications there are two main types of information design; paper-based and digital information. As technology is ever changing, healthcare is continually being transitioned from traditional paper documents to digital and online resources. This paper presents the findings of a study involving 26 participants who are familiar with Activity of Daily Living charts, and used three scenarios requiring them to complete both a paper ADL and a digital ADL. An evaluation was undertaken to discover if there were any 'human errors' in completing the paper ADL and also looked for similarities/ differences through using the digital ADL. We also analyzed the variability of the decisions made by all subjects. Results illustrate that 22 participants agreed that the digital ADL is better, if not the same as a paper based ADL. Further positives include the added benefit of the digital ADL being easy to use and also that the final calculation is done automatically.

Keywords: Activity of Daily Living · ADL · Digital

1 Introduction

There are currently two main types of information design within medical applications; paper based and digital information. Most hospital records, medicine charts, health and wellness charts and patient records are still predominantly paper based and are therefore prone to "human error" [1]. In order to investigate the design for reducing the amount of human error, comparisons and evaluations will take place between paper based charts and the same charts in digital format. This study therefore aims evaluate the usability of the Barthel ADL in paper format and then reproduced the same ADL digitally.

The paper based chart used for the study is the Barthel Index [2]. The Barthel Index Activity of Daily Living (ADL) essentially measures the functional disability of an individual through calculating their performance in 10 activities of daily living [3]. These activities are; mobility indoors, transfers, stairs, toilet use, bladder, bowels, bathing, grooming, dressing and feeding [4]. A therapist would score each activity

© Springer International Publishing Switzerland 2015
C. Bodine et al. (Eds.): ICOST 2014, LNCS 8456, pp. 249–254, 2015.
DOI: 10.1007/978-3-319-14424-5_29

based on assessing the individual. The total calculation is out of 20 and the higher the score, the more independent the individual is in various aspects of daily living. Specific activities of daily living, such as household chores, gardening, stair climbing, walking and cycling are now acknowledged as a major health resource, and activity encouraged by both health professionals and the government [5]. With the population living far longer than their ancestors, it is important that elderly people can continue to live a healthy and independent life as possible [6]. Therefore, it is important to create and design tools that offer the best method of recommended care to each individual under assessment of an ADL.

2 Related Work

The Patient Competency Rating Scale (PCRS) has the primary purpose to evaluate self-awareness following traumatic brain injury [7]. The PCRS is a 30-item self-report evaluation tool which involves the subject using a 5-point Likert scale to rate their level of difficulty in a range of tasks and activities. The subject's replies are compared to those of a relative or therapist who scores the subject on the identical tasks. Impaired self-awareness may be incidental from variation between the two scores, such that the subject overrates their abilities compared to the other informant [7]. Additionally, the Katz Index of Independence in Activities of Daily Living, frequently referred to as the Katz ADL, is the most appropriate evaluation tool to assess functional status as a measurement of the subject's ability to carry out activities of daily living indepen-dently. Clinicians typically use the assessment to spot issues in performing activities of daily living and to structure care as needed [8]. The index ranks capability of per-forming in the six activities of bathing, dressing, toileting, transferring, continence, and feeding. Subjects are given a yes/no for independence in each of the six activities. A score of six illustrates full function, four illustrates moderate impairment, and two or less indicates severe functional impairment [8].

3 Methods

Web-based tools are becoming common place within society today. They can offer fast, free services to help with tasks which previously would have required more time and money to complete [9]. In healthcare specifically, a number of systems have been developed to help train and educate medical staff. ECGSIM [10] is one such tool that allows trainees to visualise the effects of a patient having a heart attack, without the presence of an ill patient in ward. Similarly, Bond *et al.* [11] have developed a system that illustrates the effects of electrode misplacement when positioning leads for an ECG recording. Both of these tools were developed and created freely online, and in essence can help train medical staff in a safe and simulated environment.

The digital ADL was created as an online platform, as this allows data from a large group of users to be stored simultaneously [12]. The key advantage of designing the digital ADL online, is that it does not require any additional 'extras' to be bought and installed. The digital ADL is freely available 24/7 and can run on a desktop PC or a handheld tablet device. The development was completed through using Adobe Dreamweaver and coded in (Hypertext Preprocessor) PHP and (Hypertext Markup Language) HTML5. In order to allow multiple users to log in and write comments, PHP session variables were created at the start of the index page [10]. This allows the reviewer to distinguish between each participants selections as details are sent to a back end MySQL database for further analysis. The use of HTML5 was for the overall layout and design of the digital ADL, including the colour scheme and for resizing the layout for compatibility with smaller devices.

An evaluation of both the digital and paper based ADL was undertaken by 26 final year undergraduate students studying for the degree of BSc (Hons) Occupational Therapy. The study was granted ethical approval by the research ethics committee and took place in March 2014 at the University of Ulster. All participants have had prior experience in working with paper based ADLs, with only one participant having been exposed to a digital/online ADL whilst on placement. Before commencing the study all participants were given six documents including; a consent form, three scenarios (two to be completed online using the digital ADL and one to be completed on paper), a printed version of the Barthel ADL, an instruction sheet and post study questionnaire. The study aim was to evaluate the usability of the barthel ADL in paper format and then reproduced the same ADL digitally in a web browser. The objectives are as follows:-

1. Discover if the same conclusion/outcome is met from the information presented on paper and the same information displayed electronically.
2. Discover if clarity/resolution is an issue between the information displayed electronically and those which are paper based.
3. To investigate if there is a difference of the amount of errors being made through both reading and writing the details onto the paper based and digital forms.
4. To determine the subjectivity and variance when using the Barthel assessment.

Simulated scenarios were written as vignettes, in that it's a short, impressionistic scene that focuses on one moment or gives a particular insight into an idea or setting. The scenarios presented for interpretation are not being used in any recording that will affect patient treatment. The group was shown a brief introductory presentation as to what the research involved and how to use the digital ADL. After participants were given login credentials, they could start the study. Once logged into the digital ADL, participants were directed to an initial question page were they answer a series of questions including gender, age and occupation. The page has been validated ensuring that all information must be entered before progressing to the digital ADL.

The digital ADL was designed following the paper version of the Barthel Index of Activities of Daily Living. There are 10 activities and each user must select only one option for each, based on the scenarios provided. Once the user submitted their selections, a calculation was displayed along with a recommendation. The recommendation is based on the score/calculation of the digital ADL and varies in scale between 0–5, 6–10, 11–15 and 16–20. If a user saw a score of four for example, they would receive the recommendation of, "Individual has great difficulty completing tasks independently and is already dependant on help for everyday tasks". Further help and assistance is required. In comparison, if a user's calculation returned a total of 16 the following recommendation would be displayed. "User is able to complete most tasks independently, limited further help is required". The higher the score, the more independent the individual is deemed capable.

After the user completed the digital ADL using the first scenario, they were prompted to return to the same page for the final time. They would then complete the second simulated scenario through the digital ADL before filling out a paper based Barthel ADL using the third and final scenario.

4 Results

Results indicate that overall, there was a lot of subjectivity and variation between participants in each of the three scenarios. The first scenario (completed online) as shown in Fig. 1, illustrates a highest calculation of 8/20 whilst at the lower end of a scale a total of 2/20 (range = 6). The second scenario as depicted in Fig. 2, demonstrates a maximum calculation of 19/20 and a lowest total of 10/20 (range = 9).

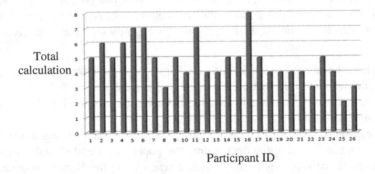

Fig. 1. The total calculation from scenario 1 illustrates a range of results from each of the participants. Overall, one participant scored eight, three participants scored seven, two participants scored six, eight participants scored five and four respectively, three participants scored three and one participant scored two. The mean is 4.76, the standard deviation is 1.42 and the variance is 2.

The third and final scenario was completed by all participants on paper. This is the method that all participants are familiar with and would have been taught how to score and interpret the various activities of the Barthel index throughout the degree program. The maximum calculation was 19/20 and the lowest was 13/20 (range = 6). The total calculation from scenario 3 demonstrates fluctuating results from each participant. Overall, three participants scored 19, eight scored 18, two scored 17, eight scored 16, two scored 15, one scored 14 and one scored 13. The mean for scenario 3 is 17, the standard deviation is 1.58 and the variance is 2.5.

Upon completion of the study, participants were invited to complete a post study questionnaire, answering a series of questions and invited to leave any other comments or suggestions. Analysis shows that 26 participants took part in the study, however only 25 returned the paper based ADL. There were 25 females and 1 male in the study

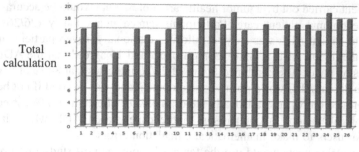

Fig. 2. The total calculation from scenario 2 similarly illustrates a wide range of results from each participant. Overall, two participants scored 19, five scored 18, six scored 17, five scored 16, one scored 15, one scored 14, two scored 13, two scored 12 and two scored 10. The mean is 15.73, the standard deviation is 2.60 and the variance is 6.76.

group, with ages between 22–45 years old. Seven participants agreed that using the digital ADL is better than on paper, 15 agreed that the ADL form is the same as on paper and four agreed that the ADL is not as good as on paper.

Further feedback indicates that participants liked how the total calculation was done automatically at the end of the ADL, rather than having to calculate the figure manually. Additionally when looking at the paper based scenarios, results show that 10/25 participants had made errors; either by miscalculating the total, or changing their original score for various activities. Participants agreed that the digital ADL makes it easier to change options, rather than simply scoring out on paper, which can look unprofessional. Furthermore, participants felt that by using the digital ADL it benefited the environment with less paper work to print out and photocopy; as well as taking less time to complete. Recommendations included the option of a comment area were therapists can make additional details/notes, as well as allowing the digital ADL to be saved and viewed at a later date, which would expedite trend analysis.

5 Conclusion

To conclude, in this study we are aware that the two main types of information design within medical applications are paper based and electronic. Most hospital records, medicine charts and patient records are still predominantly paper based and are therefore prone to "human error" [1]. In light of this, an investigation has taken place into the design for reducing the amount of human error, between a paper based ADL and the same ADL created digitally.

The digital ADL was developed as an online platform as this offers the best method of data capture for a large group of participants all together [3]. The aim of the study was to evaluate the usability of the barthel ADL in paper format and then reproduce the same ADL digitally.

Results indicate a wide variance among participants for each activity and each scenario, respectively. The variability was so significant that we cannot guarantee that an assessment carried out by a junior healthcare professional would be accurate enough to facilitate optimal patient care. Participants agreed unanimously (26/26) that the layout of the digital ADL was easy to follow. Additionally, seven participants agreed that using the digital ADL is better than on paper and 15 agreed that the ADL form is the same as on paper. The combined figure of 23/26 indicates that 88 % of participants felt that the digital ADL was a positive development and was as good if not better than the ADL printed on paper. Statistically the digital ADL offered a 100 % correction rate in the total calculation, in comparison to the paper based ADL where it is more common for users to make mathematical calculation errors.

Future developments would use the feedback from the post study questionnaire to further enhance the digital ADL. Improvements would include the facility to add a comment/note section at the bottom of the digital ADL, and offer the functionality to save and print out the scores. This would enable various therapists and practitioners to have an identical copy of an individuals results.

References

1. McDowell, S.E., Ferner, H.S., Ferner, R.E.: The pathophysiology of medication errors: how and where they arise. Br. J. Clin. Pharmacol. **67**(6), 605–613 (2009)
2. Mahoney, F.I., Barthel, D.W.: Functional evaluation: the Barthel index. Md State Med J. **14**, 61–65 (1965)
3. Anonymous, Title of measure: Barthel index of activities of daily living. http://www.rtog.org
4. Roley, S.E., DeLany, J.V., Barrows, C.J., et al.: Occupational therapy practice framework: domain & practices, 2nd edition. Am. J. Occup. Ther. **62**, 625–683 (2008)
5. Füzéki, E., Banzer, W.: Activities of daily living and health. Public Health Forum **21**(2), 4. e1–4.e4 (2013). doi:10.1016/j.phf.2013.03.002
6. Naeem, U., Bigham, J., Wang, J.: Recognising activities of daily life using hierarchical plans. In: Kortuem, G., Finney, J., Lea, R., Sundramoorthy, V. (eds.) EuroSSC 2007. LNCS, vol. 4793, pp. 175–189. Springer, Heidelberg (2007)
7. Kolakowsky-Hayner, S.: The Patient Competency Rating Scale. The Center for Outcome Measurement in Brain Injury (2010). http://www.tbims.org/combi/pcrs
8. Mary Shelkey, M.: Wallace, M.: Katz Index of Independence in Activities of Daily Living (ADL) The Hartford Institute for Geriatric Nursing, New York University, College of Nursing (2012)
9. Bochicchio, M.A., Longo, A., Vaira, L.: Extending Web applications with 3D features. In: 2011 13th IEEE International Symposium on Web Systems Evolution (WSE), pp. 93–96 (2011). doi:10.1109/WSE.2011.6081825
10. Van Oosterom, A., Oostendorp, T.: ECGSIM: an interactive tool for studying the genesis of QRST waveforms. Br. Med. J. **90**, 165 (2004)
11. Bond, R.R., Finlay, D.D., Nugent, C.D., Moore, G., Guldenring, D.: A simulation tool for visualizing and studying the effects of electrode misplacement on the 12-lead electrocardiogram. J. Electrocardiol. **44**(4), 439–444 (2011)
12. Martin, E.S., Finlay, D.D., Nugent, C.D., Bond, R.R., Breen, C.J.: An interactive tool for the evaluation of ECG visualisation formats. In: Computing in Cardiology Conference (CinC), 22–25 September 2013, pp. 779–782 (2013)

CALONIS: An Artificial Companion Within a Smart Home for the Care of Cognitively Impaired Patients

Yorick Wilks[1], Jan M. Jasiewicz[2(✉)], Roberta Catizone[1],
Lucian Galescu[1], Kristina M. Martinez[3], and Deborah Rugs[2]

[1] Florida Institute for Human and Machine Cognition, Ocala, FL, USA
[2] HSR&D/RR&D Center of Innovation on Disability and Rehabilitation
Research (CINDRR), James A. Haley Veterans' Hospital, Tampa, FL, USA
jan.jasiewicz@va.gov
[3] Defense and Veterans Brain Injury Center, James A. Haley Veterans' Hospital,
Tampa, FL, USA

Abstract. The paper describes a prototype Embodied Conversational Agent or Companion, called CALONIS, for a brain-injured Veteran with severe cognitive impairment. The CALONIS project is a sub-project of the larger Tampa VA SmartHome implementation initiative. CALONIS is intended to provide increased engagement, diversion and assistance beyond the usual mechanisms of providing assistance through text based prompting and interactions. We hope to eventually integrate CALONIS fully into the next generation of the Tampa VA SmartHome in which the SmartHome itself becomes a fully interactive and intelligent electronic caregiver. The project began with a Wizard-of-Oz version of CALONIS but even at this early stage we appear to have achieved high levels of patient engagement as well as in relation to the caregiver. The full CALONIS prototype is based on the Senior Companion project, originally developed as part of a large-scale EU project [1].

Keywords: Companion · Artificial agent · Carer · Engagement · Smart home · Wizard of Oz · Spoken dialogue system

1 Introduction

The paper describes a prototype Embodied Conversational Agent (ECA) or Companion called CALONIS, (Latin for Roman soldier's servant) for a brain-injured Veteran with severe cognitive impairment, who must have 24-hour care and has significant difficulty engaging with other people, including the spouse. The objective is to see whether CALONIS is able to provide some form of improved engagement, diversion and assistance. We also suggest that if CALONIS is able to engage the Veteran there may be some possibility of using CALONIS as a therapeutic tool and perhaps to supplement cognitive assessments. The CALONIS project is a sub-project of the Tampa VA SmartHome (SH) initiative [2, 3] which aims to explore the integration of an intelligent virtual affective agent into future versions of the SH: a Smart Home that is able to have a dialogue with a patient and form a relationship. We argue that a conversational

© Springer International Publishing Switzerland 2015
C. Bodine et al. (Eds.): ICOST 2014, LNCS 8456, pp. 255–260, 2015.
DOI: 10.1007/978-3-319-14424-5_30

partner that knows something about the Veteran would increase the likelihood that the Veteran will engage with the Smart Home. The CALONIS project is an effort to give the VA SH a personality. Others (e.g. [4]) have discussed the issues concerning long-term relationships with automated caregivers, usually in the context of the elderly, but the issues there are not fundamentally different from those we are concerned with here with our patients.

2   The VA SmartHome

In 2010 the Tampa Polytrauma Transitional Rehabilitation Program (PTRP) began to integrate advanced tracking technologies throughout the whole facility to develop an immersive Smart Home environment [2]. The SH utilizes a Gerontechnology model-based real-time tracking and location-aware system that functions as a 'cognitive prosthesis' [2]. Monitored behaviors include falls, wandering, sustained inactivity, social isolation, and patient safety (proximity to hazards). The SH uses a Ubisense ultra-wideband (UWB) Real-time Location System (RTLS). Veterans wear small tags that function like a radio beacon. Sensors installed throughout the facility pick up the beacon signals emitted by the tag. The patient's position is calculated via triangulation methods. The accuracy of RTLS is between 8 to 16 inches, depending on sensor configuration, sensor coverage and other environmental factors such as building construction materials (e.g. steel versus wood frame walls). The system can monitor an unlimited number of individuals. In 2012 the VA PTRP SH project began to implement the same system into individual homes, in order to support Veterans with TBI and their caregivers. The objective of this implementation effort was to reduce caregiver burden and delay institutionalization for as long as possible. In 2013–2014 the SHs are also being installed in rural North Florida and South Georgia – primarily to assist elderly Veterans. At the time of writing four homes are currently operational, two are scheduled for installation and two more Veterans are being interviewed for selection. All tracking and interaction data from the PTRP and every home are continuously collected and stored on a centrally located secure server. The plan is to implement the CALONIS dialogue system within the next version of the PTRP SH – although not all SHs will have this feature enabled, depending upon its appropriateness for the Veteran to use CALONIS.

3   Wizard of Oz Experiments

One challenge in deploying ECAs with brain-injury patients is whether they would accept and engage with the technology. Somewhat similar issues arise in connection with the use of such technology by the elderly, who may also exhibit some form of cognitive impairment (see [4]). The Wizard of Oz (WOZ) technique [5] is a widely used method of studying user experience in the early stages of the development process, and is one where the user believes himself to be talking to a computer but is in fact talking to a person. We decided from the start that the user interface for the CALONIS system would be based on speech and avatars alone. We implemented this interface for the WOZ system, using a realistic avatar constructed using the SitePal architecture (www.sitepal.com). The animated character is visualized in a browser window via an embedded Flash object. The text-to-speech capability is provided by a Nuance (www.nuance.com) engine, using a state-of-the-art voice model.

Following [6], we define engagement as "the process by which individuals in an interaction start, maintain and end their perceived connection" with the ECA. WOZ experiments can give us clues mostly about the maintenance part. Considering first the non-verbal channel, we monitored whether the patient directed his gaze towards the WOZ, turned away from facing the WOZ, got up, etc. We also considered the length of each interaction session. Our observations are that the patient was able to sustain interactions for about 45–60 min with only minimal periods of time when he exhibited behaviors indicating loss of engagement. For the most part of these sessions the patient's gaze was directed intently at the WOZ avatar.

Secondly, verbal communication also provides strong clues to engagement. Prior to the WOZ experiments we recorded a face-to-face interview with the patient, with content similar to what we then tested in the first WOZ session. By comparing the two, we found that the patient responded far better to the WOZ system than when responding to the same utterances from a person. This was confirmed by the quantity and quality of answers in response to open-ended questions being greater for the WOZ than for the same human conversation. The patient's wife/caregiver said she would like to have had those conversations with him, as she indicated his responses were beyond conversational exchanges between the two of them. During one of the WOZ sessions, and in the wife/caregiver's hearing, he stated he was not married. This interchange illustrates the potential ethical problems that may arise when the patient and caregiver are having separate, not overheard, conversations with an ECA, and the issue of what should not be reported back from the patient to the caregiver. In addition, it is a project design requirement that the caregiver finds CALONIS acceptable and not any kind of interference in the relationship between caregiver and patient.

During the WOZ sessions, the wizard and the patient were located in separate rooms. An occupational therapist supervised the whole session ensuring that the patient did not become overly agitated or distressed. The caregiver was also present, to support Patient X, but was discouraged from making any gestures, or giving any other form of verbal or non-verbal cues to the patient. The interactions were designed to be both flexible and structured because we wanted to elicit every opportunity for Patient X to engage in a free flowing dialogue, much like any two-way conversation between human beings. Having a scripted dialogue would run the risk of sounding like a therapy session or interrogation, and would probably lead to disengagement. Therefore we wanted to make sure that the interaction was as natural as possible. Here is a brief sample of the WOZ (called *Ava*) interaction with Patient X when he has agreed to a game of Twenty Questions:

Ava: *Do you think I know who your person is?*
Patient X: *Do I what? No, you don't know him.*
Ava: *Have I heard of your person?*
Patient X: *I don't know who you've heard of.*
Ava: *I've heard of famous people.*
Patient X: *Then–*

Ava: *Is your person famous?*
Patient X: *Not really.*
Ava: *Ah, that's too bad. I won't be able to guess your person.*
Patient X: *Why not? Why not?*
Ava: *Because I've never heard of him. Right?*
Patient X: *I guess.*
Ava: *OK, I give up. Who is your person?*
Patient X: *My dad.*

4 The CALONIS System

The CALONIS system, currently under development, is based on a Senior Companion ECA developed as part of a large-scale EU project [1]. The Senior Companion was designed as a dialogue system to converse with an older person, eliciting knowledge from them about their past through the medium of photographs, thereby building a knowledge-base about the user's life; it also provided diversion, news, jokes, etc., to increase its attractiveness as a conversation partner. The Companion was intended as a partner for a specific individual and not a generic conversation device. Its value was in the knowledge of its user's habits, choices and preferences. The technical basis of the Companion platform, also used in this prototype, included off-the-shelf speech recognition (ASR) and text-to-speech (TTS), along with an original content extraction method, based on Information Extraction, and face recognition from photos. In addition, it used a dialogue management model based on semantic networks in a single stack, as well as real time access to web information and a semantic web style inference system. It also had a model of emotion representing the emotional state of the user as a point in a two-dimensional space corresponding to classical representations of emotional space (e.g. in [7]); however, the emotional state tracking feature was highly experimental and was not fully tested in the Senior Companion prototype. We refer the reader to [8] for further details on the architecture and the implementation of the Senior Companion.

CALONIS is a Companion adapted for a quite specific type of user: a patient with Traumatic Brain Injury (TBI) with impaired executive functioning, short-term and long-term memory problems, and difficulty initiating and maintaining conversations. The purpose of CALONIS is to achieve some level of relationship with the patient, a "stickiness", by any means, and to use this to remind them of upcoming appointments or simple routines such as taking out the trash, brushing their teeth, or calling a friend. CALONIS is not designed essentially for therapeutic purposes, although early results indicate the possibility that the system may be beneficial for use as a therapeutic tool. Engagement is the first essential property of such a system (with reports of some encouraging first evidence as we noted) since everything else depends on that: useful assistance in everyday life, as a therapeutic tool and even to supplement cognitive assessments. If a higher level of engagement can be achieved with CALONIS than with a human psychologist, this option would then make long and arduous tests more tolerable and the results more valuable.

5   Future Work

In the CALONIS prototype we can distinguish immediate goals and possibilities (to be installed in the current prototype) from longer-term ones. The nature of Patient X makes certain aspects of computer dialogue management easier than in the standard case: for example, mixed initiative is hardly necessary since the patient is happy for the system to monopolize the conversational initiative; he never initiates any topic at all. Utterance repetition that might lead to boredom is less of an issue with a patient with impaired short-term memory. At the moment we are testing substitution of the prototype within the WOZ environment – the classic Turing test scenario of substituting a computer for a person to see if anyone notices – to see if the measures of engagement shift at the point of substitution. It is clear that an initial study with one patient does not allow us to generalize, and we do not; indeed, other patients may well have different cognitive abilities and be able to show conversational initiative, which is the situation the original Companion was designed for.

We shall also start to deploy the original Companion scenario of discussion of images of the patient's past to see if any recall is possible from such conversations with the system. In the current implementation of CALONIS we show images of the patient's family (with written permission from the patient's spouse). An important issue here will be the consistency, and possibly truth (as defined by the caregiver) of the "memories" so elicited, since Patient X will always reply something, even if quite random, as well as the consequent patient well-being, as defined by his willingness to continue interacting.

In the longer term, we will incorporate dialogues between the Companion prototype and the caregiver, although separately and not as three-way dialogues, since the problems associated with multi-party speech make that impractical. However, the ability to conduct some form of dialogue with both patient and caregiver is an ideal test bed for ethical issues of the limits on "cross information" transfer between them. A more adventurous goal will be the incorporation of a more systematic person-model within CALONIS, modeling the patient, the caregiver and their respective beliefs about each other of the kind set out in [9] and which we have implemented in other projects. A key assumption of such a system is that machine belief is defined by the possibility of holding alternate belief structures; in that sense an ATM does not _have beliefs_ as it has only a single possible view of the state of my bank account. This fits closely with McDermott's [10] claim that ethical belief is defined (as a necessary feature of machine agents to be ethical) by the possibility of contemplating alternative courses of action between which an agent must choose.

Acknowledgments. This work is supported by grants from the U.S. Department of Veterans Affairs and Ubisense PLC.

The views, opinions, and/or findings contained in this article are those of the authors and should not be construed as an official position, policy or decision of the Departments of Defense or Veterans Affairs unless so designated by other official documentation.

References

1. Wilks, Y.: Introducing artificial companions. In: Wilks, Y. (ed.) Close Engagements with Artificial Companions: Key Social, Psychological, Ethical and Design Issues. John Benjamins, Amsterdam (2010)
2. Jasiewicz, J., Kearns, W., Craighead, J., Fozard, J.L., Scott, S., McCarthy, J.: Smart rehabilitation for the 21st century: the Tampa smart home for veterans with traumatic brain injury. J. Rehabil. Res. Dev. **48**(8), xii–xvii (2011)
3. Kearns, W., Jasiewicz, J.M., Fozard, J., Webster, P., Scott, S., Craighead, J., Bowen, M.E., McCarthy, J.: Temporo-spatial prompting for persons with cognitive impairment using a smart wrist-worn interface. J. Rehabil. Res. Dev. **50**(10), vii–xiii (2013)
4. Bickmore, T.W., Caruso, L., Clough-Gorr, K., Heeren, T.: 'It's just like you talk to a friend' – relational agents for older adults. Interact. Comput. **17**(6), 711–735 (2005)
5. Dahlbäck, N., Jönsson, A., Ahrenberg, L.: Wizard of Oz studies – why and how. In: Proceedings of the 1st International Conference on User interfaces, IUI '93 (1993)
6. Sidner, C.L., Lee, C., Kidd, C.D., Lesh, N., Rich, C.: Explorations in engagement for humans and robots. Artif. Intell. **166**(1–2), 140–164 (2005)
7. Marsella, S., Gratch, J., Petta, P.: Computational models of emotion. In: Scherer, K.R., Bänziger, T., Roesch, E. (eds.) A Blueprint for an Affectively Competent Agent: Cross-Fertilization Between Emotion Psychology, Affective Neuroscience, and Affective Computing. Oxford University Press, Oxford (2010)
8. Wilks, Y., Catizone, R., Worgan, S., Dingli, A., Moore, R., Field, D., Cheng, W.: A prototype for a conversational companion for reminiscing about images. Comput. Speech Lang. **25**(2), 140–157 (2011)
9. Wilks, Y., Ballim, A.: Liability and consent. In: Narayanan, N., Bennun, T. (eds.) Law, Computers and Artificial Intelligence. Ablex, Norwood (1990)
10. McDermott, D.: Why ethics is a high hurdle for AI. In: Proceedings of North American Conference on Computers and Philosophy (NA-CAP), Bloomington, Indiana (2008)

Author Index

Printed in the United States
By Bookmasters